RACE, RACISM, AND HIGHER EDUCATION

Drawing upon current debates on inequalities in higher education, particularly those of race and class, and based on a Bourdieusian discussion of the relational nature of different capitals and competition for such capitals, this must-read text explores how Black and minority ethnic (BME) students navigate the university and the relational competition for capitals and status.

With original accounts of the experiences of BME students in higher education, this book draws on interviews with 58 students across three different universities to further understand experiences of how BME students navigate the predominantly White spaces of UK universities. It explores how racial inequalities continue to persist in higher education and demonstrates that greater attention needs to be made to the transitions made, not just into higher education, but from higher education. It evidences how types of support offered by different universities to different types of students ensure systemic disadvantages are reinforced and that career outcomes are embodied and legitimised in students in the practices fostered by their university.

Identifying that racism is not a new phenomenon in UK higher education but that it has adapted to changing socio-economic conditions, this is a must-read book for anyone working in higher education or with an interest in the experiences of BME students through the higher education system.

Kalwant Bhopal is a professor of education and social justice and director of the Centre for Research on Race and Education at the University of Birmingham, UK.

Martin Myers is a sociologist of education in the Centre for Research in Educational Leadership and Management at the University of Nottingham, UK.

Society for Research into Higher Education Series

Series Editors:

Rachel Brooks, *University of Surrey, UK*

Sarah O'Shea, *Curtin University, Australia*

This exciting new series aims to publish cutting edge research and discourse that reflects the rapidly changing world of higher education, examined in a global context. Encompassing topics of wide international relevance, the series includes every aspect of the international higher education research agenda, from strategic policy formulation and impact to pragmatic advice on best practice in the field.

Titles in the series:

The Social Production of Research
Perspectives on Funding and Gender
Edited By Sandra Acker, Oili-Helena Ylijoki, Michelle K. McGinn

Researching Social Inequalities in Higher Education
Access, Diversity and Inclusion
Edited by Vikki Boliver and Nadia Siddiqui

Higher Education, Place and Career Development
Learning from Rural and Island Students
Rosie Alexander

Race, Racism and Higher Education
Ethnic Minority Students' Transitions to and From University
Kalwant Bhopal and Martin Myers

For more information about this series, please visit: https://www.routledge.com/ Research-into-Higher-Education/book-series/SRHE

RACE, RACISM, AND HIGHER EDUCATION

Ethnic Minority Students' Transitions to and From University

Kalwant Bhopal and Martin Myers

Routledge
Taylor & Francis Group

LONDON AND NEW YORK

Designed cover image: Getty Images

First published 2025
by Routledge
4 Park Square, Milton Park, Abingdon, Oxon OX14 4RN

and by Routledge
605 Third Avenue, New York, NY 10158

Routledge is an imprint of the Taylor & Francis Group, an informa business

British Library Cataloguing-in-Publication Data
A catalogue record for this book is available from the British Library

ISBN: 978-0-367-55802-4 (hbk)
ISBN: 978-0-367-56296-0 (pbk)
ISBN: 978-1-003-09721-1 (ebk)

DOI: 10.4324/9781003097211

Typeset in ITC Galliard
by KnowledgeWorks Global Ltd.

Given the carnage wreaked upon Gaza since October 2023, some of the concerns raised about social justice in this book feel less significant. On 18 April 2024, the United Nations expressed its concern about the unfolding scholasticide in Gaza. The term 'scholasticide' refers to the systemic obliteration of education through the arrest, detention, or killing of teachers, students, and staff, and the destruction of educational infrastructure. We therefore dedicate this book to the memory of universities and schools destroyed since 2023 and to the academics, teachers, support staff, students, and pupils who have been killed. As educators, who care about social justice and humanity, the lesson of the Gaza scholasticide will remain on our curriculum forever.

The authors
3 October 2024

CONTENTS

ACKNOWLEDGEMENTS

We would like to thank all the students who participated in this research. It was a great pleasure to have such enlightened conversations about your experience of university life.

We would also like to thank Claire Pitkin for her valuable, early contributions as a researcher on the project.

1

INTRODUCTION

Policy designed to improve social mobility and implement an agenda of 'widening participation' for under-represented groups within UK higher education has been a staple of successive governments since New Labour's commitment to increase the higher education student participation rate to 50% (DfES, 2003; NAO, 2002). Subsequent Coalition and Conservative governments[1] persisted with 'widening participation', often framed within neoliberal ideological narratives conflating increased marketisation and 'choice' with the potential for improving identifiable problems of diversity and equity within higher education institutions (HEIs) (Ball et al., 2001; Furedi, 2010).

More recently the Conservative Government has reframed its approach to addressing issues of social mobility within a *Levelling Up* policy agenda (Gov.UK., 2022) that looks to invest in regions that have been left behind. The authors of the Levelling Up white paper, then Secretary of State for Levelling Up, Housing and Communities, Michael Gove, and the head of the government's Levelling Up Taskforce, Andrew Haldane, note this policy is driven by economic, social, and moral drivers. Although higher education is acknowledged as both a factor within levelling up strategies and also embedded within the metrics of regional disparities, it has been suggested the white paper does not fully recognise the contribution universities could make (Kernohan, 2022). Perhaps felicitously, one unforeseen consequence of the 2021 Research Excellence Framework was a slight but noticeable shift of research power (the indicator of how research funding will be distributed) away from London and the South towards the Midlands and the North.

Reflecting global patterns of change to higher education, the UK has seen both the advent of mass higher education and a move towards a more knowledge-driven economy having a significant bearing on graduate transitions

DOI: 10.4324/9781003097211-1

into the labour market (Marginson, 2016). Such structural change 'shapes the ways in which the relationship between formal educational experience and subsequent returns are regulated' (Tomlinson, 2017, p. 7). The analysis of levelling up suggests a complex pattern of pushes and pulls within regional economies that have tended to reproduce stagnation of less affluent areas whilst securing the affluence of London and the Southeast. Education plays multiple roles in this process. The identification of schools struggling to attract high-quality teachers to deindustrialised or seaside towns, for example, compounds the poorer outcomes for cohorts of pupils less likely to access universities and secure a first-class degree, a qualification that can be shown to correlate with a greater likelihood of moving to London or the Southeast to secure higher-paid employment.

How effective Levelling Up will be in reality remains to be seen, though early indicators such as the abrupt cancelation of HS2 train links to the Northwest suggest the commitment to its implementation is distinctly fragile. Regardless of its long-term prospects, the evidence that the Levelling Up agenda has highlighted about regional disparities highlights the failure of widening participation initiatives since New Labour. Despite significant increases in numbers of students entering higher education, structural inequalities determined by social class and ethnicity affecting university entrance continue to exist (Bhopal, 2018; Reay, 2018). Similar inequalities are also found within the labour market (EHRC, 2016). These inequalities, it should be noted, are not just the consequence of regional disparity but are recognisably endemic throughout higher education.

Consequently, universities have introduced measures to address such inequalities including monitoring institutions in their drive to improve access for disadvantaged students (Office for Fair Access, 2017), and the recently introduced Race Equality Charter to address the Black and minority ethnic (BME) attainment gap (AdvanceHE, n.d.). Widening participation initiatives often assume the initial access to a university place will significantly impact students and enable them to overcome disadvantages associated with their social and ethnic background. However, there is a growing recognition that disadvantage is also present throughout all sectors of higher education and is reflected in outcomes for graduates as they enter the labour market (Bhopal, 2018; Bhopal & Myers, 2023; Brown, 2014). Such outcomes are framed within a 'complex, interlinked and multidimensional nature of the factors' (Mountford-Zimdars et al., 2015, p. 24) including but not limited to aspects of students' experiences before attending university, whilst studying at university and following graduation (Bathmaker et al., 2016). Much like the evidence base for the Levelling Up agenda, it is noticeable that the processes that create disadvantage are not one-off problems that require one-off fixes. Rather these are processes that create the context for the same disadvantages to happen in the future. They are often understood as systematic institutional failings, such as institutional racism or the reproduction of bias towards middle-class interests, but also, often underestimate the scale and complexity of disadvantage.

In our research, we have consistently identified whole ecologies of disadvantage in which the past, present, and future of individual experience are entwined within complex webs of disadvantage and marginalisation (Bhopal et al., 2020). In this book, we draw upon empirical research with 58 final-year undergraduate BME[2] students to argue that greater attention needs to be paid to the transitions made, not simply *into* higher education but *from* higher education into employment and/or further study, and importantly, how the former process impacts on the latter. We evidence how types of support offered by different universities to different types of students ensures systemic disadvantages are reinforced. Career outcomes are embodied and legitimised in students in the practices fostered by their university. Using a Bourdieusian discussion of the relational nature of different capitals and competition for such capitals (Bourdieu, 1993; Bourdieu & Wacquant, 1992), we argue that students develop a range of practices, which we describe as a 'specialisation of consciousness'. These practices are fashioned by both their personal *habitus*, their individual dispositions and characteristics shaped by experience and personal history and by the 'conditionings' inherent within institutions that foster the reproduction of such *habitus* (Bourdieu, 1990).

'Specialisation of consciousness' shaped individually and institutionally mirrors structural inequalities associated with ethnicity and consequently limits further the outcomes of BME students from poorer, non-traditional backgrounds. It represents the narrowing of educational practice for BME students and legitimises the repetition of similar patterns of inequality during students' transition *out of* university into jobs, internships, or further education. Despite policy making that identifies and claims to redress inequality, our findings suggest there is little effective change. The ecological structure in which the modern university functions maintains its racist, classist integrity.

Aims of the book

At the heart of this book are the voices of BME students who participated in a research project in which they discussed their university experiences. The research was conducted at a time marked by increasing numbers of non-traditional students, increasing personal debt incurred by students, a fragmentation of the labour market, and a backdrop of raising awareness of racism and inequality within universities. The aims of the research were to analyse BME students' experiences in higher education with a specific focus on class and gender and to explore how students experience and navigate the space of the university. We draw upon current debates on educational inequalities, in particular those of race, class, and gender, and, using Bourdieu's key concepts of *habitus*, capitals, and field (Bourdieu, 1990), explore how students participate in the relational competition for capitals and status. We argue that BME students experience, accept, and *legitimise* processes that limit their expectations, opportunities, and outcomes. We describe the processes that determine this educational limiting for BME students as a 'specialisation of consciousness'.

The research and methodology

A total of 58 interviews were conducted over an 18-month period between 2016 and 2018 with final-year BME undergraduates studying on social science and humanities degrees. We were particularly interested to examine whether type of university had a significant impact on student experiences. We selected students from three different types of universities to participate in the study: Plate Glass, post-1992, and Russell Group.

Plate Glass universities are institutions originally established in the 1950s, and then in the 1960s in response to the expansion of universities recommended by the Robbins Report (1963). In contrast to the *red brick* appearance of older traditional universities, the architectural design of the period often resulted in campuses dominated by concrete and expanses of *plate glass* (Beloff, 1968) hence their nomenclature. Post-1992 universities are former polytechnics that were granted university status after the Further and Higher Education Act (1992). Post-1992 universities tend to focus more on teaching than research and often score lower in league tables compared to other universities.

Whilst Plate Glass and post-1992 are essentially descriptive of the characteristics of these institutions, the Russell Group is a self-selecting mission group of 24 research-intensive universities (Russell Group, n.d.). They tend to be long-established institutions that score highly in league tables and have a global impact on social, economic, and cultural factors. They produce more than two-thirds of world-leading research and their economic output is more than 32 billion UK pounds per year (Russell Group, n.d.). Like other HE Mission Groups, they formed to protect their member's interests including the potential economic impacts of university expansion. More recently, they have pursued policies in relation to changes in research funding and students fees (Filippakou & Tapper, 2015). They have consequently been criticised as a protectionist, self-promoting enterprise (Boliver, 2015; Watson, 2014). Members of the Russell Group include the universities of Oxford, Cambridge the London School of Economics and Political Science, and Imperial College, London.

The post-1992 university chosen for our research was located on the South Coast in a large city. It is a public university with approximately 25,000 students the majority of which are undergraduates (20,000) and it employs approximately 2000 academic staff. It has five faculties which are divided into

29 different departments. The university has achieved a gold Teaching Excellence Framework TEF[3] award, a bronze Athena Swan[4] award, and is a member of the Race Equality Charter.[5] As part of its student body, the university has slightly more males (54%) than females and the majority of students are White (68%). A total of 27% of students are from a BME background, the majority of which are Asian (10%) and Black (9%). Academic and research staff are more likely to be male (55%) and White (75%), with only 14% from a BME background with the majority from an Asian (5%) and Black background (2%). Professional and support staff are more likely to be female (66%) and White (85%). Only 5% of professional and support staff are from a BME background.[6]

The Plate Glass University is a public research university located on the outskirts of a large inner city in the southeast of England. It consists of approximately 15,000 students of which 11,000 are undergraduates. The university has three academic colleges and three research institutes. A total of 58% of students are from BME backgrounds (higher than the 22% average; 35% from Asian backgrounds and 15% from Black backgrounds). It holds a silver TEF award, a bronze Athena Swan award, and is not a member of the Race Equality Charter. Total numbers of staff are more likely to be male (51%) than female, and White (71%) with 29% of staff from BME backgrounds (18% Asian and 5% Black).

The Russell Group university was located in the midlands on the outskirts of a major city. It is a public research-intensive university and regularly ranks in the top 100 in the *QS World Rankings*. It is one of the wealthiest of the 24 Russell Group universities with an endowment of approximately £120.4 million. The university has approximately 35,000 students of which 23,000 are undergraduates. It has six academic colleges which consist of 38 different departments. The majority of all staff at the university are female (52%), 78% are White, and 22% of staff are from a BME background (in line with the average of 22%; of which Asian staff are the majority group at 10%). The majority of students are White (54%), with 17% of students from a BME background of which 6% are Asian and 4% are Black. The university holds a gold TEF award, a bronze Athena Swan award, and is a member of the Race Equality Charter mark.

Of the total 58 interviews, 18 were conducted with respondents at the post-1992 university, 22 at the Plate Glass university, and 18 at the Russell Group university. Of the total sample, 34 respondents were female and 24 were male. All respondents were 'home' rather than 'international' students and were asked to self-identify their ethnicity. A total of 18 respondents self-defined as Black, 21 as Indian, 6 as Pakistani, 3 as Bangladeshi, 1 as Vietnamese, 1 student identified as Asian Other/Mauritius, 6 students identified as mixed Black/White, 1 as mixed Chinese/White, and 1 as mixed Indian/White. We asked respondents to identify their parents' occupational status and whether one or both parents had attended university. We used this definition to determine the social class background of respondents. Twenty-three of our respondents said one or both of their parents went to university, and the majority of respondents described themselves as working class.

Once ethical clearance was obtained, access to students was gained via heads of departments and programme leaders. We contacted each of the universities via the heads of departments and asked them if they wanted to take part in the research. Once they agreed, we met with programme leaders to discuss the research. Programme leaders agreed to ask final-year students (third years) to participate in the research. If students agreed, they contacted the researchers.

All interview invitations included a participant information sheet which outlined the study aims, as well as a consent form which was signed and returned to the researcher. Participants were told they could withdraw from the study at any time and without giving an explanation for their reasons. None of the students who agreed to participate withdrew from the study. The research was conducted in line with the university research policies, the British Educational Research Association ethical guidelines, and the General Data Protection Regulation (GDPR) regulations.

Interviews focussed on examining students' expectations of what they intended to do after they had finished their final year and addressed factors they felt would impact upon their decision-making, covering finance, family support, job availability, location, and university support. Respondents were asked about processes of exclusion and discrimination they faced whilst at university. The interview also included questions about the types and level of support received by students at their institution when exploring and discussing their options after graduation. Thirty-six interviews were conducted face to face, 16 via Skype, and 6 via telephone. All of the interviews were digitally recorded and later transcribed.

The interview data were analysed by a process of 'thematic analysis' which enabled the generation of codes and development of themes as outlined in our research aims and objectives. To ensure accuracy, interview analyses were cross-checked by all three members of the research team, which enabled an analysis of the frequency of different themes within the whole context of the interview. As Namey et al. state, 'Thematic analysis moves beyond counting explicit words or phrases and focusses on identifying and describing both implicit and explicit ideas. Codes developed for ideas or themes are then applied to raw data as summary markers for later analysis' (2008, p. 138). Thematic analysis enabled the research team to code and categorise the data into themes so that data could be analysed based on similarities and differences (Miles & Huberman, 1994).

Theoretical framework

Bourdieu and capitals

Pierre Bourdieu's work has explored how the reproduction of social inequalities is a particular feature of educational outcomes (Bourdieu, 1988, 1998;

Bourdieu & Passeron, 1964/1979, 1977). In particular, he provides a complex analysis of a continuing relationship between individuals' dispositions and characteristics that are learned and practised across the life-course intersecting with access to resources and the expectations and practices of institutions.

Drawing on a Bourdieusian discussion of the relational nature of different capitals and competition for such capitals (Bourdieu, 1993; Bourdieu & Wacquant, 1992), we argue that BME student ethnicity is significant in shaping a range of practices we describe as 'specialisation of consciousness'. These practices are fashioned by *habitus*, individual student dispositions and characteristics, and by the 'conditionings' inherent within institutions that foster the reproduction of such *habitus* (Bourdieu, 1990). Du Bois describes the 'peculiar sensation' (2007, p. 8) of discomfort for Black identities framed within 'double consciousness'; using a Bourdieusian lens, in which individuals are complicit with the inequalities produced by their institutional fields, we explore how BME students framed themselves with less overt discomfort despite experiencing discrimination. In order to address both the individual *sensation* of discrimination and its institutional origins, we deploy the term 'specialisation of consciousness' to suggest individuals' awareness, acceptance, and ability to work within personal and institutional inequalities and the processes of its production. In this book, we argue that ethnicity, which as demonstrated is significant in determining types of university attended, degree class, and poorer employment outcomes, is a key factor in shaping student experience whilst *at* university.

Reflecting wider sociological accounts (Bourdieu, 1990; Weber, 1968) of decision-making processes, research on graduate transitions has tended to challenge assumptions that educational and employment-related decisions are necessarily neutral and rational (Ball et al., 2001). Decisions around future participation in education, training, and employment are framed by young people's wider cultural experiences and social networks of influence – such as familial, community, and peer relations (Bhopal, 2016). Such perceptions are reinforced within differentiations between universities (Bhopal, 2018). More elite institutions, such as the Russell Group, tend to *select* 'better' students, who are more likely to be White and from higher socio-economic backgrounds (Boliver, 2013). Less prestigious institutions (post-1992 universities) tend to *recruit* students often with lesser qualifications and with greater numbers from BME and lower socio-economic backgrounds (Bhopal, 2018; Bhopal et al., 2020; DIUS, 2006).

Similar stratification is also apparent in employment outcomes experienced by students from different types of institutions (Wakeling & Savage, 2015). Progression into postgraduate study is heavily skewed towards students who previously attended research-intensive universities, with a concomitant relationship towards the likelihood students will be White and middle-class (HEFCE, 2016). Black students are less likely to make the transition into postgraduate study (Bhopal & Pitkin, 2018). The complex amalgamation of status, particularly related to differently valued knowledge production; income, particularly in relation to capital reserves and research funding; and variations in outcomes for students transitioning out of universities demonstrates how the institutional capital of universities comprises an ever-evolving mix of cultural, economic, and social capitals (Myers & Bhopal, 2018; Myers et al., 2018).

Different identities develop through formal education that are largely culturally mediated through social class, gender, and ethnicity (Bhopal & Preston, 2011); these inform learners' educational and employment decisions, determined within subjective notions of their future education and labour market potentials (Macmillan et al., 2015). White middle-class students, for example, are more likely to draw upon better-quality social networks (Bourdieu, 1986; Bourdieu & Wacquant, 1992) to access employment opportunities. These students understand such social capital subjectively as a natural attribute of their identity. By contrast, Sung (2015) argues that BME identities are often shaped by racialized psychic harm. Drawing on Du Bois (2007) and Fanon's (2008) discussions of 'double consciousness', Sung argues that Black subjectivity or consciousness is perceived and framed within a White gaze that generates ideological and structural dislocation. Consequently, BME students may consider their restricted opportunities are also a 'natural' attribute of their identity.

Reay et al. (2005) have identified the significance of the *institutional habitus* of schools and colleges in which the congruency of pupil's family and peer groups impacted upon their experience of schools. They argue class is the most significant factor in these relations, though tempered by ethnicity and gender. Reay et al. (2005) conclude that middle-class or more privileged students are more likely to succeed as a consequence of *institutional habitus* being more closely aligned to personal *habitus*. Whilst our findings identify *institutional habitus*-shaping university experiences, it became clear that students' ethnicity played a significantly greater factor in determining student experiences' and outcomes. Bourdieu notes how the expansion of educational qualifications devalues their worth,

> because a qualification is always worth what its holders are worth, a qualification that becomes more widespread is ipso facto devalued, but it loses still more of its value because it becomes accessible to people 'without social value'.
>
> *(1993, p. 97)*

Greater numbers of students attending universities devalues outcomes such as the credentialised capital value of a degree. If, additionally, the individual *habitus* of BME students does not align with the institutional *habitus* of universities they will experience a further devaluation of their outcomes. This book explores the significance of ethnicity in framing student's personal dispositions and learned practices within the institutional shaping of student practice in preparation for what they would do when they left university. We argue that a 'specialisation of consciousness' is evident in which student identity is shaped by the institutional modelling of previous dispositions and behaviours. Whilst the impact of class within different institutional settings is highly significant, a more worrying finding was that within and above class differences, ethnicity overrides the experiences of BME students.

Race/racism

Critical scholarship exploring race and racism is currently under attack from politicians and media on the right in both the USA and the UK. In the USA, Donald Trump framed a populist understanding of opposition to his views on race/racism as the work of extremist Critical Race Theorists (CRT) under-mining American values. In particular, CRT was identified as the conduit for funnelling funding into race equality training in publicly funded organisations. This culminated in a 2020 Executive Order requiring 'Federal agencies cease and desist from using taxpayer dollars to fund these divisive, un-American propaganda training sessions' (Vought, 2020, n.p.). Contemporaneously, the UK government under the auspices of the Commission on Race and Ethnic Disparities (CRED) produced a widely discredited report that without naming CRT clearly identified it as an 'increasingly strident form of anti-racism thinking that seeks to explain all minority disadvantage through the prism of White discrimination' (CRED, 2021, p. 10). In the House of Commons, the Conservative Minister for Women and Equalities, Kemi Badenoch, explicitly attacked CRT describing it as a 'dangerous trend in race relations', and one irrevocably linked to, 'the anti-capitalist Black Lives Matter group' (Hansard, 20 October 2020: col 1012). Whilst it is relatively easy to dismiss these attacks as simply ideologically driven politicking designed to whip up support among the right-wing base on both sides of the Atlantic, this does not entirely explain their significance. The identification of CRT specifically is unusual, the intel-lectual work associated with CRT, for example, has been in the public domain for many years without being singled out for closer attention. Also, although CRT is one of the less esoteric academic standpoints, not least because of its willingness to privilege lived experience, it is still an academic, intellectual framing of understandings of race/racism. The current ideological attack on CRT has always therefore been an attack on ideas and intellectual work. Of significance to our research was the willingness of politicians like Badenoch to associate the intellectual grounds of CRT with popular dissent and anti-racist campaigns such as #BlackLivesMatter.

In this book, we draw upon critical scholarship, including CRT, that under-stands race/racism as significant organising practices of all aspects of society including education. Recently, CRT is often presented as a singular ideological position, notably by right-wing politicians but also by people who should know better including academics. We would identify a range of related positions and approaches many of which have been problematised and refined over time and we draw upon some of these in this book. We also recognise a body of work that maintains a critical understanding that pre-dates CRT and work that has emerged beyond its limits.

Early Black Critical scholarship, such as the work of Fanon (2008) and Du Bois (1935/2007), identified that race is a social construct. For Fanon, race was understood as a means of maintaining power imbalances in oppressive colonial societies in which violent psychological damage was inflicted on the colonised (2008). Like Fanon, W.E.B. DuBois recognised the psychological harm understandings of race inflicted upon Black people in the USA. He also identified the congruence of racism and capitalism as a means of maintaining social structures in which the interests of White people were maintained, and in particular, that the interests of White elites, such as landowners, were not threatened by the collective power of Black and White labouring classes. Throughout the Reconstruction Era, Du Bois identified how race divided the interests of the working class. Whilst White workers were not rewarded with significant economic or material benefits, they were

> compensated in part by a sort of public and psychological wage. They were given public deference and titles of courtesy because they were white. They were admitted freely with all classes of white people to public functions, public parks, and the best schools.
>
> *(Du Bois, 1935/2007, p. 607)*

We would argue that such privileging of White racial characteristics over other ethnic minorities has never gone away. In the USA and elsewhere, the same stratification of human value along racial lines continues. The processes through which this happens have constantly adapted to new circumstances to ensure that new racisms materialise to reproduce the same White supremacist outcomes. Education, including universities, is one field in which there has been a constant shifting and adaptation of practice to replicate racist outcomes. One of the key themes in our work (Bhopal & Myers, 2023) has been to understand how racism that is persistently acknowledged by universities as a problem that needs addressing still manages to survive.

Understandings of what constitutes race are neither based on natural or empirical evidence nor are they set in stone. At different times and in different places, race is understood differently and reflects the collective beliefs of a society at that moment in time. Who is, and who is not, White, for example, has often changed not least because the acquisition of Whiteness is readily identifiable as a beneficial, life-improving characteristic (Ignatiev, 1995). Du Bois's account of the Reconstruction Era is particularly useful because it shines a light on one of CRTs claims that all White people benefit from their Whiteness even if they are not personally racists,

> The emphasis in CRT is on the shared power and dominance of White interests. *All White-identified people are implicated in these relations but they are not all active in identical ways and they do not all draw similar benefits – but they* do *all benefit, whether they like it or not.*
>
> (*Gillborn, 2008, p. 34, original emphasis*)

Some of the key theoretical elements of CRT that we use to understand racism in universities are intersectionality, Whiteness as property, and interest convergence.

Intersectionality is a means of understanding how multiple forms of discrimination may overlap and have different impacts on specific groups of people. Crenshaw (1991) argued that often the approach to addressing racism or sexism is to take a top-down approach rather than concentrating on individual experiences. She demonstrates how the compounding of different types of discrimination such as racism and sexism impact differently for Black women compared to White women or for Black women compared to Black men. Crenshaw suggests 'placing those who currently are marginalized in the center is the most effective way to resist efforts to compartmentalize experiences and undermine potential collective action' (1989, p. 167). This sentiment has a particular resonance for our research because often the most marginalised students were those who experienced a range of different discriminations.

Understanding Whiteness as a form property that confers advantages, status, and privilege on its owners is a central concept within CRT (Delgado & Stefancic, 1997). It functions at both the individual and institutional levels. For individuals, it might materialise in easier access to social services or housing, and at the systemic institutional level, it might be an economic or legal structure that maintains racial hierarchies (Bhopal, 2023).

Interest convergence is the phenomenon identified by Bell (1980) of radical change being made to address evidence of racism only ever occurring when it is in the interests of White people to do so. Warmington makes the point that interest convergence happens as 'an overriding principle of the state' (2024, p. 57) because racism is inherently embedded within culture.

Structure of the book

This book explores how racial inequalities continue to persist in higher education. Chapter 2: *Transitions in and out of higher education* draws on the current literature to outline student experiences in and out of higher education. It provides a contextual and demographic background to the book by focussing on current statistical evidence (AdvanceHE, 2020; HESA, 2020) to demonstrate how students from different backgrounds experience transitions in and out of higher education. The chapter also provides a detailed comparative account of students' experiences in an international context (USA and Europe) and discussion of global trends towards mass education and marketisation of universities.

Chapter 3: *Racial inequalities in higher education* draws on the current literature to analyse how inequalities in higher education continue to persist for those from BME backgrounds. This chapter outlines how policy making on inclusion and widening participation has disadvantaged some groups over others. It explores recent statistical evidence (AdvanceHE, 2020) to examine degree attainment and outcomes, in the UK, the USA, and Europe. The chapter also includes a discussion of student and academic responses to racism and inequalities including high-profile protest movements and calls to 'decolonize the curriculum'.

Chapter 4: *University racisms: processes of exclusion* draws on qualitative data to explore students' experiences of racism, exclusion, and marginalisation in higher education. We examine how both covert and overt forms of racism work to disadvantage students from BME backgrounds – both from their peers and lecturers. Racist institutional processes are identified within the conceptual framework of 'specialisation of consciousness' to suggest that student identities are fostered that both accept and learn to legitimise their limited range of outcomes compared to their White peers. This chapter introduces a break with Bourdieu to argue that in terms of 'race/ethnicity' much that would be anticipated to be 'covert' or 'hidden persuasion' is, in fact, out in the open and 'overt'.

Chapter 5: *Money, money, money: drowning in debt* examines how students from BME backgrounds are affected by debt. It will explore how some students from poor BME backgrounds are disadvantaged in their experiences at university, resulting in poor degree outcomes and future decisions from higher education.

Chapter 6: *Family support, social capital, and resources* explores how family background affects the type of support students from BME backgrounds receive. It examines how students from wealthy and middle-class backgrounds receive greater levels of support (financial and emotional) compared to those from poorer backgrounds.

Chapter 7: *Institutional support: who gets it and why?* examines different types of support students receive from different universities. It explores the role that universities play in supporting students from BME backgrounds and discusses how students from specific backgrounds in different types of universities are able to access support which advantages them when they make decisions about their transitions from higher education.

Chapter 8: *Fears of the future: labour market inequalities* draws on students' aspirations for the future and examines the choices available to them when they transition out of the labour market. This chapter argues that students from some BME backgrounds are better equipped than others to make the transition out of the labour market.

Chapter 9: *'Specialisation of consciousness'* brings together the findings from all previous chapters and argues that students from BME backgrounds remain disadvantaged in their experiences in higher education. It explores how some students develop a 'specialisation of consciousness' that, firstly, limits their educational and employment outcomes and, secondly, produces students who understand their opportunities are limited but accept the process as a reality of twenty-first-century education and life. The chapter concludes by discussing how policymaking should address longstanding inequalities and the prospects for change.

Notes

1 The 2010 general election resulted in a hung parliament in which the Conservative and Unionist Party won the most parliamentary seats but not enough to command a majority; consequently, they formed a Coalition government with the Liberal Democrats. General elections in 2015, 2017, and 2019 were all won by the Conservatives; however, 2017 was also another hung parliament leading to a confidence and supply arrangement between the Conservatives and the Democratic Unionist Party.
2 In this book, we use the term BME to refer to individuals from Black and minority ethnic backgrounds as used in the Census (2011). We are aware of the limitations of the term, particularly that BME groups are not homogenous and that there are differences *within* and *between* BME groups. We use and understand the term BME to signify individuals from a visible minority with a shared experience of discrimination, and for that reason, we asked our respondents to self-identify.
3 The Teaching Excellence Framework and Student Outcomes Framework assesses excellence in teaching at universities and colleges (for more details, see https://www.officeforstudents.org.uk/for-providers/quality-and-standards/about-the-tef/
4 The Athena Swan charter was introduced in 2005 to progress the position of women in science, engineering, mathematics, and medicine subjects (STEMM). Universities are awarded a bronze, silver, or gold award (for more details, see https://www.advance-he.ac.uk/equality-charters/athena-swan-charter).
5 The Race Equality Charter was introduced in 2016 and works to improve the representation and progression of BME staff and students in higher education. Universities are awarded a bronze or silver award. Fourteen institutions currently hold a bronze award (for details see, https://www.advance-he.ac.uk/equality-charters/race-equality-charter).
6 All data on the three universities have been taken from public university documents.

References

AdvanceHE. (2020). *Statistical report: Students*. AdvanceHE.
AdvanceHE. (n.d.) *Race Equality Charter*. Retrieved September 13, 2024, from https://www.advance-he.ac.uk/equality-charters/race-equality-charter
Ball, S. J., Davies, J., Davis, M., & Reay, D. (2001). 'Classification and judgement': Social class and the 'cognitive structures' of choice. *British Journal of Sociology of Education*, 23(1), 51–72.

Bathmaker, A. et al. (2016). *Higher education, social class and social mobility*. Palgrave.

Bell, D. A. (1980). Brown v. Board of education and the interest-convergence dilemma. *Harvard Law Review, 93*(3), 518–533.

Beloff, M. (1968). *The plateglass universities*. Secker and Warburg.

Bhopal, K. (2016). *The experiences of black and minority ethnic academics: A comparative study of the unequal academy*. Routledge.

Bhopal, K. (2018). *White privilege: The myth of a post-racial society*. Policy.

Bhopal, K. (2023). Critical race theory: Confronting, challenging, and rethinking white privilege. *Annual Review of Sociology, 49*(1), 111–128.

Bhopal, K., Myers, M., & Pitkin, C. (2020). Routes through higher education: BME students and the development of a 'specialisation of consciousness'. *British Educational Research Journal, 46*(6), 1321–1337.

Bhopal, K., & Myers, M. (2023). *Elite universities and the making of privilege: Exploring race and class in global educational economies*. Routledge.

Bhopal, K., & Pitkin, C. (2018). *Investigating higher education institutions and their views on the race equality charter*. UCU.

Bhopal, K., & Preston, J. (2011). *Intersectionality and race in education*. Routledge.

Boliver, V. (2013). How fair is access to more prestigious universities? *British Journal of Sociology of Education, 64*(2), 344–364.

Boliver, V. (2015). Are there distinctive clusters of higher and lower status universities in the UK? *Oxford Review of Education, 41*(5), 608–627.

Bourdieu, P. (1986). The forms of capital. In J. Richardson (Ed.), *Handbook of theory and research for the sociology of education* (pp. 241–258). Greenwood.

Bourdieu, P. (1988). *Homo academicus*. Polity.

Bourdieu, P. (1990). *The logic of practice*. Polity.

Bourdieu, P. (1993). *Sociology in question* (Vol. 18). Sage.

Bourdieu, P. (1998). *The state nobility: Elite schools in the field of power*. Stanford University Press.

Bourdieu, P., & Passeron, J. (1964/1979). *The inheritors: French students and their relation to culture*. Chicago University Press.

Bourdieu, P., & Passeron, J. (1977). *Reproduction in education, society and culture*. Sage.

Bourdieu, P., & Wacquant, L. (1992). *An invitation to reflexive sociology*. University of Chicago Press.

Brown, M. (2014). *Higher education as a tool of social mobility: Reforming the delivery of HE and measuring professional graduate output success*. Centre Forum.

Commission on Race and Ethnic Disparities. (2021). *Commission on racial and ethnic disparities: The report*. HMSO.

Crenshaw, K. (1991). Mapping the Margins: Intersectionality, Identity Politics, and Violence against Women of Color. *Stanford Law Review, 43*(6), 1241–1299.

Delgado, R., & Stefancic, J. (Eds.) (1997). *Critical white studies: Looking behind the mirror*. Temple University Press.

DfES. (2003). *The future of higher education*. The Stationery Office.

DIUS. (2006). *Statistical release: Participation rates in higher education, academic years 2000-2007*. HMSO.

Du Bois, W. E. B. (2007). *The souls of black folk*. OUP.

Du Bois, W. E. B. (1935/2007). *Black reconstruction in America: An essay toward a history of the part which black folk played in the attempt to reconstruct democracy in America, 1860-1880*. Oxford University Press.

Equality and Human Rights Commission (EHRC). (2016). *Healing a Divided Britain: The need for a comprehensive race equality strategy*. EHRC.

Fanon, F. (2008). *Black skin, white masks*. Pluto Press.

Filippakou, O., & Tapper, T. (2015). Mission groups and the new politics of British higher education. *Higher Education Quarterly, 69*(2), 121–137.

Furedi, F. (2010). Introduction to the manifestation of higher education and the student as consumer. In M. Molesworth et al. (Eds.), *The manifestation of higher education and the student as consumer* (pp. 1–8). Taylor and Francis.

Further and Higher Education Act 1992. HMSO.

Gillborn, D. (2008). *Racism and education: Coincidence or conspiracy?* Taylor & Francis.

Gov.UK. (2022). *Levelling Up the United Kingdom.* Retrieved September 13, 2024, from https://assets.publishing.service.gov.uk/media/62e7a429d3bf7f75af0923f3/Executive_Summary.pdf

Hansard. (2020). *Black History Month, 20 October, col 1012.* Retrieved September 16, 2024, from https://hansard.parliament.uk/Commons/2020-10-20/debates/5B0E393E-8778-4973-B318-C17797DFBB22/BlackHistoryMonth

HEFCE. (2016). *Student statistics.* HMSO.

HESA. (2020). *Student statistics.* HMSO.

Ignatiev, N. (1995). *How the Irish became white.* Routledge.

Kernohan, D. (2022). What's in the levelling up white paper for universities? Retrieved June 21, 2022, from https://wonkhe.com/blogs/whats-in-the-levelling-up-white-paper-for-universities/

Macmillan, L. et al. (2015). Who gets the top jobs? The role of family background and networks in recent graduates' access to high-status professions. *Journal of Social Policy, 44*(3), 487–515.

Marginson, S. (2016). "High participation systems of higher education. *The Journal of Higher Education, 87*(2), 243–271.

Miles, M., & Huberman, M. (1994). *Qualitative data analysis: An expanded sourcebook.* Sage.

Mountford-Zimdars, A., et al. (2015). *Causes for differences in student outcomes.* HEFCE/Kings College.

Myers, M., & Bhopal, K. (2018). *Access to elite universities* [Unpublished paper]. University of Birmingham.

Myers, M., Bhopal, K., & Pitkin, C. (2018, April 10–12). *Transitions from higher education: Identity, access, support and decision-making* [Paper presentation]. British Sociological Association, Northumbria University, Newcastle Upon Tyne.

Namey, E., et al. (2008). Data reduction techniques for large qualitative data sets. In G. Guest & K. M. MacQueen (Eds.), *Handbook for team-based qualitative research* (pp. 137–162). Rowman Altamira.

NAO. (2002). *Widening participation in higher education in England.* The Stationary Office.

Office for Fair Access. (2017). *Outcomes of access agreements monitoring for 2015-16.* OfS.

Reay, D. (2018). *Miseducation.* Policy.

Reay, D., David, M., & Ball, S. (2005). *Degrees of choice: Social class, race and gender in higher education.* Trentham Books.

Robbins, L.C. (1963). Higher Education Report. (1963). HMSO.

Sung, K. (2015). Hella ghetto!': (Dis)locating race and class consciousness in youth discourses of ghetto spaces, subjects and schools. *Race Ethnicity and Education, 18*(3), 363–395.

The Census. (2011). ONS. https://www.ons.gov.uk/census/2011census Retrieved 28 October 2024

Tomlinson, M. (2017). Introduction: Graduate employability in context: Charting a complex, contested and multi-faceted policy and research field. In M. Tomlinson & L. Holmes (Eds.), *Graduate employability in context* (pp. 1–40). Palgrave Macmillan.

Vought, R. (2020). *M-20-34 memorandum for the heads of executive departments and agencies 4 September.* Executive Office of the President, Office of Management and Budget.

Wakeling, P., & Savage, M. (2015). Entry to elite professions and the stratification of higher education in Britain. *The Sociological Review. 63*(2), 290–320.

Warmington, P. (2024). *Permanent racism: Race, class and the myth of postracial Britain.* Policy Press.

Watson, D. (2014). *Only connect': Is there still a higher education sector?* Higher Education Policy Institute.

Weber, M. (1968). *Economy and society* (G. Roth & C. Wittich, Trans.). University of California Press.

Web references

Russell Group. (n.d.). *Who we are.* Retrieved September 16, 2024, from https://russellgroup.ac.uk/about/our-universities/

2

TRANSITIONS IN AND OUT
OF HIGHER EDUCATION

This chapter explores the changing demographics of UK universities and provides a comparative account of international contexts (USA and Europe). It argues that global trends towards mass education and the marketisation of universities are misrecognised as drivers of social mobility. The expansion of student numbers relates directly to the corporate practice of universities in which students are framed as consumers and higher education is sold as an individual asset rather than a collective public good. Rather than addressing inequity educational economies emerge in which ingrained inequalities are reproduced that maintain the status of dominated and dominant groups.

The twenty-first-century university

In the UK, there is a substantial body of statistical evidence highlighting how the demographic characteristics of the student body have changed dramatically (AdvanceHE, 2023; HESA, 2024). This provides the context for the experiences of participants in our research. In the UK, there are now more students in higher education than at any previous time and these numbers include more students from lower income households and more ethnic minority students. At first sight, more students attending university and gaining degrees is a positive narrative; however, it is not quite the educational success story that might be imagined. There is clear evidence that students from different backgrounds often experience very different outcomes when entering higher education and later when entering the job market. Patterns of inequality that are readily evidenced before students reach university are repeated in their later lives. Participants in our research readily identified such failings outlining how race and class both impacted their futures and how the university was

DOI: 10.4324/9781003097211-2

not a space in which radical transformations of social mobility were likely to occur.

Despite identifying the reproduction of inequity within the university, students whose backgrounds unfairly impacted their outcomes remained committed to their institutional experience. In a Bourdieusian sense, this acceptance of arbitrary outcomes as somehow natural (i.e. that Whiteness or affluence aligned with specific educational outcomes and aspirations) could be understood in terms of *doxa*. That is their experience of being university students included ingrained sets of beliefs about their natural place in the world based upon socially acceptable and socially constructed norms about the fields they inhabited that were recognised as being self-evident. Students recognised a '*sense of limits*' (Bourdieu, 1977, p. 164) within the university in which the benefits of acquiring a degree were constrained by personal attributes such as class or ethnicity. Bourdieu argues the recognition of the '*sense* of limits implies *forgetting* the limits', the acceptance of a limiting social structure goes unchallenged as dominated individuals and groups perform being dominated selves. In other words, all students whether they are disadvantaged or advantaged by their status understand their respective standing to be their natural place in the world. Furthermore, within wider society, this is an understanding that is accepted as legitimate.

The dramatic expansion of student numbers sits within a discourse that celebrates this as a moment when educational inequalities are being addressed, despite the simultaneous clear evidence that access to university and degree outcomes remain inequitable. This is not a strikingly new phenomenon. An analysis of the post-war settlement and 1944 Education Act would readily identify similar types of discourse; the sentiment of addressing inequitable school opportunities by the tripartite system being matched by evidence that the 'new' school system replicated 'old' inequalities. The repetition of inequalities feeds the social construction of a discourse in which school pupils or university students from dominated groups always understand that they are only able to attain lesser rewards than those from the dominant classes. Examples of such discourse being generated in new contexts include the persistent attempts at maintaining a narrative that selective, grammar schools are a means to provide working-class students with meritocratic opportunities and the equally persistent myth that White working-class pupils are the most disadvantaged group. The first of these examples perpetuates the narrative that the best working-class students will succeed through education whilst creating schools that actively benefit wealthier, more privileged families. The second sediments the narrative that in a post-racial Britain, education has mostly benefited ethnic minorities. The continuing emergence of such narratives creates the limits to what can be achieved as self-evident truths. Despite the fallacy of such narratives, the evidence of their essential untruthfulness remain forgotten and unchallenged within public discourse.

Student demographics in the UK

A number of broad patterns are discernible in the demographics of UK education that broadly map national social, cultural, economic, and political changes. In addition, these changes broadly reflect global trends towards increased school and educational provision. The most significant and noticeable change has been the progressive extension of educational opportunities to increasing numbers of pupils and students throughout all sectors of education. The nineteenth century saw increasing state involvement in the oversight of schooling including the introduction of compulsory schooling to the age of 12 and local school boards, followed in 1902 by the replacement of school boards with local education authorities (UK Parliament, 1870, 1902). The school leaving age rose to 14 in 1918, 15 in 1947, and 16 in 1972 (Bolton, 2012). As of 2008 although the school leaving age remained at 16, in England, participation in education (e.g. continued secondary education or training) was raised to 18 years (Gov.UK, 2008). This requirement does not apply to the other Home Countries. Allied to these changes, the state has increasingly determined the types of school provision; notably, the introduction of the tripartite system of grammar, technical, and secondary modern schools following the 1944 Education Act and the later shift towards comprehensive schools (Department for Education and Science, 1965). As a direct consequence, the number of pupils in schooling has risen from around 5.5 million in 1900 to 8.8 million in 2010 (Bolton, 2012). At the same time, school students have progressively left school at a later age and with higher numbers of qualifications.

The extension of education by the state is not unique to the UK. In the USA, a similar transition towards state schooling, a professionalised teaching body and legislation requiring school attendance, has also emerged from the 1870s to the present day (Kober, 2020). This is a process driven, as in the UK and other developing nations, by increasing industrialisation and technological developments, the centralisation of populations within new growing urban centres, and the recognition of education as a universal feature of citizenship (Mclaughlin, 2000. More generally, the rights of all children to an education has been recognised as a global human right in Articles 28 and 29 of the United Nations Convention on the Rights of the Child (UN, 1989).

Just as the UK school population has grown, so too the numbers of school pupils progressing into tertiary education and completing undergraduate and postgraduate degrees has also progressively increased. This again often reflects the involvement of the state both as a regulator and funder of higher education and also as a consequence of social policy responding to contemporary social, economic, and political changes. For example, following both World Wars schemes to support former servicemen resulted in increased numbers of students (Bolton, 2012; Green et al., 2020). More significantly, policy changing the status of institutions such as polytechnics to universities (Gov.UK, 1992) and calls to increase participation in higher education to above 50% of the school population have significantly increased numbers of graduates (Department for Education and Skills [DfES], 2003; NAO, 2002). The twenty-first century has seen an unprecedented expansion in the numbers of students attending universities and being awarded undergraduate degrees. In addition and as a consequence of universities becoming more market-orientated, there has been an expansion in the provision of higher degrees including a sharp rise in professional doctorates (Westphal & Ilieva, 2022).

The increasing student population has also been accompanied by a number of significant demographic shifts in terms of ethnicity, gender, and socio-economic background. This diversity is reflected not just in transitions into higher education but also transitions from higher education into the labour market or postgraduate study (Bhopal et al., 2020). The following sections will outline demographic data by ethnicity and gender.

Ethnic inequalities in higher education

Data collected since 2006 show that the number of pupils from all ethnic groups admitted to university has increased (AdvanceHE, 2023). Between 2003/2004 and 2018/2019 there was a significant increase of 73.4% in the numbers of students identifying as Black and minority ethnic (BME). Asian and Black students saw the most significant growth, whilst the numbers of Chinese students decreased slightly (AdvanceHE, 2020).

White pupils are the least likely to progress to university, whilst Chinese and Asian students are most likely to do so. Whilst the failure of White students to progress to university has been widely commented upon (UK Parliament, 2021), it disguises significant other trends suggesting that ethnic minority students are systematically disadvantaged. Within the broad pattern of increasing student numbers, those from ethnic minorities have tended to attend less prestigious universities. The Higher Education Statistics Agency (HESA) identifies high-, medium-, and low-tariff universities based on an equal third split of university admissions tariffs (HESA, 2023a). In all, 34.9% of White students were offered a place at a high-tariff institution compared to 18.5% of Black students; at the same time, 49.6% of Black students went to low-tariff universities compared to 27.7% of White students (HESA, 2023a). Higher tariff institutions tend to be the most selective universities with more prestigious reputations. Compounding these differences, the numbers of minority ethnic students attending the most elite and prestigious universities are even more starkly differentiated (Bhopal & Myers, 2023).

There is also evidence that ethnic minority students time at university is marked by experiences of racism. This is most identifiable in the *attainment gap* between White and ethnic minority students. The attainment gap is a measure of the different outcomes between similar students entering and leaving university (e.g. a comparison of students who enter university with the same grades). Across the entire university sector in 2017/2018, there was a 13% 'gap' in the likelihood of ethnic minority students obtaining a first or 2:1 degree classification compared to White students (Universities UK, 2019). One university, Canterbury Christ Church, had an attainment gap of over 41% (Adams, 2019). Although the attainment gap is evident between White and *all other* ethnic groups, there are also differences within the BME category, with Black students being the least likely to receive a first or 2:1 (Black African 23.3%, Black Caribbean 19.2%, and other Black 24.4%). The gap was narrower for students from Chinese (4.4%), Indian (4.8%), and mixed backgrounds (4.8%) (AdvanceHE, 2020, p. 129). AdvanceHE (2023, p. 127) noted that following the COVID-19 pandemic, 'the gaps between the proportions of White qualifiers and qualifiers from Black, Asian, and minority ethnic backgrounds awarded a first/2:1 recorded for 2021/22 increased from those reported for 2020/21 across each of the detailed ethnicity categories except for Chinese qualifiers'. This 'widening' of the gap was particularly pronounced amongst Black Caribbean (63.9% of who were awarded a first/2:1) and White qualifiers (83.0%, a difference of 22.6 percentage points and an increase of 3.0 percentage points since 2020/2021).

Following graduation, White students are more likely to be in 'sustained employment, further study or both' (measured 1, 3, 5, and 10 years after graduation), and Black, Asian, and other ethnicities are more likely to be unemployed than their White peers (HESA, 2023b; Gov.UK, 2023). However, Chinese, Indian, and other Asian groups tend to earn higher salaries than their White counterparts across the same period, whilst Bangladeshi, Black Caribbean, and Pakistani graduates earn less (AdvanceHE, 2020). The Destination of Leavers from Higher Education survey identified that greater percentages of Black (16%), Asian (16%), and other (17%) students progressed to further study, compared to 14% of their White peers.

Gender inequalities show that within every ethnic group females outnumber males, the greatest being amongst the Black students with 60.2% women, compared to 53.3% in the Asian category (AdvanceHE, 2020, p. 199). The degree awarding gap was the greatest between Black men (54.5% received a first or 2:1) compared to White women (82.9% received a first or 2:1), this is a difference of 28.4 percentage points. The BAME awarding gap also widens with age, with an 18.1 percentage point difference in the proportion of White and BAME qualifiers aged 36 and over, which is more than double the difference amongst those aged 21 and under (7.6 percentage points) (AdvanceHE, 2020, p. 199).

The inequalities that BME students experience are mirrored in the experiences of academics working in higher education institutions. UK BME staff are more likely to be on fixed-term contracts (31.4%) compared to White staff (27.7%) and more likely to be employed on precarious zero-hours contracts (Myers, 2022). They are underrepresented at the highest contract level and overrepresented at the lowest with only 3.1% of BME staff who are heads of institutions, compared to 96.9% White (AdvanceHE, 2020, p. 132). Amongst the professoriate, 90.9% of professors are White compared to 9.1% BME (3.6% Asian, 2.2% Chinese, 1.2% mixed, 1.3% other, and only 0.6% Black) (AdvanceHE, 2020).

What these data show is that throughout higher education, there is a consistent pattern of inequality that relates to ethnicity. Whiteness emerges as a quality or characteristic that is associated with better educational outcomes. This is nuanced by the interplay of other characteristics such as class, gender, or disability, but Whiteness remains a key characteristic in determining who benefits the most from education. In this sense, Whiteness can be understood as a property that benefits other disadvantaged groups as well as advantaged groups. And, by the same token, being Black or Asian and not possessing Whiteness acts to limit outcomes.

Commuter students

Commuter students tend to be those who travel to their main study location from their family residence. There has been a long-held view that the student experience of the UK university system should be characterised by young people moving away from home for the first time. For instance, historically from the 1950s to the 1980s the number of students living in the parental home declined as HE expanded and new universities were founded with a 'residential ethos' (Maguire & Morris, 2018, p. 14). However, this trend started to change in the early 1990s as polytechnics were converted to university status and with further massification of HE in the late 1990s and 2000s; the proportion of students living at home increased, as documented in data collected by both local authorities and more recently by the HESA (National Union of Students [NUS], 2015).

The increase in numbers of commuter students has led to calls for universities to address their needs more closely by adapting their welcome and induction activities, offering information and advice about commuting, revising assessment activities and models to meet commuter students' needs, developing an online commuter support community, and providing enhancement and extra-curricular activities during the day or early evening to increase accessibility for those returning home after their time on campus (Maguire & Morris, 2018; Thomas & Jones, 2017). However, this has largely not been the case in practice.

Commuter students are more likely to be from disadvantaged and BME backgrounds and be the first in their family to attend university (Donnelly &

Gamsu, 2018; Woodfield, 2014). Christie (2007) notes that since the 1990s, changes to university funding, including the transition to tuition fees, student loans, and greater parental contributions, have significantly increased the numbers of commuter students from less affluent or ethnic minority families. This has been exacerbated because these families are less able or willing to incur debt than middle-class families and often more likely to want to remain in their local areas (Pokorny et al., 2016). Even in the early years of the changes to university funding, the impact was well-documented with such students labelled 'contingent choosers' (Ball et al., 2002, p. 336), because their choice of university was limited by a range of constraints and expectations that were not shared with more affluent families with prior experience of attending university. This has been shown to be the case specifically for Bangladeshi and Pakistani girls who want to stay at home for cultural and religious reasons and are more likely to attend their local university (Bhopal, 2010; Gibbons & Vignoles, 2012; Khambhaita & Bhopal, 2013).

There is evidence to suggest that being a commuter student has the potential to 'materially affect their ability to succeed in higher education' (Maguire & Morris, 2018, pp. 9–10). Commuter students often find it harder to engage in social activities, particularly at the beginning of their studies, compared to peers living in halls of residence (Hordósy, 2023). At the same time, the culture of many higher education institutions reinforces a conventional model of student engagement, assuming that the majority of students live on campus. Recent research suggests barriers faced by commuter students when trying to engage in an effective university learning experience, including timetabling and access to facilities and technology, and the lowest perception of value for money (Neves & Hillman, 2018; Thomas, 2023). This may also be impacted by the likelihood that commuter students are more likely to be from working-class and BME backgrounds and they are also more likely to be working part-time during their studies (Southall et al., 2016; Thomas & Jones, 2017; Woodfield, 2014).

One consequence of specific difficulties associated with being a commuter student, such as having less access to peer support networks (Maguire & Morris, 2018; Thomas & Jones, 2017), is that it may affect students' self-confidence, academic outcomes, and resilience (Briggs et al., 2012; Holton & Finn, 2018; Pokorny et al., 2016; Walton & Cohen, 2011). Artess et al. (2014) also argue that commuter students are disadvantaged when securing graduate-level employment, as they may be limited by the same geographical boundaries and how far they wish to travel for employment.

Global perspectives

Student demographics in the USA

Recent statistics suggest that the population in the USA has become more racially and ethnically diverse, this is also reflected in the increase in the numbers of BME groups entering higher education. However, as in the UK, there are differences in attainment and outcomes for students from minority groups. In 2018, a total of 16.6 million students enrolled at American universities, of these 8.7 million students were White, 3.4 million were Hispanic, 2.1 million were Black, 1.1 million were Asian, 647,000 were of two or more races, 120,000 were American Indian/Alaska Native, and 45,000 were Pacific Islander (National Center for Education Statistics, 2020).

Ethnic differences

Similar to trends seen in the UK, the number of students from some minority ethnic backgrounds has increased, such as those from Hispanic backgrounds, students from two or more races, and those from an Asian background – with the latter group's enrolment increasing by 6% to 1.1 million students (National Center for Education Statistics, 2020). This was in contrast to a decrease in the enrolment of White students (20%) and Black students (21%) from 2010 to 2018. However, despite an overall increase in the percentage of Hispanic, Black, Asian, and other minority ethnic adults achieving a high school diploma or higher level of qualification, gaps in attainment continue to be greater at higher education level (US Department of Education, 2019). Furthermore, whilst bachelor's degree attainment for students from ethnic minorities has risen over time, the attainment gap has more than doubled between White and Black students, as well as between White and Hispanic students (US Department of Education, 2019).

Institution type

Similar to trends in the UK, patterns in college enrolments indicate significant variations across institution types in the USA – public, for-profit, and private, non-profit – with White students more typically enrolling in private, non-profit institutions compared to Black and Hispanic students. The percentage of students enrolled at for-profit institutions was highest amongst Black students and lowest amongst Asian students. This mirrors evidence in the UK to suggest that elite universities are dominated by White students, with Black African American and Latino students continuing to be underrepresented in elite universities, including at Harvard, Brown, and other selective institutions (Reardon et al., 2012).

A key difference between admissions in the US and the UK, however, is in relation to affirmative action. Many US institutions – including private and public universities – developed and implemented policies to address discrimination based on both race and gender. There is evidence suggesting that there are significant benefits for all students when such an approach to admissions is taken (Lieberman, 2005; Lowery et al., 2006), with an increase in racial understanding between diverse groups (Chang, 2000; Gurin et al., 2002) and reduced intergroup prejudice for students from all racial backgrounds (Hurtado, 2005).

Recently, however, and against the backdrop of Republicans bringing pressure to bear on other issues such as diversity training in state departments and the teaching of Critical Race Theory, affirmative action was found by the Supreme Court to violate the equal protection principle of the Fourteenth Amendment. The Supreme Court made its ruling based on two legal challenges: *Students for Fair Admissions v. Harvard*, 2023 and *Students for Fair Admissions v. University of North Carolina*, 2023 (Supreme Court of the United States 2023).

This represents a significant shift in ideological understandings about the role and purpose of universities. In the 1970s, the Supreme Court judged a diverse student body fell within the scope of academic freedoms and as such was protected by the First Amendment to the American Constitution (Auboussier et al., 2023). Doytcheva notes the often 'wilful decoupling' (2021, p. 2) of diversity and migration policies particularly within colour-blind narratives and a consequent discourse in which the promotion of socially just causes retains a voice, but one that is simultaneously stymied in a practical sense by the protections afforded to maintaining universal nationalist characteristics. Drawing upon Foucault, Doytcheva characterises the language and narratives of diversity work as a form of immigration governmentality. In the context of Trump's America (and previously during Obama's presidencies), the increasing hostility to immigration including literal wall-building along the Mexican border seems to have fostered political contexts in which it is no longer necessary to pay lip service to diversity as a credible form of idealism (let alone retain any value as an invisible form of governmentality). In this new political landscape, diversity policies became inextricably linked to anti-American values. The logic of defining affirmative action as a violation of equality rights seems premised on an increasingly insular understanding of who can be a citizen with access to rights defined primarily by normative White understandings of society. Promoting opportunity for non-Whites requires policy that creates bureaucratic walls to exclude the same ethnic categories the state is keen to exclude from the Republic. Similar ideological narratives are increasingly evident in the UK where Critical Race Theory and criticisms of British imperialism have been cited as subjects that should not be taught because they pose a threat to British values.

Key figures relating to student success, including retention rates, completion, and degree attainment indicate that students from all ethnic backgrounds have lower graduation rates at for-profit institutions when compared to public and private, non-profit institutions. Specifically, the graduation rate for Black students was 20% at for-profit institutions, 41% at public institutions, and 45% at private non-profit institutions amongst the first-degree, full-time cohort.

When considering degree completion across all students entering college, completion is lower amongst Black and Hispanic students compared to White and Asian. In the USA, nearly half of Asian students who enrol for college education complete a bachelor's degree within six years, compared to 36% of White students and only 17% of Black and Hispanic students (US Department of Education, 2019).

Employment outcomes

As in the UK, racial and ethnic inequalities continue in the labour market; individual earnings are correlated with college completion, race, and ethnicity, whilst an increased demand for skilled workers continues to disadvantage those without college degrees (US Department of Education, 2019). Such inequalities contribute to socio-economic disadvantages across different ethnic groups. Whilst higher education has been shown to influence social mobility in the USA (Warikoo, 2018), the unemployment rate for college graduates is 2.5%, which is approximately half of the national average. The USA (as in the UK) continues to show racial and ethnic disparities in higher education enrolment and attainment, as well as gaps in earnings and employment for communities of colour (Bureau of Labor Statistics, 2020).

Student demographics in Europe

Recent evidence suggests an increase in student numbers attending universities in Europe (European University Association [EUA], 2019). As a result, the student population has become more diverse resulting in students from different ethnic and socio-economic backgrounds attending European universities (Sursock, 2015). Similar to the widening participation agenda in the UK, many institutions have taken steps to find new ways to enable those from under-represented backgrounds to secure a place in higher education (EUA, 2019; European Commission, 2019).

In 2017, across the EU member states, there were 19.8 million students in tertiary education, of which 7.4% were following short-cycle tertiary courses, 61% were studying for bachelor's degrees, 27.7% for master's degrees, and 3.8% for doctoral degrees (Eurostat, 2019). Specifically, Germany, the most populous EU member state, had 3.1 million tertiary education students, the highest number in the EU and equivalent to 15.6% of the EU-28 total. In 2017, women accounted for 54% of all tertiary students in the EU-28, with close to three-fifths of all tertiary students in Sweden, Slovakia, Poland, and Estonia being women. Women were also a majority cohort across all other EU member states, with the exception of Greece (accounting for 48.6%) and Germany (accounting for 48.5%) (Eurostat, 2019).

Despite an increase in the diversity of students attending European universities, there is a lack of monitoring of student ethnicity. One of the key goals of the 2017 European Commission's Renewed European Union agenda for higher education has been a commitment to increasing social inclusion in education. However, despite this, many European countries are failing to consistently monitor the ethnic and socio-economic background of students (European Commission, 2019). The lack of such data is problematic when evaluating widening participation initiatives, as well as analysing attainment and student outcomes. However, recent evidence from the Bologna Process Implementation (European Commission, 2018) which aims to create more comparable and compatible education systems across Europe to support widening participation initiatives confirms that students from low socio-economic backgrounds and those from migrant communities are underrepresented in higher education in European universities.

Degree outcomes in Europe (similar to the UK and USA) suggest that students with higher levels of education are more likely to be in employment. Between 2013 and 2023, the highest employment rates were recorded for 20-to-34-year-olds who had graduated with a tertiary education, with lower employment rates recorded for those with an upper secondary or postsecondary non-tertiary education (Eurostat, 2024).

The global market

The changing composition of the student body both in the UK and internationally needs to be contextualised against the massification of the global higher education system. Since the late 1970s, academic life has seen significant changes as 'policies of marketisation' have become the norm across universities, more closely reflecting the managerial models of private corporations (Furedi, 2011). Those advocating marketisation legitimise this process by arguing that the increased availability of higher education has led to a more flexible and efficient system, offering better value for money and operating in response to the needs of society, including the economy and students (Barnett, 2011). Typical indicators of marketisation across the sector include institutional autonomy, institutional competition, and the provision of information to assist students, now viewed as consumers, to make their choice(s) within an educational market (Brown, 2011). This may include, but not be limited to, institutional rankings and other metrics used to aid consumer choice and an increase in dedicated resources by universities to develop marketing and branding to attract prospective students (Tomlinson, 2017a).

Globally, the USA is often viewed as being the most marketised system, with institutions having a high degree of autonomy and substantial competition amongst a range of institutions. As discussed by Brown, the system in the USA reflects 'a liberal entry regime and means that [...] students have a wide range of choices' (Brown, 2011, p. 17). Overall, in the USA, there is a vast private sector consisting of not-for-profit and for-profit universities and colleges.

The UK HE sector has also positioned itself in a similar way to the USA, with a considerable drive to attract students and to secure research funds across a range of autonomous institutions (Furedi, 2011). The introduction of tuition fees in 1998, following the Dearing Report (1997), was another step towards marketisation, with institutions' funding and financial security becoming increasingly dependent on student numbers (Meek, 2000). Similarly, Australia, Canada, and New Zealand find themselves with a significant degree of marketisation across their systems, including competition for research funding and securing fee-paying students (Connell, 2013).

Other European systems also indicate a significant degree of competition amongst providers. A driving factor for creating a more diverse market in Europe has been the European Union's aspiration to modernise higher education systems in order that they can make an effective contribution to the development of their societies and be able to compete with other prestigious higher education systems globally (Sporn, 2003). The development and implementation of the Bologna Process, the commitment to ensure comparability in the standards of higher education qualifications, has also contributed to the introduction of elements of marketisation across continental Europe (Brown, 2011). Elsewhere, however, including in Nordic countries the move towards a free market has been more limited, where institutions continue to align themselves with their public support for higher education institutions and students (Brown, 2011).

The marketisation of universities in the UK

The move towards the marketisation of universities in the UK can be linked back to changes in policy in the 1980s. Higher education in England, specifically, began to reflect the concept of the 'market' with the introduction of the 1988 Education Act, which saw the freeing of polytechnics and HE colleges from local authority control, enabling them to increase student recruitment for the first time (Bathmaker, 2003). The Act also outlined that rather than universities and colleges receiving unconditional public subsidies, instead they were to be regarded as 'suppliers of services under contract to the state and other purchasers' (Williams, 2016, p. 134). During the 1990s, the financial crisis across the sector resulted in debate over where the responsibility should lie for funding students' tuition fees. The establishment of the Dearing Committee and subsequent report (Dearing Report, 1997) concluded that students should make a direct contribution to the cost of their education, which was reflected in the introduction in 1998 by the Labour government of an initial tuition fee of £1k per year[1] (Shattock, 2012). In addition, maintenance grants were replaced by student loans to be repaid on a deferred basis when entering the employment market (Bolton, 2022). Despite opposition to fees from within the Labour Party during their second term in office they successfully passed the Higher Education Act 2004. This allowed universities to determine the level of fees they would charge students with an overall cap of £3000 per annum and also made provision for students to take a tuition loan to cover this new cost. When introduced in 2006, most universities charged the maximum amount of £3000 (Hubble & Bolton, 2018). As a concession to MPs who opposed these measures, then Business Secretary Peter Mandelson agreed there should be a review of the impact of these changes after three years. In 2009, Mandelson appointed the crossbench peer John Browne to lead the Independent Review of Higher Education Funding and Student Finance[2] (Gill, 2009).

The Browne report, 'Securing a sustainable future for higher education' (Gov.UK, 2010), represents a striking moment in which New Labour's pursuit of a marketised higher education economy emerges fully formed. Perhaps, ironically, this moment in the dying days of the third Labour government was not enacted by Labour but by the incoming Coalition government. Perhaps even more ironically the only political party who campaigned in the 2010 election to oppose the introduction of increasing fees on students, the Liberal Democrats, were themselves in government and forced to patch together a deal with the Conservative party to abstain from voting down its recommendations. Based on the Browne report the cap on student tuition fees was raised to £9000 (and again in 2017 to £9250). Minister for Universities and Science, David Willets, claimed that universities would only set their fees at the maximum amount in exceptional circumstances; however, as with the previous cap in 2006, nearly all universities immediately opted to charge the highest amount possible. The Browne report made the case for three key areas crucial to the future of higher education. Firstly, to increase participation including by students from lower income households, secondly to improve and preserve minimum standards of quality, and finally to ensure the sustainability of the sector by allowing it to grow to meet demand. These objectives are essentially framed as the goal of a competitive educational market; the report's concluding remarks note,

> Our proposals are designed to create genuine competition for students between institutions, of a kind which cannot take place under the current system. There will be more investment available for the institutions that are able to convince students that it is worthwhile. This is in our view a surer way to drive up quality than any attempt at central planning.
>
> *(Browne, 2009, p. 56)*

To do so, they recommended quality control of higher education to ensure minimum standards are maintained and that students are provided with more information about what universities can deliver. In respect of the latter requirement, the Teaching Excellence Framework (TEF) was introduced by the Office for Students in 2016 to provide a ranking system for universities in which their teaching is awarded gold, silver, or bronze awards. In effect fulfilling a perceived need for students who are consumers of education to identify the best and the worst quality of teaching available in the university marketplace. Significantly, the introduction of the TEF has not seen a market emerge in which tuition fees vary depending on the quality of the educational offering. This might suggest that the cap on tuition fees is currently set at too low a figure and that on the supply side universities are unable to pitch a rational economic offering to a market in which demand is high (e.g. the long-term value of a degree from both a bronze or a gold institution might be worth more than the current £9250 price, and therefore the cap acts to put a brake on competition). Alternatively, the TEF rankings may have far less of an effect on reputational status; an elite university receiving a silver or bronze award may feel a little dent to their ego, but the value of their degree in the real-world marketplace is unlikely to be diminished. This raises questions about what measures would be effective for students as consumers if the educational economy was opened to market forces. It is not too far-fetched to imagine the University of Oxford or the London School of Economics (LSE), for example, being able to charge greatly higher fees based on the cachet of their degrees. This would be a politically unpalatable approach not least because it would immediately price many consumers out of an 'elite' education. However, it is worth noting that both prior to the introduction of free-market logic and since, many elite universities maintain their reputation for excluding poorer students or students from ethnic minorities (Bhopal & Myers, 2023). It is not immediately clear that the marketisation of universities and the understanding of students as their consumers has radically impacted upon pre-existing inequalities.

When the cap on fees was raised to £9250 in 2017, it was widely assumed this would be an amount that would rise in the future reflecting inflationary economic drivers. However, this has not been the case. No doubt this reflects the unpopularity of high fees amongst the electorate, exacerbated in part by the growing numbers of students and their parents having to make financial contributions and/or incur significant debt. Raising fees has also been constrained by the extraordinary impact of Brexit, COVID-19, and inept political management of the economy, all of which have impacted families' economic security. Consequently, the level of fees that looked excessive in 2017 is now widely cited by vice chancellors as being too low to make it economically viable to educate undergraduates (Busby, 2023; Weale, 2023). This has partly been offset by the rise in postgraduate university offers and the ability of many universities, particularly those identifiably high in university rankings, to recruit wealthy international students willing to pay significantly higher fees (Bhopal & Myers, 2023).

The impact of policy-based and statutory changes during this period and the earlier shift towards a concept of customer-provider relationships in higher education between students and universities, changes both the day-to-day relationship between students and universities and also the public understanding of the purpose of a university education. Since the 1870s, education was traditionally understood as a 'public good', with the need for a skilled and highly educated population as a rational economic strategy to deliver practical benefits to the national economy. However, the marketisation of higher education as 'something which is privately funded, consumed and utilised for future economic return' (Tomlinson, 2017a, p. 4) increasingly situates its value as an individual's own accumulation of capital. In other words, the university degree becomes a 'private good' within an educational economy in which the student invests their economic capital to generate a future return. In this context, students become individual consumers of education, and a new economic relationship between the demand for specific educational outcomes (better employment prospects, for example) impacts on universities now positioned as commercial suppliers of these potential outcomes. The value of university degrees is no longer understood as a collective social benefit but simply as an individual asset. The move towards marketisation has often been couched as a means to remedy the discrepancy in costs and benefits of acquiring a degree. Prior to the introduction of student fees, the costs of students' being awarded degrees were imposed on society as a whole including the 50% of the population who do not go into higher education, do not benefit individually from its identifiable rewards but still have to pay their taxes. The validation of a narrative in which degrees equate to individual rather than collective value informed the wider political debate about who should pay for education. The UK was one of the first of the Organisation for Economic Cooperation and Development (OECD) countries to adopt such 'new public management policies' (Deem, 2001, p. 10), its pattern of marketisation has since been emulated across the globe.

The consequences of these fundamental changes to the system in the UK were both ideologically damning for those who had long considered higher education a public good, and long-lasting for the sector as competition has become the norm (Lynch, 2006; Nixon et al., 2018). The rapid expansion of student numbers and competition to attract high-fee paying students – for example, international students – in addition to universities being encouraged to compete for income generated through research meant that by the end of the noughties there 'could be little doubt that British universities were, to all intents and purposes, commercial institutions' (Williams, 2016, p. 135), responsible for meeting largely private interests (see also Rutherford, 2005). The Department for Business Innovation & Skills (2016), itself, identified that the sector has undergone a rapid and significant transformation over the last 30 years as higher education provision has come to include a more diverse range of providers. Nixon et al. (2018) discuss that in an era of academic capitalism, there is no sign of marketisation diminishing; especially with the uncapping of undergraduate student numbers in 2015 and the removal of the fee cap for 'high-rating' higher education institutions (such as Oxbridge and the Russell Group). These further changes reinforced the commitment of the current government to continue the marketisation of university education in the UK. Overall, the British system has changed to a 'knowledge-based service industry of medium and large enterprises with diverse missions, profiles and character' (Foskett, 2011, p. 25), forming a significant aspect of the economic profile of the UK, as well as a key contributor to the global service sector. Universities themselves have become part of a system in which they are 'measured' through a system of rankings. In this system, the marketization of universities means that parents can 'choose' the best university for their children, to ensure 'value for money'. Marginson states, 'The criteria used to determine each institution's position in the ranking system become meta-outputs that each institution must place on priority. In that manner, rankings begin to define what "quality" means and they shape its subsequent evolution' (2007, p. 97).

Following the Higher Education and Research Act (Gov.UK, 2017), the regulatory body, the Office for Students (OfS) was introduced in January 2018 to, 'ensure that every student, whatever their background, has a fulfilling experience of higher education that enriches their lives and careers' (OfS, 2018a). The OfS was charged with ensuring that regulatory frameworks which include 'sector recognised standards' are met for those attending higher education institutions in England. This includes 24 'conditions of registration' and 'key performance measures' that all higher education providers must meet. The OfS regulates providers to ensure that these conditions are met, and if they are not, they have a responsibility to intervene (OfS, 2018b). Other measures include the introduction of the Teaching Excellence and Student Outcomes Framework, which assesses excellence in teaching and student outcomes. Institutions are awarded a gold, silver, or bronze award based on an assessment of their teaching quality and student outcomes (OfS, 2018c). The OfS also monitors Access and Participation Plans for higher education institutions to ensure that they are addressing equality of opportunity for all students (OfS, 2018d).

Graduate transitions

Whilst the benefits for the British economy of having a marketised sector may be apparent, what does mass education and the marketisation of universities mean for our students and graduates? Alongside growing demand and promoting choice amongst prospective consumers, the student body itself as previously highlighted has diversified significantly at the same time (Foskett, 2010). As the system has expanded, there has been an increasing focus through government policy on demonstrating a strong commitment to inclusion and equity, seeking to increase diversity in social class, gender, ethnicity, and age profiles across the higher education sector. Specifically, a drive by the New Labour government to improve social mobility and a commitment to achieve a 50% participation rate in higher education (DfES, 2003) led to the 'widening participation' agenda to increase the numbers of young people from marginalised groups entering higher education. This has been consistently promoted by consecutive governments, with the Coalition and Conservative governments continuing to commit to 'widening participation'. This action, however, has typically been within a neo-liberal framework, conflating increased marketisation and student choice with the potential for addressing issues of inequity within universities (Brown, 2011; Connell, 2013; Marginson, 2016).

Despite the increases in numbers of students entering higher education, including those from minority groups, structural inequalities linked to social class and ethnicity in higher education continue to persist (Reay, 2018). Tomlinson (2017b) argues that the higher education system is ideologically driven by the notion that investment in education should result in tangible returns. This includes the potential for increased salaries securing better-rewarded employment in the labour market often characterised as *graduate careers*. However, as discussed, students from marginalised groups specifically those from BME communities continue to be disadvantaged both in their experiences and their educational outcomes (Bhopal, 2018), despite regulatory measures introduced by the OfS (2018a) and the introduction of equality initiatives such as the Race Equality Charter (AdvanceHE, n.d.). These same experiences and outcomes are then repeated upon transitioning into the labour market.

The assumptions that attending university will have a positive impact on life chances and social mobility can and should be challenged. We argue that too often outcomes depend on the type of student. White, middle-class students are likely to benefit from higher education to a greater extent when they enter the labour market than Black, Pakistani or Bangladeshi, Gypsy, Roma or Traveller students. This outcome suggests that going to university is not a means of generating upward social mobility for the most disadvantaged groups. Whilst the marketisation of universities may have resulted in greater choice and higher levels of access to higher education for underrepresented groups, higher education continues to be a system that reproduces disadvantage, ensures those from White, middle-class backgrounds succeed whilst those from BME groups fail.

Notes

1 This amount was calculated to be around 25% of the full cost of teaching. Fee waivers were available for students from low-income families.
2 Browne was joined by David Eastwood, vice chancellor of the University of Birmingham, Julia King, vice chancellor of Aston University, as well as Michael Barber, head of McKinsey's Global Education Practice, Diane Coyle of the Enlightenment Economics consultancy firm, Rajay Naik, board member of the Big Lottery Fund, and Peter Sands, chief executive of Standard Chartered bank.

References

Adams, R. (2019, March 29). Universities must do more for black students, warns watchdog. *The Guardian.* Retrieved September 18, 2024, from https://www.theguardian.com/education/2019/mar/29/english-universities-show-gaps-in-black-students-attainment-data-reveals?CMP=share_btn_url

AdvanceHE. (2020). *Equality + higher education: Students statistical report.* AdvanceHE.

AdvanceHE. (2023). *Equality + higher education: Students statistical report.* AdvanceHE.

AdvanceHE. (n.d.). *Race equality charter.* September 13, 2024, from https://www.advance-he.ac.uk/equality-charters/race-equality-charter accessed

Artess, J., McCulloch, A., & Mok, P. (2014). *Learning from futuretrack: Studying and living at home.* BIS Research Paper 167. Department for Business, Innovation and Skills.

Auboussier, J., Doytcheva, M., Seurrat, A., & Tatchim, N. (2023). Diversity in discourse: Contexts, forms and devices. *Words. The Languages of Politics, 131*(2023), 9–26.

Ball, S. J., Reay, D., & David, M. (2002). 'Ethnic choosing': Minority ethnic students, social class and higher education choice. *Race Ethnicity and Education, 5*(4), 333–357.

Barnett, R. (2011). The marketised university: Defending the indefensible. In M. Molesworth, M. Scullion, & R. Nixon (Eds.), *The marketisation of higher education and the student as consumer* (pp. 39–51). Taylor & Francis.

Bathmaker, A. (2003). The expansion of higher education: A consideration of control, funding and quality. In S. Bartlett & D. Burton (Eds.), *Education studies. Essential issues* (pp. 123–137). SAGE Publications.

Bhopal, K. (2010). *Asian women in higher education: Shared communities.* Trentham.

Bhopal, K. (2018). *White privilege: The myth of a post-racial society.* Policy Press.

Bhopal, K., & Myers, M. (2023). *Elite universities and the making of privilege: Exploring race and class in global education economies.* Routledge.

Bhopal, K., Myers, M., & Pitkin, C. (2020). Routes through higher education: BME students and the development of a 'specialisation of consciousness'. *British Educational Research Journal. 46*(6), 1321–1337. https://doi.org/10.1002/berj.3634

Bolton, P. (2012). *Education: Historical statistics SN/SG/4252.* House of Commons Library.

Bolton, P. (2022). *The value of student maintenance support.* House of Commons Library.

Bourdieu, P. (1977). *Outline of a theory of practice.* Cambridge University Press.

Briggs, A. R. J., Clark, J., & Hall, I. (2012). Building bridges: Understanding student transition to university. *Quality in Higher Education, 18*(1), 3–21.

Brown, R. (2011). The march of the market. In M. Molesworth, M. Scullion, & R. Nixon (Eds.), *The marketisation of higher education and the student as consumer* (pp. 11–24). Taylor & Francis.

Bureau of Labor Statistics, US Department of Labor. (2020). *The Economics Daily,* Rising educational attainment among Blacks or African Americans in the labor force, 1992 to 2018. https://www.bls.gov/opub/ted/2019/rising-educational-attainment-among-blacks-or-african-americans-in-the-labor-force-1992-to-2018.htm

Busby, E. (2023, November 14). Universities trapped in 'triangle of sadness', says vice-chancellor. *The Independent.* https://www.independent.co.uk/news/education/universities-russell-group-fees-ratings-b2447110.html

Chang, M. (2000). Improving campus racial dynamics: A balancing act among competing interests. *Review of Higher Education, 23,* 153–175.

Christie, H. (2007). Higher education and spatial (im)mobility: Nontraditional students and living at home. *Environment and Planning A, 39*(10), 2445–2463.

Connell, R. (2013). The neoliberal cascade and education: An essay on the market agenda and its consequences. *Critical Studies in Education, 54*(2), 99–112.

Dearing Report. (1997). *Higher education in the learning society.* HMSO.

Deem, R. (2001). Globalisation, new managerialism, academic capitalism and entrepreneurialism in universities. Is the local dimension still important? *Comparative Education, 37*(1), 7–20.

Department for Business Innovation & Skills. (2016). *Higher education: Success as a knowledge economy.* HMSO.

Department for Education and Science. (1965). *Circular 10/65 (1965): The organisation of secondary education.* Department for Education and Science.

Department for Education and Skills. (2003). *The future of higher education.* HMSO.

Donnelly, M., & Gamsu, S. (2018). *Home and away – Social, ethnic and spatial inequalities in student mobility.* The Sutton Trust.

Doytcheva, M. (2021). Diversity as immigration governmentality: Insights from France. *Social Sciences, 10*(7), 237.

European Commission. (2018). *Bologna Process and the European higher education area.* https://ec.europa.eu/education/policies/higher-education/bologna-process-and-european-higher-education-area_en

European Commission. (2019). *Social inclusion policies in higher education: Evidence from the EU Overview of major widening participation policies applied in the EU 28.* https://ris.utwente.nl/ws/portalfiles/portal/135881389/jrc_117257_social_inclusion_policies_in_higher_education_evidence_from_the_eu.pdf

European University Association. (2019). *Diversity, equity and inclusion in European diversity, equity and inclusion in European higher education institutions- Results from the INVITED project.* https://eua.eu/resources/publications/890:diversity,-equity-and-inclusion-in-european-higher-education-institutions-results-from-the-invited-project.html

Eurostat. (2019). *Tertiary education statistics.* https://ec.europa.eu/eurostat/statistics-explained/index.php?title=Tertiary_education_statistics

Eurostat. (2024). *83.5% of recent graduates employed in 2023.* https://ec.europa.eu/eurostat/web/products-eurostat-news/w/ddn-20240821-1 Retrieved 28 October 2024

Foskett, N. (2010). Global markets, national challenges, local strategies; The strategic challenge of internationalisation. In F. Maringe, & N. H. Foskett (Eds.), *Globalisation and internationalisation in higher education: Theoretical, strategic and management perspectives.* Continuum Press.

Foskett, N. (2011). Markets, government, funding and the marketisation of UK higher education. In M. Molesworth, M. Scullion, & R. Nixon (Eds.), *The marketisation of higher education and the student as consumer* (pp. 25–38). Taylor & Francis.

Furedi, F. (2011). Introduction to the marketisation of higher education and the student as consumer. In M. Molesworth, M. Scullion, & R. Nixon (Eds.), *The marketisation of higher education and the student as consumer* (pp. 1–8). Taylor & Francis.

Gibbons, S., & Vignoles, A. (2012). Geography, choice and participation in higher education in England. *Regional Science and Urban Economics, 42,* 98–113.

Gill, J. (2009, November 29). Lord Browne to lead fees review. *Times Higher Education*. Retrieved December 14, 2022, from https://www.timeshighereducation.com/news/lord-browne-to-lead-fees-review/409011.article

Gov.UK. (1992). Further and Higher Education Act. HMSO.

Gov.UK. (2010). *Securing a sustainable future for higher education: an independent review of higher education funding & student finance*. Retrieved September 20, 2024, from https://assets.publishing.service.gov.uk/media/5a7f289540f0b62305b856fc/bis-10-1208-securing-sustainable-higher-education-browne-report.pdf

Gov.UK. (2008). Education and Skills Act. The Stationery Office.

Gov.UK (2017). Higher Education and Research Act. HMSO.

Gov.UK. (2023). *Work and study after higher education*. Retrieved September 18, 2024, from https://www.ethnicity-facts-figures.service.gov.uk/education-skills-and-training/after-education/destinations-and-earnings-of-graduates-after-higher-education/latest/

Green, L., Laqua, D., & Brewis, G. (2020). Student funding and university access after the great war: The scheme for the higher education of ex-servicemen at Aberystwyth, Liverpool and Oxford. *British Journal of Educational Studies*, 68(5), 589–609.

Gurin, P., Dey, E., Hurtado, S., & Gurin, G. (2002). Diversity and higher education: Theory and impact on educational outcomes. *Harvard Educational Review*, 72, 330–366.

Higher Education Statistics Agency (HESA). (2023a). *Table 27 - UK domiciled first year students by ethnicity and higher education provider tariff grouping 2014/15 to 2021/22*. Retrieved September 18, 2024, from https://www.hesa.ac.uk/data-and-analysis/students/table-27

Higher Education Statistics Agency (HESA). (2023b). *Graduate Outcomes 2021/22: Summary Statistics - Graduate activities and characteristics*. Retrieved September 18, 2024, from https://www.hesa.ac.uk/news/13-06-2024/sb268-higher-education-graduate-outcomes-statistics/activities

Higher Education Statistics Agency (HESA). (2024). *Higher Education Student Statistics: UK, 2022/23*.Retrieved September 18, 2024, from https://www.hesa.ac.uk/news/08-08-2024/sb269-higher-education-student-statistics

Holton, M., & Finn, K. (2018). Being-in-motion: The everyday (gendered and classed) embodied mobilities for UK university students who commute. *Mobilities*, 13(3), 426–440.

Hordósy, R. (2023). 'I've changed in every possible way someone could change'– transformative university transitions. *Research Papers in Education*, 38(2), 187–207.

Hubble, S., & Bolton, P. (2018). *Higher education tuition fees in England* (Briefing Paper 8151). House of Commons Library.

Hurtado, S. (2005). The next generation of diversity and intergroup relations research. *Journal of Social Issues*, 61(3), 595–610.

Khambhaita, P., & Bhopal, K. (2013). Home or away? The significance of ethnicity, class and attainment in the housing choices of female university students. *Race, Ethnicity and Education*, 18(4), 535–566.

Kober, N. (2020). *History and evolution of public education in the US*. Centre on Education Policy.

Lieberman, R. (2005). *Shaping race policy: The United States in comparative perspective*. Princeton University Press.

Lowery, B., Unzueta, M. M., Knowles, E. D., & Atiba Goff, P. (2006). Concern for the in group and opposition to affirmative action. *Journal of Personality and Social Psychology*, 90(6), 961–974.

Lynch, K. (2006). Neo-liberalism and marketisation: The implications for higher education. *European Journal of Educational Research*. 5(1), 1–17. https://journals.sagepub.com/doi/10.2304/eerj.2006.5.1.1

Maguire, D., & Morris, D. (2018). *Homeward bound: Defining, understanding and aiding 'commuter students'*. Higher Education Policy Institute.

Marginson, S. (2007). Global university rankings. In S. Marginson (Ed.), *Prospects of higher education: Globalisation, market competition, public goods and the future of the university* (pp. 79–100). Sense Publishers.

Marginson, S. (2016). High participation systems of higher education. *The Journal of Higher Education, 87*(2), 243–271.

Mclaughlin, T. (2000). Citizenship education in England: The Crick report and beyond. *Journal of Philosophy in Education, 34*(4), 541–570.

Meek, V. (2000). Diversity and marketisation of higher education: Incompatible concepts. *Higher Education Policy, 13*, 23–39.

Myers, M. (2022). Racism, zero-hours contracts and complicity in higher education. *British Journal of Sociology of Education, 43*(4), 584–602.

NAO. (2002). *Widening participation in higher education in England*. The Stationery Office.

National Center for Education Statistics. (2020). *Status and trends in the education of racial and ethnic groups*. Retrieved September 19, 2024, from https://nces.ed.gov/programs/raceindicators/index.asp

National Union of Students. (2015). *Reaching home: Policy and practice for students living in the parental home*. NUS UK.

Neves, J., & Hillman, N. (2018). *Student academic experience survey*. AdvanceHE/HEPI.

Nixon, E., Scullion, R., & Hearn, R. (2018). Her majesty the student: Marketised higher education and the narcissistic (dis)satisfactions of the student consumer. *Studies in Higher Education, 43*(6), 927–943.

Office for Students. (2018a). *Our strategy*. https://www.officeforstudents.org.uk/about/our-strategy/

Office for Students. (2018b). *How we measure success*. https://www.officeforstudents.org.uk/about/our-strategy/how-we-measure-success/

Office for Students. (2018c). *About the Teaching Excellence Framework (TEF)*. https://www.officeforstudents.org.uk/advice-and-guidance/teaching/about-the-tef/

Office for Students. (2018d). *Access and participation plans*. https://www.officeforstudents.org.uk/advice-and-guidance/promoting-equal-opportunities/access-and-participation-plans/

Pokorny, H., Holley, D., & Kane, S. (2016). Commuting, transitions and belonging: The experiences of students living at home in their first year at university. *Higher Education, 74*, 1–16.

Reardon, S., Baker, R., & Klasik, K. (2012). *Race, income and enrolment patterns in highly selective colleges 1984–2004*. University of Virginia Tech. http://hdl.handle.net/10919/92633

Reay, D. (2018). *Miseducation*. Policy.

Rutherford, J. (2005). Cultural studies in the corporate University. *Cultural Studies, 19*(3), 297–317.

Shattock, M. (2012). *Making policy in British higher education 1945–2011*. Open University Press.

Southall, J., Wason, H., & Avery, B. (2016). Non-traditional, commuter students and their transition to higher education – a synthesis of recent literature to enhance understanding of their needs. *Student Engagement and Experience Journal, 5*(1), 1–15.

Sporn, B. (2003). Management in higher education: Current trends and future perspectives in European colleges and universities. In R. Begg (Ed.), *The dialogue between higher education research and practice* (pp. 97–108). Kluwer Academic Publishers.

Supreme Court of the United States. (2023). *Students for Fair Admissions, Inc. v. President and Fellows of Harvard College*. Retrieved September 19, 2024, from https://www.supremecourt.gov/opinions/22pdf/20-1199_hgdj.pdf

Sursock, A. (2015). *Trends 2015: Learning and teaching in European universities*. European University Association.

Thomas, L. (2023). Being a student or becoming a graduate? Contemporary student experiences through the lens of 'commuters'. In C. Baik & E. R. Kahu (Eds.), *Research handbook on the student experience in higher education* (pp. 466–481). Edward Elgar Publishing.

Thomas, L., & Jones, R. (2017). *Student engagement in the context of commuter students*. The Student Engagement Partnership.

Tomlinson, M. (2017a). Introduction: Graduate employability in context: Charting a complex, contested and multi-faceted policy and research field. In M. Tomlinson, & L. Holmes (Eds.), *Graduate employability in context* (pp. 1–40). Palgrave Macmillan.

Tomlinson, M. (2017b). Student perceptions of themselves as 'consumers' of higher education. *British Journal of Sociology of Education*, *38*(4), 450–467.

UN. (1989). *The United Nations convention on the rights of the child*. Retrieved December 14, 2022, from https://www.ohchr.org/en/instruments-mechanisms/instruments/convention-rights-child

UK Parliament. (1870). Elementary Education Act The Stationery Office.

UK Parliament. (1902). *The Education Act*. The Stationery Office.

UK Parliament. (2021). *The forgotten: How White working-class pupils have been let down, and how to change it*. Retrieved September 18, 2024, from https://publications.parliament.uk/pa/cm5802/cmselect/cmeduc/85/8502.htm

Universities UK. (2019). *Black, Asian and minority ethnic student attainment at university: #Closing the Gap*. Universities UK\National Union of Students.

US Department of Education. (2019). *Status and trends in the education of racial and ethnic groups 2018*. Retrieved September 19, 2024, from https://nces.ed.gov/pubsearch/pubsinfo.asp?pubid=2019038

Walton, G., & Cohen, G. (2011). A brief social-belonging intervention improves academic and health outcomes of minority Students. *Science*, *331*, 6023.

Warikoo, N. (2018). *The diversity bargain: And other dilemmas of race, admissions and meritocracy at elite universities*. University of Chicago Press.

Weale, S. (2023, May 31). Funding model for UK higher education is 'broken', say university VCs. *The Guardian*. https://www.theguardian.com/education/2023/may/31/funding-model-for-uk-higher-education-is-broken-say-university-vcs

Westphal, J., & Ilieva, J. (2022). *Global demand for UK postgraduate degrees*. UUK.

Williams, G. (2016). Higher education: Public good or private commodity? *London Review of Education*, *14*(1), 131–142.

Woodfield, R. (2014). *Undergraduate retention and attainment across the disciplines*. Higher Education Academy.

3

RACIAL INEQUALITIES IN HIGHER EDUCATION

As discussed in the previous chapter there have been year-on-year increases in the numbers of UK-domiciled Black and minority ethnic (BME) students attending university since the 1990s reflecting broadly consistent cross-party support for a policy designed to increase student numbers (AdvanceHE, 2020; HEFCE, 2017). Throughout this same period, a range of inequalities related to race have been evident in the HE sector including students experiencing racism from peers and academics (Fazackerley, 2020), BME students being less likely to attend the more prestigious, selective universities (Bhopal & Myers, 2023), high dropout rates for Black students (Universities UK and the National Union of Students [UUK/ NUS], 2019), an ethnocentric curriculum (Atkinson et al., 2018), and a persistent attainment gap in the outcomes for all BME groups compared to their White peers. One direct consequence of these factors is that BME students entering the employment market often do so with a lesser degree obtained from a less prestigious university and this results in them securing less-rewarding jobs. The Office for Students found that only 52% of HE providers have one or more outcomes targets specifically aimed at BME students (2018, p. 9). The total amount of targets is 154, and of these, only 19 explore additional student criteria; 8% focus on progression, and just over a third focus on the BME achievement gap. The same report found only 30% of providers planned to introduce targeted measures to address the inequalities experienced by BME students. These patterns of racist outcomes have happened against a backdrop of changing equalities policy in the UK which to a large extent has identified the need to address racial inequality.

DOI: 10.4324/9781003097211-3

Race, racism, and UK policy

The most significant moment in UK policy making in respect of race and racism was the publication of *The Stephen Lawrence Inquiry* report (Macpherson, 1999) commonly referred to as the *Macpherson Report*. The inquiry investigated and published evidence of the London Metropolitan Police's flawed investigation of the murder of Stephen Lawrence due to institutional racism within the police. The unprovoked murder of Stephen Lawrence, a Black teenager by a White racist gang in southeast London in 1993, was a particularly brutal example of racist violence. Despite the police securing evidence of the murderers' identities, they were not successfully prosecuted. In a surprising move, the Daily Mail published the names and photographs of five members of the gang on their front page against the headline 'MURDERERS. The Mail accuses these men of killing. If we are wrong, let them sue us' (Daily Mail, 14 February 1997). Growing public outrage eventually led to the commissioning of the inquiry into Stephen Lawrence's death. Gillborn (2008) identifies three key elements of the report's findings that highlight a marked shift in understandings of how racism should be understood and addressed by policymakers in its findings. Firstly, it defines racism in terms that resonate with anti-racists by focussing on racist outcomes rather than attempting to identify racist intent behind the actions that led to those outcomes. Consequently, the report condemns the racism of both individuals and organisations and provides the argument for defining 'institutional racism' as,

> The collective failure of an organisation to provide an appropriate and professional service to people because of their colour, culture, or ethnic origin. It can be seen or detected in processes, attitudes and behaviour which amount to discrimination through unwitting prejudice, ignorance, thoughtlessness and racist stereotyping which disadvantage minority ethnic people.
>
> *(Macpherson, 1999, 6.34)*

By doing so, it moved beyond earlier explanations of racism, such as those presented in the *Scarman Report*'s inquiry into policing of the 1981 Brixton riots (Scarman, 1981) that identified racism as the work of individuals, typically identified as *a few bad apples* within an organisation. Secondly, Gillborn identifies a shift in whose perception of racism counts, in essence, it is not the police or any other institution's role to define whether a racist incident has occurred, instead the report recommends adopting the following definition,

> A racist incident is any incident which is perceived to be racist by the victim or any other person.
>
> *(Macpherson, 1999, 45.17)*

Finally, Gillborn notes that the report recommends that its recommendations should apply beyond just the Metropolitan Police Service to all government organisations and in particular within education. The emphasis on education included specific recommendations including a requirement for all schools to keep a record of racist incidents. The vast majority of the recommendations made by Macpherson were implemented and its overarching findings informed equalities policy at the time. Its recommendations underpinned the changes made in the Race Relations (Amendment) Act 2000 (Gov. UK, 2000) and later included within the Equality Act (Gov.UK, 2010).

Drawing on the Macpherson findings that all public bodies should be responsible for addressing and combating racism (EHRC, 2019), the Race Relations (Amendment) Act (2000) placed a statutory duty on public bodies (including schools, colleges, and higher education institutions) to work towards the elimination of unlawful racial discrimination and promote equality of opportunity and positive race relations. The Race Relations (Amendment) Act (2000) was replaced by the 2010 Equality Act. This act of parliament was passed in the last weeks of the New Labour government, bringing together and superseding a wide range of equalities legislation, including the Race Relations Act. It included anti-discrimination legislation for 'race' amongst a number of other 'protected characteristics' including disability, age, sex, sexual orientation, and religious beliefs. The act also included, and to some extent, its over-arching ethos seemed premised upon including socio-economic inequalities; however, this one element was not brought into force. The Equality Act makes specific reference to its application to education including higher education and highlights universities should not discriminate against any protected characteristics in respect of enrolment and participation.

Despite its lineage in policy drawing upon Macpherson's definitions of racism there have been some significant criticisms of the enactment of the Equality Act in relation to addressing racism in higher education. Pilkington (2011, 2013) has argued that by bringing together a wide range of issues within a single piece of legislation this has diminished the significance of race and racism within university equality and diversity practice. 'Race' is effectively in competition with other protected characteristics such as gender or disability which may be regarded as more significant and therefore take priority within a 'hierarchy of oppression' (Bhopal, 2023, p. 326) or maybe assumed to have been dealt with because a university is seen to be engaging in a generic programme of equality and diversity measures. The implementation of the Equality Act within universities has also been identified as often overly bureaucratic and framed by institutions as primarily an auditing process (Lewis et al., 2012). By doing so, it becomes a *tick-box exercise* ensuring the university can produce evidence of addressing racism rather than actually working to address racism.

In August 2016, the Conservative Prime Minister, Theresa May commissioned a Race Disparity Audit (Cabinet Office, 2017) that would,

> look into racial disparities in our public services that stretches right across government. It will highlight the differences in outcomes for people of different backgrounds, in every area from health to education, childcare to welfare, employment, skills and criminal justice.
>
> *(May, 2017)*

This audit seemingly built on the comments made by Theresa May during her first speech as prime minister outside Downing Street when she acknowledged there was a need to address racial inequalities in order that all British citizens could benefit from the equal opportunities. The initial findings of the audit were slightly reticent when discussing universities (Cabinet Office, 2017) focussing on a narrow cut of their data indicating that Indian and Chinese children were more likely than White children to go to university. However, the audit continued to collate and publish data, and in doing so confirmed much pre-existing research of the existence of racial inequalities in higher education. In 2019, the Department for Education announced,

> Universities will now be held to account on how they will improve outcomes for underrepresented students, including those from ethnic minority backgrounds, through powers of the Office for Students, who will scrutinise institutions' Access and Participation plans. All universities will now have to publish data on admissions and attainment, broken down by ethnicity, gender and socio-economic background, to shine a spotlight on those making good progress and those lagging behind.
>
> *(Department for Education [DoE], 2019)*

Significant concerns about the work of the Race Disparity Audit have been raised in relation to the audit data being conceptualised within Feagin's *White racial frame* (2013), with the language used when implementing policy based on the audit erasing racism as a cause of racial inequalities,

> In so doing, the RDA acts to de-legitimise and conceal anti-racism as part of the solution, thereby preventing the naming of actions which would be transformative. It is not difficult therefore to imagine the true aim of the RDA, in variance with its purported aim of enacting change, is to *appear* active whilst effectively obfuscating the real issues (racism as the cause of inequities) thereby also effectively circumventing actions which would bring about real change to the race disparities revealed by the statistics (anti-racism).
>
> *(Smith, 2023)*

As becomes increasingly obvious, successive policies to address race and racism have often appeared to retrench back from the anti-racism at the heart of the Macpherson report. This became most apparent when Boris Johnson became prime minister and announced in July 2020 the introduction of a new *Commission on Race and Ethnic Disparities* (CRED),

> This cross-government Commission will examine inequality in the UK, across the whole population. The Commission will be inclusive, undertaking research and inviting submissions where necessary. It will set a positive agenda for change.
>
> *(PM's Office, 2020)*

From the outset, serious questions were raised about CRED's remit, which seemed explicitly positioned to dispel evidence of institutional racism. The commission itself was established and members were recruited by a long-standing advisor to Johnson and head of the policy unit at 10 Downing Street, Munira Mirza. Mirza has in the past refused to accept the existence of institutional racism and has claimed inquiries into racial inequalities have fostered a 'culture of grievance' (Gedalof, 2023; Walker et al., 2020). This mirrored comments made by the prime minister that CRED would *change the narrative* of how racial inequalities should be understood in the UK away from a *sense of victimisation*. Mirza appointed Tony Sewell as chair of the Commission, a former journalist, teacher, and academic. Previously, Sewell contributed to a special issue of *Prospect* magazine edited by Mirza that discussed the 'failings of multiculturalist policies' in the UK arguing that, 'Race is no longer the significant disadvantage it is often portrayed to be' (Mirza, 2010). Tony Sewell's contribution to the issue argued poor educational outcomes for Black boys were not a consequence of 'institutional racism' but rather, 'They have failed their GCSEs because they did not do the homework, did not pay attention and were disrespectful to their teachers' (Sewell, 2010).

Amongst others, the Muslim Council of Great Britain argued that Sewell was not well-placed to lead the Commission because he was 'keen on downplaying race disparities' (BBC, 2020). When the report was published in 2021 it found no evidence of institutional racism raising serious doubts about the Conservative government commitments to tackle racism in society (CRED, 2021; Runnymede Trust, 2021). Instead, it identified racism in terms of individual acts of racial prejudice characterised as abhorrent but not systematic or a true reflection of British society. It represented a marked return to the discredited, pre-Macpherson accounts of racism that 'reproduced a colour-blind racial grammar', one that in 2024 was, 'a postracial artefact: a depiction of an "open" Britain in which problems of race and racism had largely evaporated' (Warmington, 2024, p. 76). The report itself became increasingly discredited upon publication, not least because many of the people quoted as giving evidence to the commission expressed concern that their views were misrepresented and, in some cases, claimed they were not aware they were contributing to the review.

(White unequal) Inclusive policy making in higher education

Despite significant quantitative and qualitative evidence documenting the BME attainment gap and the persistent inequalities experienced by BME students there has been little change in the sector in advancing race equality. One development has been the introduction of the Race Equality Charter (REC) in 2014 to address racial inequalities for staff and students in higher education. Modelled on the Athena Swann Initiative but focussing on race rather than gender inequalities to improve the representation, progression, and success of BME staff and students in HE (see AdvanceHE, n.d.; Bhopal & Jackson, 2013). Unlike the mandatory legislative requirements of the Equality Act (Gov.UK, 2010), the REC is a voluntary programme that relies upon vice chancellors and university senior managers choosing to invest in the initiative.

Critics of the REC have argued that whilst it addresses inequalities in higher education, it still works to perpetuate White hegemonic structures and 'exists within a framework of White privilege and a normative culture of Whiteness, which does not specifically address structural frameworks which disadvantage BME groups' (Bhopal & Pitkin, 2020, p. 13). In some respects, the REC is a bureaucratic enterprise through which institutions are required to demonstrate evidence they have audited practice rather than evidence successful outcomes. In effect, an archetypal tick-box exercise. Bhopal and Pitkin (2020) argue that diversity policies such as the REC are a response to the global marketization of higher education in which 'badges' such as the REC mark are used as signs to display inclusion and diversity to attract students, despite higher education institutions failing to address issues such as the BME attainment gap or lack of BME staff in senior decision-making roles in their own institutions.

Policy making such as the REC works to reinforce White supremacy for the interest of White groups (Bhopal & Pitkin, 2018; Decuir & Dixson, 2004; Garcia & Guerra, 2004; Hu-DeHart, 2003; Iverson, 2007) through the '*enactment* of policy', and securing a badge from the REC becomes a performative institutional practice and 'a ritual part of organisational interests; rather than addressing entrenched racial inequalities' (Bhopal & Pitkin, 2020, p. 14, original emphasis, see also Picower, 2009). Consequently, such policies reproduce existing racial inequalities rather than challenging the institutional and structural racism that continues to disadvantage BME staff and students in higher education institutions (Bhopal, 2018; Kalev et al., 2006).

Critics of inclusive policy making argue that policy intended to address racial inequalities works from the premise that Whiteness and White privilege are the norm (Delgado, 1995; Ladson-Billings & Tate, 1995) and such policy making actually addresses the perception of racism rather than the actual racism experienced by people of colour (Myers, 2018; Myers & Bhopal, 2017). Scholars in the UK have argued that policy making aimed to address racial inequalities is used instead to 'display' a picture of inclusion and further marginalise people of colour without addressing racial inequalities (Bhopal, 2020; Gillborn, 2006, 2008; Preston, 2018; Warmington, 2012, 2024). Gillborn goes even further to argue that, '...education is an act of White supremacy... policy assumes and defends White supremacy through the priorities it sets, the beneficiaries it privileges and the outcomes that it produces' (2008, p. 63). He argues that policy making aimed to address racial inequalities but fails to do so is a deliberate act of racism, 'shaped by long established cultural, economic and historical structures of racial domination, the continued promotion of policies and practices that are known to be racially divisive testifies to a *tacit intentionality* in the system' (Gillborn, 2008, p. 65, our emphasis). Critical Race Theory also suggests that White groups only support and tolerate advances of equality for people of colour if their own positions are not threatened and if they benefit to a greater extent from such advances (Guy-Sheftall, 1993; Ladson-Billings, 2009). Derrick Bell characterised White groups support for such social change, and accrual of benefits from them, as *Interest Convergence* (Bell, 1980).

Considering the arc of policy from the Macpherson Report to the publication of the CRED report there is a very clear sense of anti-racist gains being persistently eroded. Warmington (2024) describes the Macpherson report as a 'contradiction-closing case', in its current policy context it is used as the evidence that inequality has been addressed and that calls for further change are unwarranted. Warmington argues that 'contradiction-closing cases' play a key function in interest convergence; they 'exist in a space between interest convergence and interest divergence. They are enacted in instances where interest convergence exists: we have addressed the issue; let's move on' (2024, p. 91). The gains that were made through Macpherson were the consequence of an extraordinary moment when White politicians understood they had to do something dramatic to address the outrage of racist killers being allowed to freely walk the streets by a racist police force. In the retrenchment of White interests, such as publication of the CRED report, the Macpherson report itself is cited as evidence for the claim that the UK is a post-racial society. Within universities the same retrenchment occurs as policy initiatives addressing racial inequalities are reinvented as the means to audit equality practice rather than deliver on its aims. These are systemic, structural processes by which explicit evidence of racism, such as attainment gaps, never needs to be remedied. The narrative of action taking place to address racism invariably given prominence over the evidence that these actions are failing.

Ways forward?

Universities UK and the National Union of Students jointly suggested that significant change is needed in the higher education sector to address the inequalities that BME students face on a daily basis (UUK/NUS, 2019). Whilst there is a body of evidence to show that the persistence of racial inequalities continues year on year, there is little indication from higher education institutions of how they intend addressing such inequalities (see Bhopal, 2018). UUK/NUS (2019) argue that change is needed in five areas including by providing strong leadership; having open conversations about race and culture; creating and developing racially diverse, inclusive environments for students and staff; providing and analysing evidence; and exploring what works to make significant changes in the sector. The failure of higher education institutions to tackle these inequalities indicates they stem from structural and institutional racism embedded within higher education. Too often universities approach equality and diversity work from a 'deficit model' which assumes the individual student is to blame for his/her achievements, rather than examining and interrogating the systems that are designed to set BME students up for failure (Bhopal, 2018; Hopkins, 2011; Richardson, 2008, 2015; Smith, 2017; Woolf et al., 2008). In some respects, this is a consequence of the myth of meritocracy in action; university reputations are premised on their adherence to meritocratic principles, in which, if admissions or academic outcomes were skewed by a students' race, class, or gender, it runs counter to the basic principles of university education. A critical race theory perspective would of course identify the obvious evidence that universities do skew their admissions and degree outcomes based on ethnicity. For universities to redress racial inequalities therefore becomes deeply problematic because it involves acknowledging they are institutionally racist. Addressing a 'deficit' in students is another way of avoiding addressing the structural disadvantages of universities themselves. This promotes the meritocratic narrative of individual students taking responsibility for their own success or failure whilst ignoring evidence that BME students are systematically disadvantaged.

Other issues that need to be addressed in higher education include the failure amongst many academic staff to recognise factors which affect BME students in higher education. These include a lack of awareness amongst academics that a BME attainment gap is a consistent feature of all UK university outcomes and consequently indicates a lack of recognition of the actions needed to address the issue (HEA, 2012). A lack of BME role models in higher education has also been identified including the low number of BME academics in senior positions. This reinforces the notion that higher education is a White space reserved for Whites only. It has an adverse effect on the experiences of BME students in which they are less likely to feel a sense of belonging (Bhopal, 2016, 2018; Thomas, 2012; UUK/NUS, 2019).

There is evidence to suggest that some BME students have limited access to information, advice, and guidance when applying for universities, with some lacking the cultural capital to navigate the application process and the selection of different types of universities (Bhopal, 2018; Field & Morgan-Klein, 2012). Research has found that many BME parents, particularly those of first-generation students, are unaware of the processes involved in applying for university and for high-tariff universities (such as Oxbridge) which stipulate different admissions criteria, deadlines, and application procedures to the standard Universities and Colleges Admissions Service (UCAS) model (Bhopal et al., 2020; Bhopal & Myers, 2023). This is one of the reasons BME students are more likely to study locally and choose post-1992 rather than higher tariff universities (Bhopal, 2018; Neves & Hillman, 2019).

Decolonising the curriculum?

In addition to racism and Whiteness working to exclude BME students at all levels of their educational experiences through policies and practice, it is also perpetuated through the curriculum (Mahmud & Gagnon, 2020; Tate & Bagguley, 2017; Tate & Page, 2018).

BME students often describe the higher education curriculum as being designed to be exclusive rather than inclusive by taking a Eurocentric perspective (Bhopal, 2018; Mahmud & Gagnon, 2020; NUS, 2015) leading to calls to *decolonise the curriculum*. Whilst decolonising the curriculum is often understood by universities as a relatively simplistic task in which the names of non-white authors are appended to reading lists; more radical voices, particularly from the Global South, have identified the need to go further and dismantle colonial perspectives and the holistic racist structures underpinning universities (Heleta, 2016; Le Grange, 2016; Luckett & Shay, 2017; Pillay, 2018).

In the UK, the recognition of the predominance of a Eurocentric curriculum in higher education has led to attempts to decolonise the curriculum (Andrews, 2020; Stevenson, 2012). Much of this work has focussed on developing reading lists which historically have been skewed towards White scholars and Western perspectives to the exclusion of voices from the Global South (Altbach, 2016; Connell, 2018; Romero, 2017; Tickner, 2013). By including more diverse and marginalised voices, students receive a broad range of perspectives in their teaching and learning experiences whilst at university, which challenges colonialism and imperialism (Le Grange, 2016; Phillips & Archer-Lean, 2018). An inclusive curriculum can also help to ensure that the voices, histories, and experiences of marginalised groups are represented (Wolff, 2016) and the experiences of scholars of colour are acknowledged and included (Bhambra et al., 2018; Connell, 2018). Bird and Pitman (2019) argue that universities must be transparent and have informed discussions on how to approach decolonising the curriculum, what it means, and how reading lists can be used to reflect this

(Whitsed & Green, 2016). Beyond the reading list, other more radical movements often led by students have emerged including 'Why is my curriculum White'? (NUS, n.d.), 'Why isn't my professor Black?' (UCL, 2018), #Liberate-MyDegree (NUS, 2015), 'I too am Oxford' (Henriques & Abushouk, 2018).

Conclusions

Many higher education institutions lack a clear understanding of how to support BME students. They often fail to acknowledge the existence of racism as a systemic feature of higher education; practice designed to address racial inequality often perpetuates deficit models and racist stereotypes; there is little understanding of how to introduce targeted measures to address the inequalities; the curriculum remains largely Eurocentric; BME students are rarely involved in the implementation of interventions; and many universities do not have effective policies in place to deal with implicit bias racism or effectively deal with complaints about racism. On the one hand, all of this is well-known and reflects the consistent findings of many researchers working in the field and acknowledged in policy focussed on implementing change. On the other hand, however, it can often feel as though within universities these issues are less readily acknowledged. In part, this reflects the function of policy, both national policy and policy implemented by universities themselves. At the national level, equality policy can be understood to produce an illusion of the UK as a post-racial society. In universities, equality policy produces an illusion that change is always happening. In reality, systematic racism persists in society generally and in the experiences and outcomes of students studying at university. In the next chapter, we explore how the students in our research experienced these same issues.

References

AdvanceHE. (2020). *Equality + students statistical report 2020*. AdvanceHE.

AdvanceHE. (n.d.). *Race equality charter.* https://www.advance-he.ac.uk/equality-charters/race-equality-charter#:~:text=Advance%20HE's%20Race%20Equality%20Charter,Minority%20Ethnic%20staff%20and%20students

Altbach, P. G. (2016). *Global perspectives on higher education*. Springer.

Andrews, K. (2020). Blackness, empire and migration: How black studies transforms the curriculum. *Area, 52*(4), 701–707.

Atkinson, H., Bardgett, S., Budd, A., Finn, M., Kissane, C., Quershi, S., Saha, J., Siblon, J., & Sivasundaram, S. (2018). *Race, ethnicity and equality in UK history: A report and resource for change*. Royal Historical Society.

BBC. (2020, July 16). *Charity boss Tony Sewell to head government race commission.* https://www.bbc.co.uk/news/uk-politics-53428248

Bell, D. (1980). Brown v Board of Education and the Interest Convergence Dilemma. *Harvard Law Review, 93*(3), 518–533.

Bhambra, G. K., Gebrial, D., & Nişancıoğlu, K. (2018). Introduction: Decolonising the university? In G. K. Bhambra, D. Gebrial, & K. Nişancıoğlu (Eds.), *Decolonising the university* (pp. 1–18). Pluto Press.

Bhopal, K. (2016). *The experiences of black and minority ethnic academics: A comparative study of the unequal academy.* Routledge.

Bhopal, K. (2018). *White privilege: The myth of a post-racial society.* Policy Press.

Bhopal, K. (2020). Confronting white privilege: The importance of intersectionality in the sociology of education. *British Journal of Sociology of Education, 41*(6), 807–816.

Bhopal, K. (2023). 'We can talk the talk, but we're not allowed to walk the walk': The role of equality and diversity staff in higher education institutions in England. *Higher Education, 85*(2), 325–339.

Bhopal, K., & Jackson, J. (2013). *The experiences of BME academics in higher education* (EPSRC Research Report). University of Southampton.

Bhopal, K., & Myers, M. (2023). *Elite universities and the making of privilege: Exploring race and class in global educational economies.* Routledge.

Bhopal, K., Myers, M., & Pitkin, C. (2020). Routes through higher education: BME students and the development of a 'specialisation of consciousness'. *British Educational Research Journal, 16*(6), 1321–1327. https://doi.org/10.1002/berj.3634

Bhopal, K., & Pitkin, C. (2018). *Investigating higher education Institutions and their views on the race equality charter.* UCU.

Bhopal, K., & Pitkin, C. (2020). 'Same old story, just a different policy': Race and policy making in higher education in the UK. *Race, Ethnicity and Education, 23*(4), 530–547. https://www.tandfonline.com/doi/full/10.1080/13613324.2020.1718082

Bird, K., & Pitman, S. (2019). How diverse is your reading list? Exploring issues of representation and decolonisation in the UK. *Higher Education, 79*, 903–920.

Cabinet Office. (2017). *Race disparity audit.* HMSO.

CRED. (2021). *Commission on racial and ethnic disparities: The report.* HMSO.

Connell, R. (2018). Decolonizing sociology. *Contemporary Sociology: A Journal of Reviews, 47*(4), 399–401.

Daily Mail. (1997, February 14). MURDERERS. The Mail accuses these men of killing. If we are wrong, let them sue us. P1.

Decuir, J., & Dixson, A. (2004). So when it comes out, they Aren't that surprised that it's There': Using critical race theory as a tool of analysis for race and racism in education. *Educational Researcher, 33*(5), 26–31.

Delgado, R. (1995). *Critical race theory: The cutting edge.* Temple University Press.

Department for Education. (2019). *Universities must do more to tackle ethnic disparity.* https://www.gov.uk/government/news/universities-must-do-more-to-tackle-ethnic-disparity

Gov.UK. (2010). Equality Act 2010. HMSO.

Equality and Human Rights Commission (EHRC). (2016). *Healing a divided Britain: The need for a comprehensive race equality strategy.* EHRC.

Equality and Human Rights Commission (EHRC). (2019). *Tackling racial harassment: Universities challenged.* EHRC.

Fazackerley, A. (2020, July 7). It's not banter, it's racism: UK students accuse universities of brushing complaints aside. *The Guardian.* https://www.theguardian.com/education/2020/jul/07/its-not-banter-its-racism-uk-students-accuse-universities-of-brushing-complaints-aside

Feagin, J. R. (2013). *The white racial frame. Centuries of racial framing and counter-framing* (2nd ed.). Routledge.

Field, J., & Morgan-Klein, N. (2012). The importance of social support structures for retention and success. In T. Hinton-Smith (Ed.), *Widening participation in higher education: Casting the net wide?* (pp. 178–192). Palgrave.

Garcia, S., & Guerra, P. (2004). Deconstructing deficit thinking: Working with educators to create more equitable learning environments. *Education and Urban Society, 36*(2), 150–168.

Gedalof, I. (2023). Eviscerating equality: Normative whiteness and conservative equality policy. *Critical Social Policy*, *43*(2), 257–276.

Gillborn, D. (2006). Rethinking white supremacy: Who counts in "WhiteWorld" [Special issue: *Rethinking Race and Class in a time of ethnic Nationalism and The New Imperialism* (eds) McLaren, P and Jarmillo, N.]. *Ethnicities*, *6*(3), 318–340.

Gillborn, D. (2008). *Racism and education: Coincidence or conspiracy?* Routledge.

Guy-Sheftall, B. (1993). A black feminist perspective on transforming the academy: The case of Spelman College. In S. M. James, & A. P. A. Busia (Eds.), *Theorizing black feminisms: The visionary pragmatism of black women* (pp. 77–89). Routledge.

Heleta, S. (2016). Decolonisation of higher education: Dismantling epistemic violence and eurocentrism in South Africa. *Transformation in Higher Education*, *1*(1), 1–8.

Henriques, A., & Abushouk, L. (2018). Decolonising Oxford: The student movement from Stuart Hall to skin deep. In H. S. Mirza and J. Anday (Eds.), *Dismantling race in higher education: Racism, whiteness and decolonising the academy* (pp. 297–309). Springer.

Higher Education Academy (HEA). (2012). *Black and minority ethnic student degree retention and attainment*. www.heacademy.ac.uk/knowledge-hub/blackand-minority-ethnic-student-degree-retention-andattainment

Higher Education Funding Council for England (HEFCE). (2017). *Higher education in England: Students*. HEFCE.

Hopkins, P. (2011). Towards critical geographies of the university campus: Understanding the contested experiences of Muslim students. *Transactions of the Institute of British Geographers*, *36*, 157–69.

Hu-DeHart, E. (2003). The diversity project: Institutionalizing multiculturalism or managing differences?. *Academe*, *86*(5), 39–42.

Iverson, V. (2007). A policy discourse analysis of US land-grant university diversity plans [Unpublished PhD thesis]. University of Maine.

Kalev, A., Dobbin, F., & Kelly, E. (2006). Best practices or best guesses: Assessing the efficacy of affirmative action and corporate diversity polices. *American Sociological Review*, *71*(4), 589–617.

Ladson-Billings, G. (2009). The evolving role of critical race theory in educational scholarship. *Race, Ethnicity and Education*, *8*(1), 115–119.

Ladson-Billings, G., & Tate, W. (1995). Toward a critical race theory of education. *Teachers College Record*, *97*(1), 47–68.

Le Grange, L. (2016). Decolonising the university curriculum. *South African Journal of Higher Education*, *4*(2), 111–132.

Lewis, T., Everson-Rose, S., Powell, L., Matthews, K., Brown, C., Karavolos, K., Sutton-Tyrrell, K., Jacobs, E., & Wesley, D. (2012). Chronic exposure to everyday racism. *Health Psychology*, *32*(7), 810–819.

Luckett, K., & Shay, S. (2017). Reframing the curriculum: A transformative approach. *Critical Studies in Education*, *61*(1), 50–65.

Macpherson, W. (1999). *The Stephen Lawrence inquiry: Report of an inquiry by Sir William Macpherson of Cluny*. HMSO.

Mahmud, A., & Gagnon, J. (2020). Racial disparities in student outcomes in British higher education: Examining mindsets and bias. *Teaching in Higher Education*, *28*(2), 254–269. https://doi.org/10.1080/13562517.2020.1796619

May, T. (2017). *Prime minister orders government audit to tackle racial disparities in public service outcomes*. PM's Office press release. https://www.gov.uk/government/news/prime-minister-orders-government-audit-to-tackle-racial-disparities-in-public-service-outcomes

Mirza, M. (2010). *Rethinking race*. https://www.prospectmagazine.co.uk/essays/54493/rethinking-race

Myers, M. (2018). Gypsy students in the UK: The impact of mobility. *Race Ethnicity and Education, 21*(3), 353–369.

Myers, M., & Bhopal, K. (2017). Racism and bullying in rural primary schools: Protecting white identities post-Macpherson. *British Journal of Sociology of Education, 38*(2), 125–139.

National Union of Students. (NUS). (2015). *Race for equality: A report on the experiences of black students in further and higher education*. National Union of Students.

Neves, J., & Hillman, N. (2019). *Student academic experience survey*. AdvanceHE/HEPI.

Office for Students. (OfS). (2018). *Topic briefing: Black and ethnic minority students*. OfS.

Phillips, S. R., & Archer-Lean, C. (2018). Decolonising the reading of Aboriginal and Torres Strait Islander writing: Reflection as transformative practice. *Higher Education Research & Development, 38*(1), 24–37.

Picower, B. (2009). The unexamined whiteness of teaching: How white teachers maintain and enact dominant racial ideologies. *Race, Ethnicity and Education, 12*(2), 197–215.

Pilkington, A. (2011). *Institutional racism in the academy: A UK case study*. Trentham.

Pilkington, A. (2013). The interacting dynamics of institutional racism in higher education. *Race, Ethnicity and Education, 16*(2), 225–240.

Pillay, S. (2018). Thinking the state from Africa: Political theory, eurocentrism and concrete politics. *Politikon, 45*(1), 32–47.

PM's Office. (2020). *Commission on Race and Ethnic Disparities: 16 July 2020*. https://www.gov.uk/government/news/commission-on-race-and-ethnic-disparities-16-july-2020

Preston, J. (2018). *Grenfell Tower: Preparedness, race and disaster capitalism*. Palgrave Macmillan.

Richardson, J. T. E. (2008). *Degree attainment, ethnicity and gender: A literature review*. Equality Challenge Unit/Higher Education Academy.

Richardson, J. T. E. (2015). The under-attainment of ethnic minority students in UK higher education: What we know and what we don't know. *Journal of Further & Higher Education, 39*(2), 278–291.

Romero, M. (2017). Reflections on "the department is very male, very white, very old, and very conservative": The functioning of the hidden curriculum in graduate sociology departments. *Social Problems, 64*(2), 212–218.

Runnymede Trust. (2021). *Statement regarding the report from the commission on race and ethnic disparities*. https://www.runnymedetrust.org/news/statement-regarding-the-cred-report-2021

Scarman, L. (1981). *The Scarman report, the Brixton disorders 10-12 April 1981*. HMSO.

Sewell, T. (2010). *Master class in victimhood*. https://www.prospectmagazine.co.uk/essays/54494/master-class-in-victimhood

Smith, H. J. (2023). The doublespeak discourse of the race disparity audit: An example of the white racial frame in institutional operation. *Discourse: Studies in the Cultural Politics of Education, 44*(1), 1–15.

Smith, S. (2017). Exploring the black and minority ethnic (BME) student attainment gap: What did it tell us? Actions to address home BME undergraduate students' degree attainment. *Journal of Perspectives in Applied Academic Practice, 5*, 48–57.

Stevenson, J. (2012). *Black and minority ethnic student degree retention and attainment*. HEA.

Tate, S. A., & Bagguley, P. (2017). Building the anti-racist university: Next steps. *Race, Ethnicity and Education, 20*(3), 289–299.

Tate, S. A., & Page, D. (2018). Whiteliness and institutional racism: Hiding behind (un) conscious bias. *Ethics and Education*, *13*(1), 141–155.

Thomas, L. (2012). *Building student engagement and belonging in higher education at a time of change*. Paul Hamlyn Foundation.

Tickner, A. B. (2013). Core, periphery and (neo)imperialist international relations. *European Journal of International Relations*, *19*(3), 627–646.

UCL. (2018). *Inclusive curriculum healthcheck*. https://www.ucl.ac.uk/teaching-learning/education-strategy/1-personalising-student-support/bame-awarding-gap-project/ucl-inclusive

UK.Gov. (2000). Race Relations (Amendment) Act 2000. HMSO.

UUK/NUS. (2019). *Black, Asian and minority ethnic attainment at UK universities: #ClosingTheGap*. UUK/NUS.

Walker, P., Siddique, H., & Grierson, J. (2020, June 15). Dismay as No 10 adviser is chosen to set up UK race inequality commission. *The Guardian*. https://www.theguardian.com/world/2020/jun/15/dismay-over-adviser-chosen-set-up-uk-race-inequality-commission-munira-mirza

Warmington, P. (2012). A tradition in ceaseless motion: Critical race theory and black intellectual spaces. *Race, Ethnicity and Education*, *15*(1), 5–21.

Warmington, P. (2024). *Permanent racism: Race, class and the myth of postracial Britain*. Policy.

Whitsed, C., & Green, W. (2016). Lessons from star trek: Engaging academic staff in the internationalisation of the curriculum. *International Journal for Academic Development*, *21*(4), 286–298.

Wolff, E. (2016). Four questions on curriculum development in contemporary South Africa. *South African Journal of Philosophy*, *35*(4), 444–459.

Woolf, K., Cave, J., Greenhalgh, T., & Dacre, J. (2008). Ethnic stereotypes and the under achievement of UK medical students from ethnic minorities: Qualitative study. *British Medical Journal*, *337*, 611–115.

4

UNIVERSITY RACISMS

Processes of exclusion

This chapter draws upon qualitative data to explore students' experiences of racism, exclusion, and marginalisation in higher education and how this affects their understanding of how they navigate the space of higher education. Throughout the research, we identified how both covert and overt forms of racism work to disadvantage students from Black and minority ethnic (BME) backgrounds both from their peers and their lecturers. The significance of race, racism, and ethnicity in framing student's personal dispositions and learned practices within the institutional shaping of student practice directly impacted students' preparation for leaving university and entering the job market.

In effect, the racist institutional practice of universities is both a continuation of prior educational racism and a means of lowering expectations and outcomes across the life course for BME students. We argue that university practice that produces these outcomes can be understood within a conceptual framework we describe as a 'specialisation of consciousness' that demonstrates how student identities are fostered so they both accept and learn to legitimise a limited range of outcomes compared to their White peers. In his account of *doxa*, Bourdieu identifies the means by which individuals conform to readily accepted understandings of power imbalances. Despite being premised on inequities that have no rational validity, they are perceived as a natural and legitimate state of affairs by both the dominated and the dominating. Consequently, inequalities are legitimised as inevitable and unchallengeable. This is a two-way process, it both conditions individuals and structures the social world.

This chapter introduces a break with Bourdieu to argue that in terms of 'race/ethnicity' much that would be anticipated to be 'covert' or 'hidden persuasion' is, in fact, out in the open and 'overt'. Consequently, the students

DOI: 10.4324/9781003097211-4

in our research both understood and commented upon their experiences of racism and also understood and commented upon the legitimacy that was attributed to such racism. They were the dominated group within universities in which White interests were doing the dominating and they did not recognise that as a normal or natural state of affairs, but they did not challenge the state of affairs. A number of students for example described accounts of #BlackLivesMatter protests in a largely positive fashion but they did not simultaneously argue they were committed to supporting the objectives of such protests or express an opinion that they were likely to be a productive activity on the part of protestors. Bourdieu hints at the potential 'conditions under which dominated visions can be constituted and prevail' through 'a practical mastery, a practical knowledge of the social world upon which nomination can exert a theoretical effect, an effect of revelation: when it is well-founded in reality, naming involves a truly creative power' (Bourdieu, 1987b, p. 16).

We argue that a 'specialisation of consciousness' in which student identity is shaped by the institutional modelling of previous dispositions and behaviours stymies even the hint of pushing back against the *doxic* imagining of the social world and in effect counters the recognition of reality as a meaningful starting point for change. In their 1999 film *The Matrix*, the Wachowski's offered a grim Baudrillardian choice between a red pill that reveals the world for what it is or a blue pill that maintains an illusion of freewill and opportunity. The students in our research described something grimmer: they both understood the inequities of the university and accepted an understanding of inequity as unchallengeable (as opposed to misrecognising the legitimacy of their social standing as a dominated class). They were, therefore, fully cognisant of the unjust nature of inequalities shaping their lives but perceived this to be an inevitable state of affairs.

Whilst the impact of class within different institutional settings is, as anticipated, highly significant, a more worrying finding was the sense that, within and above class differences, ethnicity overrides the experiences of BME students. This chapter will deploy Bourdieu's analytical tools (*habitus*, field, capitals) to unpick the very complex relational structures and processes experienced by students. It will introduce the concept of 'specialisation of consciousness' as a means to understand how race/ethnicity and racism limit student experience, expectations, and outcomes.

Ordinary racism

A common theme to emerge from the conversations we had with students at all three universities was their recognition that experiencing inequality in a university setting was not a new experience. This is hardly surprising if we accept firstly the 'ordinariness' of racism in BME lives (Delgado & Stefancic, 2017) and the historical reproductions of class inequities throughout all areas of social life (Bourdieu, 1987a). And secondly, that racism and class inequalities change and adapt over time to economic, social, and political changes (Myers & Bhopal, 2017; Savage et al., 2013). In effect, inequality is a normal experience, and an equally normal feature of inequality is that it reimagines itself in relation to social change. So, for example, when new technologies emerge with the potential to transform working lives rather than their benefit being felt collectively they are deployed to reinforce pre-existing class inequalities. Similarly, Derrick Bell's (1980) account of interest convergence identifies how ostensibly positive progress within racial politics invariably happens because it primarily benefits White groups. The *ordinariness* of racism is an indicator that it determines political and social change in a slightly different fashion to Bourdieu's account of *doxa*. The *status quo* is not recognised by individuals as their personal failings within the social world but rather as an inevitable level of inequality that is unchallengeable because it is normal. The predicament for many of the students in our research was a recognition of their lack of agency in the face of overtly recognisable inequality.

Throughout our research, it often felt odd and, at times, deeply uncomfortable that many students gave personal accounts of both experiencing inequality in their lives and at the same time quietly accepting this state of affairs. In their work on 'The Great British class survey', Mike Savage and colleagues revealed the persistent depth of British feelings felt about class in the early twenty-first century, 'social class is now a very powerful force in the popular imagination once again. People in Britain are aware of, interested in and also upset about class' (Savage, 2015, p. 5). The BME students in our research often appeared inured to their experiences of inequality, despite providing angry or upsetting accounts of life in the modern university setting they often appeared to simply accept this.

In many respects, it would be interesting to revisit the accounts of our students in the angry aftermath of the George Floyd killing which, in the short term at least, noticeably changed public perceptions of what is acceptable in the twenty-first century. The impression gained from our research is that although the significance of the event would be acknowledged, on a personal level it would not be seen as a significant moment of personal change. We have described BME students' acceptance of a limiting of their potential because of their ethnicity as a 'specialisation of consciousness' (Bhopal et al., 2020). Specialisation of consciousness is the processes by which routine and everyday habits develop that continue to normalise institutional racism for BME students. In effect, BME student dispositions are being changed, generally in ways that appear barely perceptible on a daily basis, but which, over time, positions these students' dispositions and their understanding of the world and the university within the orthodox ethos of the university. They are moulded not in the shape of pre-existing inequalities but within the shape of an ethos in which these pre-existing inequalities are able to adapt over time and still be considered normal and unchallengeable.

Some participants seemingly identified habitual behaviours emerging through their experience of university practice (and before that school), in which habit was engendered through change 'in the disposition, in the potential, in the internal virtue' (Ravaisson, 1838/2018, p. 25). In particular, their accounts resembled Ravaisson's account of the 'double law' of habit in which there is an inverse correlation between action and sensation. The 'double law'

> gives expression to our everyday experience of habit and habituation: we find that repeating a certain action leads to this action becoming more dextrous, precise and efficient; we find that sense-data that are repeatedly or continuously present to us decline in intensity after some time.
>
> *(Carlisle, 2010, p. 127)*

For BME students, their actions associated with accepting racism became increasingly routinized whilst their feelings about experiencing racism were blunted. Their embodiment of individual characteristics as habitus in the Bourdieusian sense is a 'moving equilibrium' (Crossley, 2001, p. 112); it is a dynamic process in which change, shaped by shared routine habits, impacts the individual. A sentiment voiced by several students was that 'things do not change' or that 'we always live with racism, we have to work around the world as it is'. Such comments belie the dynamism evidenced by Bourdieu and underline the slow, imperceptible movement in which the 'habitus of both the individual and the group is in a process of constant, if slow and gradual, change. And the proximate source of that change is the innovative praxis of the agent' (Crossley, 2001, p. 112). Student's actions are embodied within the racist or White supremacist ethos of the university; the process we describe as 'specialisation of consciousness'. This sense of slow and collective action usefully points to the moments of 'interest convergence' identifiable in universities happening not in respect of an immediate and specifically identifiable moment of crisis, but rather as emerging shifts in the interests of the White elites. More problematically from our analysis of BME student experience would be the likelihood of BME students becoming almost complicit in moments of interest convergence. The slow, steady collective processes ensure that those most adversely affected by change, that is designed to appear equitable rather than genuinely addressing inequality (or by change that only materialises because it has the potential to impact beneficially on the already privileged White university), are readily accepted as positive steps forward by BME students.

The emergence of forms of habitus that embody racial identities can clearly be understood within a Bourdieusian analysis of the relationship between structure and agency, and within the interplay between field, capitals, and habitus. Bourdieu's conceptual analysis mirrors the nuances of racialized identities present within his analysis of relationships between dominant and subordinate ethnic groups within colonialism for example (Bourdieu, 1962; Bourdieu &

Sayad, 1964; Go, 2013). Within Bourdieu's overarching theoretical project, the micro-analysis of racisms are subsumed within the dynamics of macro-structural processes. In these circumstances, *habitus* is integral to maintaining security and minimizing personal risks such as threats to financial security or status within the realities of institutional life (Bourdieu, 1977). It is also 'potentially racialized within an unspoken, unacknowledged framing of a White collective investment in White interests' (Myers, 2022) or in the acknowledgement by BME students that White individuals and groups are performing their racist practice as though it was unseeable. For the students in this research, it often appeared they encountered the performance of racism by the White institution and its agents as something that the institution *assumed to materialise covertly*, but which in reality was acknowledged by BME students as overt everyday, ordinary racism.

Liberal values?

Universities emerged as institutions who performed a range of liberal values. Typically they would present themselves as diverse, multi-cultural, and equitable. In their public discourse, in Mission Statements, and in accounts of the values they were committed to uphold, students were assured they could all expect to be treated similarly, to encounter the same opportunities and share in its educational rewards. However, students identified these performed aspects of the university ethos as a thin veneer obscuring patterns of racism in 'the real world'. Aaron (male, Black British, post-1992) explained how,

> Outside of the university there's racism. We all know that. It's the real world and the real world does not stop when you become a student. It still happens. It doesn't magically disappear when you walk into a lecture hall. Maybe lecturers hide it better.

Aaron's account was interesting because, on the one hand, he situated the university as another institutional site of racism in his life but also hinted at how the university ethos transformed the experience into something that was not immediately challenged. On the one hand, this reflected the ordinariness of the experience but *lecturers hide it better* suggested Aaron understood this as a concealed form of racism. Asked about how he dealt with the racism he identified, Aaron was quite reticent and fell back on describing the experience and his response as being driven by an acceptance of *the real world*. Aaron described previous experiences of racism at school largely involving name-calling between pupils and noted how it was 'not worth the effort' of complaining about these. His account of racism in schools suggested it was pitched at a low level and again reflected ordinary, everyday events. Aaron neither suggested he was scarred by these events nor did he give any impression they had caused him harm. His account seemed to fall within the institutional *doxa* (Bourdieu, 2000; Bourdieu & Wacquant, 1992) of the university, implicit patterns of individual behaviours to mirror the institutional ethos. For Bourdieu, this is the investment in 'the game' and their 'fundamental belief in the interest of the game and the value of the stakes which is inherent in that membership' (Bourdieu, 2000, p. 11). For BME students, their individual dispositions seemed cast within accepting, or performing, the institutional doxa whilst simultaneously identifying it as evidentially racist.

The sense of lecturers disguising their racism suggests their overt displays of individualised liberalism, often evidenced through their membership of a multi-cultural cadre, are necessary characteristics for academics in twenty-first-century universities. On the surface, this is borne out in the promotional literature and vision statements of universities; it is also apparent in policy directly and indirectly affecting universities. Beneath the surface, the implicit practical guidance of university guidelines and codes is the official face or institutional rhetoric of the university, which needs to be performed rather than strictly observed. Beneath the surface, the shared attributes are the 'sense of the game' (Bourdieu, 2000, p. 11), an ability to perform membership of *being a lecturer*. For Aaron and other BME students, what emerges in their dispositions and behaviours is the ability to understand both that racism is being performed by the university and that it is shielded in a very ordinary way within a lecturer's performance. It provides an ironic counterargument to arguments from the political right that universities are full of woke liberals; if anything the evidence of our research suggests wokeness is a façade that disguises old-fashioned racism (and racists).

This raises the question of whether or not a term such as 'covert racism' is useful. In the very moment of saying *lecturers hide it better*, there is an acknowledgement that racism is being disguised but also that racism is happening and recognised as such. The recognition of lecturers being adept at hiding their racism is, to all intents and purposes, the recognition of a performance of being a non-racist actor rather than non-racist. It is a performance designed to obscure racism, by redefining the parameters in which racism is performed. In other words, the label of 'covert racism' to distinguish something from an obvious and 'overt' form of racism is a misnomer; the performance is not covert, simply a different type of manifestation that within the university *doxa* is considered permissible. It is a permissible form of racism between the lecturer and the BME student that is assumed will go unnoticed, or at the very least unchallenged. This hints at an un-doxa-ish characteristic of doxa in universities: it is essentially doxa for White people.

Recognising racism

The performance of anti-racist behaviours was discussed by many students. Much like Aaron, Faiqa (female, British Pakistani, post-1992) understood her current position as a student within a broader pattern of experiences before university, and particularly when she reflected upon the experiences of her family and friends, she anticipated racism would be a significant factor in the future upon entering the employment market,

> It's very hard to pin down. It's more subtle. The lecturers can disguise their racism in universities. How they [lecturers] treat you, it carries on when you get a job. It's not as bad in universities as it is in jobs, but it's still there, and it's worse for me because I'm a Muslim.

Shelby (female, Black, Plate Glass) believed it was 'basically impossible' to evidence specific racism amongst lecturers and suggested this was a consequence of lecturers being conscious of how they presented themselves and also that lecturers and the university would generally find means to protect their own interests rather than be identified as institutionally racist. Faiqa suggested that part of her reasons for believing that individual lecturers and the university, in general, were racist was the widely held perception amongst BME students that White students were consistently getting better grades. Ironically, she described this as one example of 'covert racism'; however, her institution's 'attainment gap' was very clearly evidenced by the university. The persistence of this attainment gap across all faculties and over long periods of time suggesting structural racism within the university was both endemic and 'overt'. Similarly, Shelby also suggested it was frustrating to always be taught by White lecturers rather than BME lecturers; again the non-representation of BME teaching staff generally and specifically at higher grades was also well-evidenced by her university (as it was in all three universities where the research was conducted).

Faiqa also described the 'discomfort' many of the White lecturers appeared to demonstrate around BME students, noting

> Maybe less so around me. Because I'm small and quite smiley...but round the boys, round black boys, they keep their distance. One lecturer, she looks as though she is scared of the boys, all the time.

She felt this lecturer was performing their fear of these students rather than being genuinely scared, and by doing so, it 'makes the boys seem bad'. Consequently, ordinary and non-threatening Black students were imbued with qualities of being difficult or potentially dangerous. Whilst students should anticipate that educational space is a 'safe space' to experiment and stretch their intellectual muscles, instead they were being offered a space in which they are being labelled as disruptive, difficult, and unsuited to the opportunity. In this way, the dispositions of BME students appear shaped by an institutional White gaze that deliberately misrepresents them as problematic whilst also insisting on their acquiescence to the processes of that misrepresentation.

In Faiqa's account, intersections between ethnicity and religion and between ethnicity and gender were identified as generating different patterns of racism experienced by BME students. Intersectional identities were often cited by students to explain their experience of being a student. Daniel (male, Black British, Plate Glass) described concerns about being both Black and from a working-class background,

> I do feel generally I am at a disadvantage, definitely based on my social characteristics, so I am from a working-class background [and] I also come from a Black background, so you could say they're both a disadvantage. What I am trying to say is I do feel confident in my abilities in the future however, I do [also] feel that I am still at a disadvantage compared to someone else who is White, middle class.

This suggests that 'experience' and 'background' become embodied within the practices of individuals. BME students from lower social class backgrounds were effectively on track not just to secure less prestigious job opportunities but also to a certain extent to *accept* this state of affairs. Daniel also noted,

> There are small gestures made. Friendly advice from some of the lecturers about opportunities. But I feel on the outside. One of my [White] friends was told about the Masters programmes. There is a bursary they offer to 3rd year students. No one told me about that.

In addition, another Black student Josh who was studying at the Russell Group institution noted something similar in respect of ethnicity and gender,

> I might be out of line saying this but a lot of the opportunities, little things like being paid to attend open days or help out at an event. It is always a White girl.

Universities demonstrate a process in which the institutional logic of racist discourses constructed at an institutional level transcends the ideological consequences of producing racism, not just through university managers or lecturers but also in the 'bodies' of graduates, 'in durable dispositions to recognize and comply with the demands immanent in the field' (Bourdieu, 1990, p. 58). One repeated refrain of BME, working-class students was the need for their actions to reflect the 'reality' of their opportunities. In practice, this included the embodiment of specialised dispositions that limited their potential outcomes: they might observe and understand institutional racism but these were unchallengeable because they reflect the 'reality' of university practice. To understand their positioning, BME students adopted the perspective of the White university even though this was shaped by racism.

Equality and diversity work

In her research on work to promote equality in higher education, Sara Ahmed adopts a phenomenological standpoint to understand how institutions establish routines, behaviours, and characteristics that are embedded within the background and become 'taken for granted' (2012, p. 21). For Weber, such 'routinization' occurs as a process of domination within institutions, it is

> the need of social strata, privileged through existing political, social, and economic orders, to have their social and economic positions 'legitimized.' They wish to see their positions transformed from purely factual power relations into a cosmos of acquired rights, and to know that they are thus sanctified.
>
> *(Weber, 2009, p. 262)*

In a twenty-first-century university, such legitimisation ensures the significant voices of the university, those of vice chancellors, senior managers, and the professoriate, are rendered as authentically reflecting the liberal institutional ethos. It would be unthinkable for a vice chancellor to argue for a policy to promote the welfare and advantage of White academics, as by doing so, the same vice chancellor would be required to publicly justify an obvious impression of supporting inequality and being a racist. However, the outcomes of university policies and institutional practice do evidentially lead to racist outcomes such as attainment gaps and the underrepresentation of BME academics in senior positions. Within universities' institutional narratives what emerges is not just an explanation that racist policy is somehow not racist, but rather that an additional step is taken in which an example of racism can be both explained as not racist and done so with authority and legitimacy. Ahmed uses such an understanding of institutionalisation to explain the processes by which universities might promote their public commitment to diversity whilst avoiding addressing issues of inequality. Consequently,

> To be in this world is to be involved with things in such a way that they recede from consciousness. When things become institutional, they recede. To institutionalize *x* is for *x* to become routine or ordinary such that *x* becomes part of the background for those who are part of an institution.
>
> *(Ahmed, 2012, p. 21)*

In the public world, it is unacceptable to be racist and the identification of institutions as 'institutionally racist' has, since the Macpherson report (1999), been seen as an affront to commonly held values. Within the power dynamics of universities, in which there are sharply delineated hierarchies of status, the existence of racist practice is countered by legitimising it as non-racist. So, for example, a commitment to tackle the attainment gap is used to make the claim that an institution is not racist; it is not used to make the evidential claim that the university is in fact racist, because in order to perform an acceptable ethos of being inclusive, it has to be seen to be addressing a persistent racist outcome of the university's people and processes.

The students in our research identified such practices but also, with depressing regularity, appeared to recognise their own immersion within practices that were actively discriminating against their interests. If the purpose of institutional racism is to make racism an ordinary and normal practice so that it becomes an acceptable form of discrimination then that was not exactly what emerged in our research. In our discussions, students identified the racist practice, the racist subterfuge of rhetoric and diversity policy, and yet still did not actively challenge the *status quo*. Institutionalised racism was often contextualised as the same as the experience of racism in British society more generally. As a first-generation Black British student attending a Russell Group university, Josh characterised his experience of racism as a, 'part of growing up really'. He had experienced and learned to live with racism at school and saw this in some respects as a preparation for university life, and in a similar fashion, he described accepting racism at university as a preparation for the labour market.

Josh identified his positioning within a higher education economy shaped by money and the reproduction of status,

> Maybe the university wants me the student paying my fees and my accommodation but does not want Josh, the Black man. I feel it and my friends feel it. Even my White friends.

Josh noted the 'smokescreen' of 'Black faces and Chinese faces' in the publicity materials for his Russell Group institution and Faiqa described her post-1992 institution's high-profile commitment to equality issues as 'irrelevant' and 'just words to look better'. Faiqa made the point that her university website included many photographs of smiling female Muslim students wearing a hijab to cover their hair. These gave the impression of Muslim students comfortably engaging with a range of academic and social activities; however, she noted 'it's simply not true'. Faiqa suggested the visible markers of her ethnicity and religion were in fact viewed as deeply problematic,

> my brown skin, the headscarf, they just say look at me I'm not the same. And then, when I sit on the table with the other girls like me it's like we are doing something wrong. The more noticeable the more…I don't know the more we are not meant to be here. Every lecturer always says something

about changing places but its always us, or the Chinese table, it's never can all the White people move around.

Whereas Josh and Faiqa demonstrated incisive and deeply-help beliefs about their positioning in the university in terms of their economic contribution. Usha (female, Indian, post-1992), however, suggested such reflexive awareness was not as widely held,

> Some of my friends don't get it. They think all this money [fees] is going to open up the world for them. They think we will be this super-generation. They just suck up all that stuff. All the Black kids will be entrepreneurs. Kids off estates. From Croydon. They all want to be lawyers or on TV.

Josh, Faiqa, Usha, and other students took a cynical view of the emphasis universities placed on their adoption of equality measures, on statements of tolerance and liberalism, and on the high visibility of BME students within promotional literature. Their discussion of institutional 'diversity' or 'widening participation' practice was often framed as being part of the very processes by which racism was perpetuated. Their personal experience of diversity work in universities chimed with Bourdieu & Wacquant's (1999) notion of 'racial sociodicy'; practices that are ostensibly designed to address racial inequality are part of the processes of perpetuating racism. Doytcheva (2020) identifies the normalisation of such activity within a broader trend identified (within academic writing and cultural commentary), as a 'diversity turn' in European and American universities. Diversity framed within a broad understanding of dealing with multiple inequalities (gender, age, sexuality, for example) is situated within understanding the value of individuals within the university. Such policies emphasise, 'merit, productivity, and individual potentialities, it downplays more collective and structural sources of inequality and subordination. Instead of correcting injustices or redressing wrongs, diversity is about supporting those who contribute to the performance of the organization' (Doytcheva, 2020, p. 9). This liberal narrative of diversity resonates with students' comments about the diversity represented in promotional literature and their daily encounters with lecturers. The practice of *universities doing equality work* was noticeable to students but seemingly understood within their broader awareness of a range of bureaucratic practices that shaped everyday university life. It was no different to explanations of how to use the library or how to scan a QR code to register for class or what to do in the event of the fire alarm ringing.

Normalising Racism

The sense that students understood racism within the university as 'ordinary, not abberational – "normal science," the usual way society does business'

(Delgado & Stefancic, 2017, p. 8) underlines the accumulative nature of their understandings. They brought an awareness of the *ordinariness* of inequality and the processes that fostered inequality with them into the institution. Consequently, the internalised discomfort Du Bois or Fanon might identify became lost almost subsumed within the practice of being a student. By being complicit in the wider competition for better degrees and better jobs, BME students were accepting and working within processes that reinforced inequality despite recognising overt racist practices that impacted them. In Chapter 8, we discuss how students' experiences impact upon their expectations of entering the labour market in which similar racial inequality is a given.

One of the more significant findings in this research is the sense that what happens to BME students in universities is both a mirror of racism in British society more generally, but also a means of processing graduates to function within the constraints of such racism. The transitions that students described from school to university and their expectations of leaving university and entering the job market were inevitably framed by accounts of racial inequality. To a large extent that is not a surprising finding and if we consider the experiences of BME people generally, we would expect them to experience racism in their daily lives. The evidence base for such assumptions can be readily drawn from multiple fields including education, employment, health, criminal justice, and housing data (House of Commons, 2020; Hussain, 2023; Marmot, 2020; Rogaly et al., 2021). However, in the context of universities this seems a more significant failing.

The expansion of higher education has been premised on multiple expectations that a graduate education is beneficial to individuals and wider society. It is associated with earning higher salaries in better and more secure employment. It has been cited as a key means of addressing inequalities throughout society by offering all individuals the opportunity to benefit from upwards social mobility. Within the starkest of neoliberal accounts higher education is a place in which the individual can exercise their personal responsibility for improving their life chances. Across the political spectrum education is understood to be a 'good thing'. Young people attend university because it is a means, possibly the single most effective means, to improve their life chances.

For these arguments to hold together, it is necessary that universities are equitable in their provision of educational outcomes. If, for example, universities preferred to recruit students whose surnames began with letters earlier in the alphabet that would be as absurd as it would be discriminatory. If a student named Sharon Andrews was more likely to be recruited by a university in the first place and then more likely to graduate with a first-class honours degree than a student named Patricia Williams, because their respective surnames appeared earlier or later in the alphabet: that would be absurd. There would be no meaningful rationale for those outcomes. And yet in effect that is what happens in terms of race. We can evidence this through educational data, and in this research, we also found it evidenced in our participants' accounts.

All the arguments given for the value of education, for both individuals and society, revolve around the centrality of equality of access and opportunity. This is an argument in which the most benefits accrue to individuals by allowing them to make the most of their skills and abilities and consequently to wider society. For universities to persist with a practice that has racist outcomes ultimately disadvantages not just the individuals affected but society as a whole. For universities to persist with a practice that moulds student identities to not challenge this phenomenon suggests it is practice that is designed not to benefit society as a whole but rather to benefit particular interests. Using the concept of 'specialisation of consciousness', we argue that universities are producing processes that allow racism not just to materialise in daily life but also to adapt to social, political and economic change. It is a set of practices that are designed to cement the long-term interests of White people within educational outcomes that reward them with financial security, status, and self-belief in their right to such rewards. The *doxa* that they experience is a White *doxa*. It is a doxa that was recognised as inequitable by BME students.

References

Ahmed, S. (2012). *On being included: Racism and diversity in institutional life*. Duke University Press.

Bell, D. A. (1980). Brown v. Board of Education and the interest-convergence dilemma. *Harvard Law Review, 93*(3), 518–533.

Bhopal, K., Myers, M., & Pitkin, C. (2020). Routes through higher education: BME students and the development of a 'specialisation of consciousness'. *British Educational Research Journal, 46*(6), 1321–1337.

Bourdieu, P. (1962). *The Algerians*. Beacon Press.

Bourdieu, P. (1977) *Outline of a theory of practice* (Vol. 16). Cambridge University Press.

Bourdieu, P. (1987a). *Distinction: A social critique of the judgement of taste*. Harvard University Press.

Bourdieu, P. (1987b). What makes a social class? On the theoretical and practical existence of groups. *Berkeley Journal of Sociology, 32*, 1–17.

Bourdieu, P. (1990). *The logic of practice*. Cambridge: Polity.

Bourdieu, P. (2000). *Pascalian meditations*. Stanford University Press.

Bourdieu, P., & Sayad, A. (1964). *The uprooting. The crisis of traditional agriculture in Algeria*. Polity.

Bourdieu, P., & Wacquant, L. (1992). *An invitation to reflexive sociology*. University of Chicago Press.

Carlisle, C. (2010). Between freedom and necessity: Félix Ravaisson on habit and the moral life. *Inquiry, 53*(2), 123–145.

Crossley, N. (2001). The phenomenological habitus and its construction. *Theory and Society, 30*(1), 81–120.

Delgado, R., & Stefancic, J. (2017). *Critical race theory*. New York University Press.

Doytcheva, M. (2020). "White diversity": Paradoxes of deracializing antidiscrimination. *Social Sciences, 9*(4), 50.

Go, J. (2013). Decolonizing Bourdieu: Colonial and postcolonial theory in Pierre Bourdieu's early work. *Sociological Theory, 31*(1), 49–74.

House of Commons. (2020). *Ethnicity and the criminal justice system: What does recent data say on over-representation?* House of Commons.

Hussain, R. (2023). *An alarming rise in the numbers of BME workers in insecure work.* TUC.

Macpherson, W. (1999). *The Stephen Lawrence inquiry: Report of an inquiry by Sir William Macpherson of Cluny.* HMSO.

Marmot, M. (2020). *The Marmot review: 10 years on.* Institute of Health Equity.

Myers, M. (2022). Racism, zero-hours contracts and complicity in higher education. *British Journal of Sociology of Education*, 43(4), 584–602.

Myers, M., & Bhopal, K. (2017). Racism and bullying in rural primary schools: Protecting white identities post Macpherson. *British Journal of Sociology of Education*, 38(2), 125–143.

Ravaisson, F. (1838/2018). *Of habit.* Continuum.

Rogaly, K., Elliott, J., & Baxter, D. (2021). *What's causing structural racism in housing?* JRF.

Savage, M. (2015). *Social class in the 21st century.* Penguin.

Savage, M., Devine, F., Cunningham, N., Taylor, M., Li, Y., Hjellbrekke, J., & Miles, A. (2013). A new model of social class? Findings from the BBC's Great British class survey experiment. *Sociology*, 47(2), 219–250.

Weber, M. (2009). *From Max Weber essays in sociology.* Routledge.

5

MONEY, MONEY, MONEY

Drowning in debt

Since the 1990s, there has been a consistent emphasis within educational policy on the importance of widening participation, to increase the numbers of students from marginalised backgrounds entering higher education (Burke, 2013). This has largely been related to inequalities in the labour market, in particular, barriers to working-class and ethnic minorities entering higher status professions where a good honours degree is a basic requirement (Millburn, 2012). Whilst the number of women studying at university in the twentieth century was low, since 2000 more women have entered university every year than men. By contrast, poor access for working-class and ethnic minority children has remained largely fixed for the previous 30 years. Since the 2010s, Coalition and Conservative governments have also focussed attention more closely on geographical regions with poor rates of progression to university regardless of class or ethnic difference (Wiseman et al., 2017).

Earlier widening participation schemes focussed on providing students with financial support and outreach activities. More recently, the focus has been on improving access and participation in higher education. The publication of the government's white paper, *Higher Education: Students at the Heart of the System* (Department for Business, Innovation & Skills, 2011) outlined a new framework for widening participation and fair access for students from marginalised backgrounds. This included the National Scholarship Programme to support individuals from low-income backgrounds to enter higher education by providing bursaries from 2012 to 2015 (Connell-Smith & Hubble, 2018). In 2012, the Office for Fair Access (OFFA) developed a National Strategy for Access and Student Success in Higher Education. It was replaced by the Office of Students in January 2018 which included within its remit a focus on widening participation initiatives.

DOI: 10.4324/9781003097211-5

A significant factor affecting students' willingness and ability to access higher education in the last two decades has been the significant changes in fees paid directly by students taking out student loans. In 1998, Tony Blair's New Labour government passed the Teaching and Higher Education Act 1998 (Gov.UK,1998), which introduced annual tuition fees of £1000. New Labour persisted with their policy of transferring more responsibility for the costs of attending university when it passed the Higher Education Act 2004 (Gov.UK, 2004), which allowed fees to be increased to £3000 from 2006 onwards. Although widely supported by most universities, Universities UK and the Russell Group, concerns were raised by the vice chancellors of 15 'new' universities that the increase in fees would 'further widen the differences in resources for universities and disadvantage the majority of students' (Macleod, 2004, n.p.). These fees were often described as 'top-up' fees and the New Labour government of the time argued they represented a means by which universities could address anomalies in differences in costs associated with different courses. Both Conservative and Liberal Democrat opposition parties opposed the legislation, with Charles Kennedy leader of the Liberal Democrats stating it was, 'a poor reflection of the government of the day' (Tempest, 2004).

Despite the argument that the fees should reflect the realistic costs of teaching programmes (e.g. to be a top-up for courses that cost more to deliver), almost all universities immediately introduced the full £3000 fees across the board for all courses. In addition, the Act also established the OFFA whose main role was to ensure equal access for disadvantaged students to enter higher education. New Labour again pushed forward an agenda of further marketizing higher education in 2009 when Peter Mandelson, the Secretary of State for Business, Innovation and Skills, commissioned the *Browne Review*, which defined its role in the following terms,

> The Review will analyse the challenges and opportunities facing higher education and their implications for student financing and support. It will examine the balance of contributions to higher education funding by taxpayers, students, graduates and employers. Its primary task is to make recommendations to Government on the future of fees policy and financial support for full and part time undergraduate and postgraduate students.
>
> *(Browne Review, 2010, p. 57)*

The Browne Review was published in 2010, after a general election that saw Labour ousted and a new Coalition government of the Conservative and Liberal Democrat parties. Despite previous objections to the introduction of fees, the Coalition government acted on the key Browne recommendation to significantly increase student fees in 2012. These were capped at £9000 and provision made for outstanding student debts to be written off after 30 years.

It is worth noting the Liberal Democrats election manifesto included a commitment not to raise tuition fees, a commitment they could have delivered if they had voted against the introduction of higher fees. They chose instead to abstain from the vote and by doing so ensured the new legislation was passed. As previously, although the new £9000 figure was presented as a 'cap' on fees, almost all universities immediately adopted the full amount across all courses.

Other changes have also signalled the further transition to a marketized higher education field initially envisaged by New Labour in which students were increasingly positioned as consumers. Firstly, the removal of a cap on the number of students universities could recruit in 2015 expanded the customer base of potential students. Secondly, the introduction of the Teaching Excellence Framework (TEF)[1] in 2016 used a range of metrics to assess the teaching performance of different institutions and rank them as gold, silver, and bronze, respectively. In part, this measure was designed to provide students (and their parents), with a tool to assess the value they might derive from attending any given university. Beyond the implication that students acting as consumers would choose gold institutions over others allowing the competition of a free market to raise standards, the TEF rankings were also linked to future increases in fees. Jo Johnson, then Minister for Universities and Science, announced that only higher education institutions that were awarded a gold rating for the first year of the TEF would be able to raise their fees in 2017/2018 to £9250. In many respects, this was a contradictory position in which, somewhat ironically, the Conservative government appeared to restate an interest in the need for universities to deliver better educational outcomes as a public good requiring state intervention rather than being entirely market-led. That impression was confirmed in October 2017, when the Prime Minister, Theresa May, announced that fees would be frozen at £9250 per year.

The 2017 cap at £9250 has remained in place for successive Conservative governments (and largely unchallenged by opposition parties), reflecting a degree of pragmatic policy making. On the one hand, it is politically damaging to raise fee levels placing greater financial burdens on the demographic of voters most affected (students and their parents). On the other, increasing central funding for universities has become politically unpopular with another demographic of voters who identify, correctly given the discourse of marketisation of universities, that they will not personally gain from increasing student numbers. Such pragmatism has produced an extraordinary stasis in which the funding universities receive for home students has progressively fallen. In 2024, the Office For Students estimates 'that the "real-terms value" of income for teaching UK students (tuition fee plus teaching grant from UK public funding, per UK student) is approximately 25 per cent lower than it was in 2015-16, when adjusted for inflation over time' (Office For Students [OFS], 2024, p. 8).[2] Analysis of the consequences of this real-term decline in the value of student fees to universities reveals an increasing dependence on fees from international students to subsidise home students' education (Menzies & Smyth, 2024; OFS 2024). On average the share of tuition fees from international students at Russell Group institutions was 57.3% but is dramatically higher in other universities (Glasgow 80.7%, Imperial 78.4%, London School of Economics (LSE) 76.6%, University College London (UCL) 76.4%, Edinburgh 73.2%). The Russell Group suggests that home students are in effect subsidised by £2500 per student from international fees (Russell Group, 2024). The OFS described this as an 'increasingly precarious model' (2024, p. 10) at risk of rapid and unpredictable changes within global higher education economies. Such unpredictability has been fostered within domestic politics where an emphasis on stronger migration controls has signalled the likelihood of visa restrictions on some international students. A final irony, given their participation in the shift towards marketization, has been the calls of former ministers including Peter Mandelson (now Lord), David Willets (now Lord), and Alan Johnson (now Chancellor of the University of Hull) for increased university funding.[3]

There was a further significant change to funding arrangements in 2016 with the abolition of maintenance grants and replacement by student loans. This increasingly emphasised the responsibilities of students and their families to bear the brunt of the costs of a university education. Loans to students to cover their living costs are means-tested, and consequently, the loan available to individual students is relational to family income levels. The expectation being that middle-income and wealthier families contribute to their children's living costs at university (an expectation consistent with previous funding arrangements),[4] whilst students from poorer families became entitled to access greater loans to cover their living costs. Whilst in principle, this suggests poorer students' ability to enter university is being protected, this comes with a significant financial penalty: *when poorer students leave university, they are likely to do so with greater debts than those of students from wealthier families.* There is also evidence that students from poorer and ethnic minority families often go to less prestigious institutions than wealthier students, but in the current university economy, all institutions, regardless of their prestige or the value of their degree in the labour market, essentially charge the same level of fees. This is an economic model in which,

> the transfer of economic capital mirrors transfers of knowledge and cultural capital, and the fostering of social networks to benefit already privileged students. Put simply, students from poorer, non-traditional working-class BME backgrounds pay more and get less back.
>
> *(Bhopal et al., 2020, p. 1334)*

Widening participation policies have always been entwined within government reforms designed to make higher education institutions financially self-sufficient and reduce the public deficit (Hubble & Bolton, 2018). The shift in emphasis from central government funding of higher education to individual students has seen significant increases in student debt in the form of loans to cover both fees and living costs. Despite this, students have not been deterred from applying to university. Entry rates amongst 18-year-olds from England increased from 29.2% in 2013 to 33.4% in 2017, setting new year-on-year records. The increase in the numbers of students from disadvantaged backgrounds saw the greatest rise in numbers, up from 15.1% in 2011 and 2012 to 20.4% in 2017 (UCAS, 2017, see also Hubble & Bolton, 2018). During the COVID-19 pandemic, many A-level students reported feeling their only real option in the consequent economic climate was to progress to university, and, at the same time, the cancellation of examinations and subsequent chaos awarding grades led to larger numbers of students being granted university places (Bhopal & Myers, 2020, 2023).

Value for money?

With higher education students increasingly positioned as consumers purchasing a commodity (Brown & Carasso, 2013), this has changed attitudes about the role of universities and students' expectations about their education. Tomlinson (2014) has argued that the impact of fees shapes students' expectations of their university experience with students anticipating that their higher education institutions will be well-resourced and their degrees offer value for money. Students identify benefitting from substantial returns from their university education in terms of high expected earnings and see student loans as short-term debt in return for long-term gain (Bachan, 2014; Harrison et al., 2015). Recent research suggests that students would rather their fees be spent on teaching-related activities than those which benefit the university, such as marketing or community engagement (Hillman et al., 2018).

With considerable irony, the introduction of neoliberal policies designed to open up the 'market' for higher education through competition and increased student responsibility for covering the costs of university education has resulted in disillusionment about the value of a degree across the entire university sector. Rather than individual institutions being identified as offering poor value through metrics such as the TEF's gold, silver, and bronze awards, a general feeling that degrees do not offer value for money has emerged. The Institute for Fiscal Studies (IFS, 2017) reported that the introduction of higher student fees since 2012 had contributed to students graduating with debts of over £50,000. The abolition of grants directly contributed to higher student debt leaving English graduates with the highest levels of debt in the developed world, with students from the poorest backgrounds being the most disadvantaged. In 2017, researchers found that only 35% of students felt that their degree and experience at university was 'good' or 'very good' value for money, and the number of students who said their experience was 'poor' or 'very poor' had doubled in five years (Higher Education Policy Institute [HEPI]/ Higher Education Academy [HEA], 2017). By 2018, this figure had increased to 41%. The same survey found that Asian and Chinese students found degrees offered less value and lower levels of learning and effective teaching compared to other students. They also described how their own efforts and expectations were not matched by universities, and that universities needed to do more to offer them support (Neves & Hillman, 2019).

Inequalities

There is evidence to suggest that student experiences and outcomes in higher education vary by gender, socio-economic status, and ethnic background (Crawford & Greaves, 2015). The shift towards the current funding arrangements for degrees has been associated with positive fiscal outcomes related to the introduction of fees and access to maintenance grants (Dearden et al., 2014) but also identified with adverse impacts students' choice of institution, ability to attend, academic outcomes, and reliance on bursaries (Callender & Jackson, 2005, 2008; Dearden et al., 2011; Murphy & Wyness, 2015). Once students graduate they also experience differential outcomes in terms of wages and employment along the same axes (Belfield et al., 2018; Gov.UK, 2022).

The financial implications of fees are more likely to adversely affect students from poor and marginalised backgrounds, resulting in different student experiences and outcomes skewed by demographic characteristics (Callender & Jackson, 2008; Reay, 2018). Students from working-class and marginalised backgrounds are more likely to view student finance as a debt and a burden rather than a long-term investment (Reay, 2018), and this can be a deterrent for some groups who decide not to attend university for fear of long-term financial insecurity (Benton, 2012; Esson & Ertl, 2016; Harrison & Agnew, 2016; Wilkins et al., 2013). At the same time, richer families experience little or no financial burdens or difficulties as a result of paying student fees (Blanden & Machin, 2013). The means-testing of eligibility for loans is a particularly blunt instrument based solely on parental income and does not recognise individual circumstances. Consequently, many students are unable to draw upon additional parental support during their studies at the levels anticipated by student loan policies. They have to survive on maintenance grants in order to attend university and their studies are often impacted by term time working (Callender, 2008; Dearden et al., 2011; Hunt et al., 2004).

The impact of student debt has been shown to have a significant impact students' mental health and well-being (Gani, 2016; Marsh, 2017; Richardson et al., 2015, 2016). Students report high levels of stress associated with the financial burden of attending university (Benson-Egglenton, 2019) and suffer from anxiety and depression (Jessop et al., 2005; Johnson et al., 2009). Students who rely on work during term time also report having poorer mental health and poorer academic outcomes compared to those who do not have to work (Roberts et al., 2000).

Ethnic differences

There is very little research which has explored the impact of student loans and fees on Black and minority ethnic (BME) students. The research that does exist argues that BME groups from lower socio-economic backgrounds are sceptical of the 'value' of education and are more likely than other groups to see it as a debt rather than a long-term investment (Bhopal, 2018). Research also suggests that Asian students (particularly those from Indian backgrounds) are less likely to have taken out loans compared to their White peers (Bhopal, 2010). This may be because Asian students are less likely to spend money on entertainment compared to their White peers and they are more likely to live in the parental home (Bhopal, 2016). Religion has been shown to be a factor in whether students take out loans, with Muslim Asian students less likely to want to take out a loan compared to non-Muslim Asian students (Hussain & Bagguley, 2007).

The emphasis on individual (or family) responsibility for the costs of education has been associated with positive understandings of 'ethnic capital' in the experiences of BME students, particularly those from Asian backgrounds. Bhopal (2016) has argued that many Indian families see the economic capital that they invest in their children's education (such as paying for their loans, accommodation, and other needs), as a contribution to the status and 'worth' of the family in the community. They also understand it as a long-term investment, which pays back dividends in the form of greater social mobility and access to better jobs in the labour market. Other research has explored the importance of ethnic networks such as cultural and familial obligations which serve as a distinct form of social capital (Zhou, 2005; Zhou & Bankston, 1994). In this sense, ethnic groups provide support to their children to help with the transmission of values from one generation to the next to achieve higher social mobility and achieving high aspirations. Shah et al. (2010) argue that parents from minority ethnic backgrounds (particularly Pakistani families) demonstrate high educational aspirations for their children to ensure social mobility. Families use their ethnic capital to reinforce high aspirations and ensure successful outcomes, and so, in turn, ethnic capital through extended families becomes part of the transmission of norms and aspirations from one generation to the next. Zhou and Bankston (1994) have also argued that ethnicity as a form of social capital is important for minority groups because ethnic group membership is a basis for systems of strong, supportive social relations (Portes, 1987; Zhou, 2005; Zhou & Bankston, 1994). For minority ethnic families, the traditional close trusting ties and frequent interactions between parents, children, and extended families strengthen the extent to which social and ethnic capital are able to reinforce expectations of high academic performance (Bankston & Zhou, 2002). However, Mishra (2020) argues that students from under-represented communities often only access restricted forms of social capital from within their own communities. In addition, family obligations and lack of support from families combine with ineffective support within higher education for ethnic minorities.

The potential for forms of ethnic capital to positively impact students' experience has also been explored in relation to other intersectional inequalities, in particular the experiences of BME women students. Bhopal (2018) identified how,

> …the norms, values and networks that exist in Asian communities form part of the ethnic capital on which Asian women rely in times of financial and economic need, particularly in relation to their participation in higher education. The community and extended kin network that forms part of the ethnic capital which women draw upon is crucial to ensure access to higher education and an increase in social capital to ensure access to the labour market. (p. 518)

There remains very little research which has explored the impact of debt on BME students and their experiences whilst at different types of higher education institutions. This chapter will provide new data on such experiences and examine how students from BME backgrounds are affected by debt. It will explore how some students from less affluent BME backgrounds are disadvantaged in their experiences at university, which impacts their attainment and the future decisions available to them as they transition from higher education.

Ethnic capital: the double-edged sword of family support

In our study, students described different expectations based on their access to family support. This support was often based on family access to social and economic capital. Unsurprisingly, all students spoke about wanting to enter the labour market after graduation, rather than being unemployed, and most talked about finding full-time rewarding employment. However, as they discussed their options in more detail, different accounts emerged in which working part-time, taking a 'stop-gap' job, or unpaid voluntary work and internships were variously put forward. Students' ability to consider these as realistic career choices was primarily driven by their family's access to economic capital.

Indian students were more likely to identify access to family support to enable certain transitionary decisions. Such support was either in the form of direct financial support or often related to returning to the family home and benefiting from a more generalised availability of economic capital, Pavani (female, British Indian, Russell Group) described how she was,

> back living at home, so don't have to pay bills and don't really have to worry about that side of things. My parents are quite happy to support me and want me to get the job that I want. So it means I can travel to [name of city] or wherever to do a job without having to worry about the cost or anything.

Kirti's (female, British Indian, Plate Glass) ambition was to work in journalism, and she had identified that most of the initial routes into that field (internships, working in charity media departments, or developing experience through online blogs) were either unpaid or poorly paid. She was from London and wanted to live there, and described how her family support would ensure that she could develop her CV by,

> doing a job that will give me experience before I get the main job that I want. I know I will have to do something that I don't want to do for a while before I get the job that I want. It might even mean that I have to do some jobs without even getting paid for them and that's ok because I know I can afford to do that.

As first-generation students, both Pavani and Kirti, described, ethnic capital is associated with parental aspirations for upward social mobility. Beyond bald statements that their parents could or could not afford to support them after university, other students also provided more nuanced accounts of expectations placed upon them following university. These often conflated specific family circumstances with wider narratives that included the increasing participation of more students in higher education and fears of a precarious labour market determining students' 'realistic' choices. The seeming distinction between Indian students supported their ambitions to take more time to establish careers whilst other BME students were less well placed also disguised concerns of some Indian Students about the influence of family. Jagan (male, British Indian, Russell Group) described how a traditional expectation of the non-academic elements of the 'university experience', including his personal independence, was compromised by family expectations,

> Really it's not what I need. Going back home. It's great but the one reason I came here was to be away from home. Put some distance between us and now my choices are limited. If I get the 2.1 that helps but I still have to find a job.

Jagan and other Indian students also suggested that Indian parents often went to great lengths to ensure their children did not incur debt whilst at university. As Jagan noted this was a *double-edged sword* that often related either to students remaining at home whilst studying or returning home after they graduated. This was not universally identified by all Indian students, some of whom also gave accounts of their parents being unable to support them financially and relying upon student loans and paid work. Indian students were, however, more likely to suggest their parents felt it was their role to support them financially, in some cases with an expectation of parental support continuing until they were married. It was seen as an expected role for parents and one that some students felt helped them in their future lives but also one that made it harder for them to become independent. It was a role that parents themselves did not question and one that Bikram (male, Indian, post-1992), who identified as a working-class student from a less affluent background, still framed as an expected parental duty,

> They kind of see it as their duty, it's the way it works for us. Our parents don't just say at 18 you have to leave and that's it. It doesn't work like that for us. They continue to support us, they give us money and they don't want us to be in any debt. My cousin even got a car when he went to uni. His parents just gave it to him. They didn't want him to struggle in any way. They wanted him to focus on his studies. Money is seen as something that will get in the way of that, so if your parents can, they will provide for you. I know that in my first year my parents didn't take out a loan they paid for everything themselves and that hurt them financially so they couldn't do it for later years, but they will help me pay that back. But they paid for all my accommodation and my food.

Whilst Bikram identified the family making sacrifices in order to allow their children to complete a successful graduate degree, other students were less comfortable with the consequences. They characterised the provision of economic capital as being inevitably positioned as an ongoing factor in their social relations with their family (and wider community). Ethnic capital provided in the form of an economic resource came with multiple strings attached. For Bhakti (female, Indian, Russell Group), financial support was never an issue. Both her parents were employed in professional roles and previously attended university themselves. She described the conflicting pressures of receiving financial support from her parents which affected her sense of self and independence.

> It's great to have that financial support and I get it. I get why they [parents] want to support us, it's what all parents want to do, but it kind of feels like a struggle sometimes because it means you can't be as independent as you want to be. And it feels like I owe my parents, so I have to do things they want me to do. It can be challenging sometimes, but at the same time

I know I wouldn't be able to survive financially if I didn't have that support. All of my cousins are in the same boat, they feel it [financial support] restricts our levels of independence and that can be tricky, but at the same time they want the money and know the benefits it brings. So it's kind of give and take I suppose.

Gul (male, Plate Glass), who was from a less affluent Bangladeshi background, did not receive the same financial support from his family. However, he also explained how family expectations were determined by economic concerns,

I don't get any support from my parents or my extended family. My mum doesn't work and my dad is a chef in a restaurant and he doesn't earn much at all. My family struggle financially and if anything they want me to provide for them when I get my degree. I am the oldest and so it is expected that when I leave, I will get a good job and be able to help my family. My parents would not be able to provide me with any more money. They give me some and the rest I have to take up in loans and I work part-time.

Gul's contention that by completing a degree his family anticipated this would contribute to the whole family's security again reflects the ambiguity of ethnic capital. A narrative emerged throughout the research in which ethnic capital was a valuable source of support for individual students but one tempered by a reciprocal cost to their personal autonomy. It was generated within the expectations of families' social networks and community expectations. The social capital described by Gul and other students represented a powerful and sustained network of resources that were being continually reconstituted by students' family and community relations (Bourdieu, 1986). By doing so, students recognised they are locked in to the processes of producing relations that are profitable in terms of competing for capitals in university because that competition is itself a relational part of the process itself. In other words, their individual success was not a personal gain but a community or family profit.

Being poor

For many students, the complexities of navigating family expectations and associated ethnic capital were less of an issue. Like Gul, their families were unable to provide financial support and their most pressing concern was simply to make ends meet. In addition, students identified that *being a student* consisted of more than simply studying their degree programme and consequently their financial concerns related to their generating the finance to engage in activities related to their student experience. There was a similarity here with students who found the pressures of family expectations restricted their independence; for these students, the lack of financial resources curtailed their own expectations of personal development. The difficulty of completing university studies whilst simultaneously enjoying the university experience for poorer students was echoed by Waseem (male, Pakistani, Plate Glass),

> I have to work, I have no choice. I need that extra money. To be honest if I didn't have it, I would struggle. I need it to supplement my grant but it also means I can go out with my mates, and I wouldn't want to miss out on things like that.

Indian participants who received financial support from their parents generally did not feel the need to work. For those who did work, it was not out of necessity, but rather to complement the income they received from their grant and/or from their parents. Raj (male, Indian, Plate Glass) explained that his part-time work financed the cost of his social life but that this was a bone of contention with his parents,

> [They] don't want me to work because they keep saying I have to focus on my exams and do well, they think that is more important than having a job that will affect my studies. They see the long term benefits of the degree. If I do well now then I will be able to get a good job later. That's something they've always said to me, do well now and see the benefits later by getting a good job.

For Raj, his part-time work caused a rift with his parents not just because of the expectation that he should solely concentrate on his studies but also because it implied a break with wider cultural expectations. By pursuing a degree of independence based on his personal economic independence, there was a sense of an erosion of the impact of ethnic capital. Raj explained that sometimes he felt 'a bit guilty' about his parents' feelings, but that he was personally invested in the 'experience' of being a student. In his account, he would benefit both from this experience of greater independence as well as from future rewards in the labour market. Other students also talked about how they struggled financially at university despite the supportive role of their family. Brianna (female, Black, post-1992) spoke about how her family circumstances meant she could not receive any support from her family.

> I come from a single parent family and I am the first to go to university in my family. My mum really worked hard to ensure I got here, but she can't afford to give me any extra money. I get the full grant and sometimes when I see my peers who get given money from their families it makes me feel it is unfair because when I am out working they are working on their studies or enjoying themselves and that puts me at a disadvantage. It's simple it

just means they will do better than me because they haven't had the added burden of working. They will be the ones who get the first class degrees because they have had more time to spend on their assignments.

For Brianna, access to the forms of 'ethnic capital' identified by Indian students was essentially blocked by her family's lack of economic capital. When she discussed her mother and other family, she invariably described how much pride they felt about her achievements and their overwhelming encouragement to complete a degree. Many echoed Brianna's assessment that they were having to sacrifice their studies by working part-time to support themselves financially. They feared they spent too little time on their studies and this would adversely impact their final grades. Other students chose to stay at home rather than live independently whilst at university in order to save money. Shelby (female, Black, Plate Glass), who was a first-generation student, described how she had struggled with finances and how this impacted on her decision to stay at home,

> I stayed at home because of the cost. I knew it would be hard with taking out a loan anyway and I didn't want to have additional debt, so I decided it was better for me to stay at home. My parents also felt it would be better if I stayed at home so that I wouldn't have to worry about the financial element and could just focus on my studies.

The importance of access to financial support and inequalities was also emphasised in access to practical things such as laptops, smartphones, iPads, and books. All participants needed access to digital equipment in order to realistically continue their studies, but many highlighted their concerns about replacing them if they no longer worked or were out of date. Zainab (female, Pakistani, post-1992) said,

> Yes I have all the different gadgets that I need, that's not the problem for me. I worry about what happens when they break. If my laptop was to break, I wouldn't be able to replace it straight away and I wouldn't be able to replace it with a new one, it would have to be second hand and then that would probably break in time.

Students like Zainab recognised their lack of financial security left them vulnerable to unforeseen emergencies. The students in our research tended to position themselves in terms of either being conscious and concerned about financial vulnerability or unconcerned because they anticipated family support would resolve any short-term emergencies. The evidence that financial concerns related to feelings of lesser well-being (Benson-Egglenton, 2019) materialised in our research as accounts of insecurity about academic outcomes and about the value derived from the experience of being a student.

Futures

There were clear ethnic differences in the financial support students received from their parents and extended families. Black students from working-class backgrounds were less likely than Indian students to have access to financial and economic capital and were keen to find a job immediately upon graduation in order that they could be financially independent. Paige (female, Black British, post-1992) envisaged a career in journalism but was considering an offer to work full-time in a university administrative role that was advertised specifically for graduating students,

> I am thinking a lot about what I'm going to do when I graduate. I have been thinking about it for a long time and have applied for lots of different jobs. My first option is to get a job, maybe in journalism where there's a training scheme on offer but those are hard to get onto. I know it's going to be competitive, I may have to get a job that's not ideal. I just have to work. *I cannot afford not to work.* My parents can't support me.
>
> *(original emphasis)*

Paige identified that the option of working as an administrative assistant was both personally a disappointment in terms of her ambitions and also likely to hinder her future options. She felt her options for the future were closing down following graduation because of the more general precarity that characterised her family's economic situation.

Despite the claims of successive widening participation policies to empower students, Paige identified her background still restricted her outcomes. She characterised her family as a typical working-class family from London and made the point that in all likelihood her own future would mirror those of her parents who both held low-income jobs. Her mother had trained as a nurse but she was currently working for a care provider on a precarious contract, and her father worked in the civil service. As the first student in her family to attend university, she (and her parents) had aspirations for a more satisfying and rewarding career. She knew that accepting the poorer return of the short-term administrative role would relieve her immediate fears about supporting herself, but at the same time, it was not a move that would result in her fulfilling her career ambitions. If anything, it was likely to forestall those ambitions as she would not be gaining relevant experience to add to her CV.

One irony in Paige's account was that she identified how her university regularly advertised jobs for graduating students. Typically, these would not be characterised as the sort of jobs that Paige or her peers envisioned for their long-term career. They were essentially generic administrative roles in non-academic parts of the university. A cynical view of her university might interpret their self-interest in creating jobs solely aimed at their own graduates as a means of improving metrics, such as graduate employment rates, which could improve their position in rankings such as the TEF. A more troubling reading might note that Paige's post-1992 university was an institution that had significantly increased its recruitment of student numbers against the backdrop of HE marketisation. The university itself had expanded significantly both in terms of student numbers and also across its estate portfolio. This expansion, funded by the accrual of student debt, *reproduced the conditions of past inequitable student outcomes at a much greater scale reflecting the massification of student numbers.* There was a Kafkaesque resonance in Paige's own analysis of her situation if she became absorbed into the administrative functioning of the university,

It might mean I'm stuck here. I might never leave.

Many of the Black students, whilst keen to attend university for the long-term benefits it would bring them and/or because of the expectations placed upon them by parents and family, were also aware that the additional burden incurring debt would place them at a long-term disadvantage. Cody (male, mixed White/Black, post-1992) was aware of this but was also keen to stress the longer-term impacts of gaining a university degree.

It does seem very hard now with all the debt and on top of that the pressure of having to perform – and to do well all the time – but you know you can't give it 100% when you have to go to work at the weekends. Also the expectation from my family, they want me to do well and not waste this time. I try and look at it longer term, when I am older the stats tell me I should earn more in the long term. I think if you only thought about the debt then you wouldn't come to university.

Cody's optimism was not shared by students such as Madison (female, Black, post-1992), for whom the long-term effect of debt was a constant worry,

I find going to university a very expensive experience, the fees alone are so much and then on top of that there is the living expenses and the rent. I wanted to come to university and my parents really wanted me to come. I am the first to go, and being the oldest as well it means I have to be a role model for my younger sisters. My parents were so proud when I came here, but I wonder about the debt I will have when I leave and how I will pay it back. It worries me, because I see it as something that will just be there forever, hanging around my neck. That worries me all the time.

For many students like Madison, the opportunity offered by a university degree was tempered by their family's economic circumstances. Despite having made their way to university and despite facing the prospect of successfully graduating, they still harboured significant doubts about their future. Class and affluence were continual factors in determining student experience.

Class

We found that the social class background of respondents influenced their access to financial support. This affected their decision-making in relation to all aspects of higher education, from whether or not they applied to university in the first place to decisions about future employment or postgraduate study. There were clear correlations between those students whose parents had not attended university themselves being less likely to have access to financial support for their studies, whilst students whose parents had attended university were more likely to be in professional well-paid occupations and better placed to offer financial support. There was also a correlation between students enrolled at the Russell Group university and those whose parents had themselves been to university. Such findings are unsurprising and reflect the well-evidenced phenomenon of education reproducing social class rather redressing inequalities (Bourdieu, 1984). Our findings also highlight how the expansion of higher education is itself a process that reproduces rather than a means to redress inequality. It highlights how first-generation students are disadvantaged on multiple fronts. In the first instance, they are less likely to receive informed guidance on university options from their family, and later, having made their way to university they are likely to face greater financial pressures. In our sample, those students who attended the post-1992 university were more likely to be from working-class and less affluent backgrounds compared to those who attended the Russell Group university.

Returning to Paige's account, she described how her decision to go to university was complicated by her family's class and lack of economic capital,

> I think the fees issue is a big deal for a lot of people who are in the same situation as me, my mum didn't go to university and she doesn't have a job that is that well paid. So I have to rely more on my dad, I had to think carefully about how much going to university was going to cost me. I didn't have that choice of not being able to think about it, like I know other students who just thought ok I want to go to university and then thought about the money. For me, *I had to think about the money first*, could I afford it, could my family afford it? If they couldn't, I would not have been able to go. So those financial restrictions mean some people have more choices

and options because there are some things – like money – that they don't have to worry about.

(original emphasis)

Similarly, Victoria (female, Black/White mixed, post-1992) explained how she felt class background impacted her own and fellow students' decision-making about the future. She identified a relationship between the significance of social capital as a support mechanism and economic capital as a practical requirement,

I think your background comes into it and with that comes people's financial situations, you have to have that support to be able to go to university and that is in addition to the fees that you need. So, you have that debt and if you want to continue with a Masters you have to think about all of those things. It's not just a case of saying, oh I want to do a Masters so I can. You have to think about what that means and what that entails. Some people have those choices but others have to think about the financial burden.

Paige and Victoria both highlighted that for other students, those from more affluent backgrounds, considerations of finance were less significant. Maitri (female, Indian, Russell Group) explained the thought processes behind her choice of university and course of study. She described her family circumstances as comfortable. Her father owned a clothing factory, and her mother recently returned to work as a teacher following a period as a stay-at-home mother. Maitri explained how her mother had been to university, but her father had not and deeply regretted this as a lost opportunity. As a migrant to the UK in the 1960s, the expectations of his family were to work and provide for his family. Both parents expected all their children to go to university,

I wasn't thinking about the financial aspect, I was more concerned about the course and getting the grades I needed to get into [Russell Group university] and we didn't really discuss finance as a big deal. I knew I would have to take out a loan for the fees, but for the accommodation my parents paid for that and they give me an allowance each month. I wasn't worried about the financial aspects, my parents were keen for me to focus on passing and doing well in my 'A' level exams so that I could get the grades to get into university – and they said that as much. That was their main concern.

In many respects, Maitri described a process that aligned with expectations of the 'student as consumer'. She made decisions based on finding the best course at the best university to match her plans for the future. Being able to adopt that approach, however, was reliant upon the initial access to economic capital and a supportive family environment. Waseem (male, Pakistani, Plate

Glass) provided a similar account of his family's expectation that he solely concentrate on his studies. To facilitate this, his parents wanted him to focus on his studies and so took care of all the financial aspects for him.

> I wasn't involved in the finance, my parents took care of all of that. They said they just want me to make sure I do well on my course, so that needed to take priority. I think they felt if I had to worry about money then that would mean it would distract me from my studying, so they didn't want me to have that additional burden. Their main concern was doing well to get here and the doing well while I am here. I have grown up with it being drummed into me that it's all about getting a great education that set you up for life. In some ways, you could say it's just the Asian mentality, the Asian way.

Some students also identified another category of students, primarily within the Russell Group university, who displayed excessive wealth and lavish lifestyles. Leela (female, Indian, Russell Group) described seeing students driving into the university in expensive, new cars or wearing designer clothes,

> I see those very rich students coming in, it's mostly Asian boys who are driving the flash cars, Mercedes, but I think they must be their parent's cars. How can they afford them? But I also see some of my friends, they have the designer bags and sunglasses. Why do they need those? They're making a statement to let everyone know they have the money. But not all the students are that rich, there are many who are struggling and it's a big deal for them to come to university. You are able to see the inequalities at uni who is rich and who is not so rich.

None of the students we interviewed explicitly suggested it was wrong for other students to openly demonstrate their wealth. Rather students made clear that they understood the wider inequalities they would evidence in society were also alive and kicking in the university. The narrative that universities might be engines of social change was not one that materialised in these conversations. Students described how past inequalities shaped their access to university and time spent at university. The debts they were incurring felt more like burdens that would follow them into futures that would be similarly shaped by the same pre-existing inequalities in their lives.

Conclusions

Aspirations towards education vary across different socio-economic groups (Baker et al., 2014; Chowdry et al., 2011), and the shift towards the student-as-consumer model has had different impacts different groups of students.

Placing greater individual responsibility for the financing of a degree through student loans for both fees and living costs has inevitably created new inequalities. Our study found clear cultural differences in the expectations students have of their parents in relation to financial support and debt related to differences of ethnicity, social class, parental education and employment. The shift from recognising higher education as a public good to being valued as a commodity that can be marketized (Collini, 2012) fosters new types of inequality, but ones that predictably mirror historic patterns of racial and class marginalisation.

The role of economic capital was a significant factor for all students in our research. For many working-class or poorer students, their choices are hampered by both a lack of economic capital and fears of the consequences of incurring large debts. Perhaps the single greatest failing of the current funding arrangements for higher education is the promotion of a narrative that student loans secure equitable access. The argument that all students can complete degree study and will be rewarded equitably based on their performance regardless of their family wealth does not hold water. Not only are some students dissuaded from studying, but when poorer students do attend, they find it harder to draw upon family economic capital. Consequently, they rely more heavily on self-funding through employment, whilst simultaneously incurring greater debt in the form of student loans than other wealthier students. These circumstances create costs and benefits that continually disadvantage and advantage students throughout their study. In Bourdieu's terms, prior access to all forms of capital is a key factor in how well individuals can compete to gain more or better rewards in the future. The current funding arrangements mean that poorer students compete for their degrees with the odds stacked against them. In our research, the impact of economic capital was an overwhelming factor in students' accounts of their time at university.

Whilst the narrative of equitable access is one that does not stand up to scrutiny, strong arguments are made to suggest that ethnic minorities are the most successful groups in universities today. Access to forms of ethnic capital often being cited as being a hugely beneficial resource, but on closer examination, this is another very flawed narrative. The students we interviewed provided evidence that ethnic capital is largely only effective when aligned with economic capital. For some poorer students, this might emerge out of extended family support networks, but more generally, the economic capital needed is capital at the disposal of parents. Participants highlighted how traditional expectations of leaving home to become a student and lead more independent lifestyles were not available to them because of the expectations of parental support understood in terms of ethnic capital. For these students, ethnic capital did materialise as the financial support needed to succeed in their studies, but it came with strings attached. The financial support was premised on their relinquishing some degree of independence and choice in their lifestyles. This highlights the complex relational context in which ethnic capital can be a valuable resource but one that reproduces itself. It is neither given nor taken by individuals without the process of its production shaping both parties. One alternative, to break with the process, is to break to some degree with family and community. In doing so, echoing Bourdieu's account of *habitus clivé*, but from a perspective of ethnic transformation rather than class progression. For other students, whose families were simply unable to provide enough financial support, their own choices were more directly limited but often with similar outcomes. Students who could not afford to leave home also found expectations of more independent lives were effectively curbed.

The expectations of educational economies envisaged by successive neo-liberal governments, since New Labour, have been that a free market delivers value in two different though complementary ways. Firstly, it delivers value for money in the most basic sense that the market is understood to produce better educational offerings more cheaply. Secondly, it enriches the individual's engagement with educational economies by freeing them from relying on the state or other people to pay for or determine their educational choices. Within these arguments, student loans offer an unfettered opportunity for students to pick and choose their best options. None of these benefits have materialised in practice. Not least because the 'market' has always been rigged by caps on fee levels and the failure of measures like the TEF to fully equip students to act as consumers. *In this respect, it fails on its own terms.* In our research, what also emerged was the continuing significance of family relationships and economic capital as key determinants of BME student experience. Relationships, pressures, and expectations of students before university all rematerialise within the university. These include pre-existing inequalities, including those in schools and in the labour market, which adversely impact BME experiences inside the university. The narrative that it is BME rather than White students who have benefited most from the expansion in student numbers disguises the relational significance of economic to ethnic capital and also fails to acknowledge the ancillary costs of ethnic capital for BME students who do reap its benefits.

Notes

1 The Teaching Excellence Framework (TEF) is a national framework which assesses excellence in teaching at universities and colleges. Providers are awarded a gold, silver, or bronze rating. The TEF is managed by the Office for Students (see https://www.officeforstudents.org.uk/for-providers/the-tef/about-the-tef/).

2 It is possibly more revealing that the OFS prefaced this statement with the following explanation of inflation (presumably to aid policy-makers): 'The value of money changes over time with inflation. By adjusting past and future monetary values, we can show past money at current value – in real terms' (2024, p. 8).

3 A further irony is of course that both Lord Mandelson and Lord Willets enjoyed their time at the University of Oxford (like many of their parliamentary peers) at a

time when they were not required to pay tuition fees. Alan Johnson left school at the age of 15 and did not attend university.
4 For more detail on the impact of parental income levels on different types of students, see the Martin Lewis MoneySavingExpert website (https://https://www.moneysavingexpert.com/) which includes a range of calculators and other tools.

References

Bachan, R. (2014). Students' expectations of debt in UK higher education. *Studies in Higher Education, 39*(5), 848–873.

Baker, W., Sammons, P., Siraj-Blatchford, I., Sylva, K., Melhuish, E., & Taggart, B. (2014). Aspirations, education and inequality in England: Insights from the effective provision of preschool, primary and secondary education project. *Oxford Review of Education, 40*(5), 525–542.

Bankston, C. III, & Zhou, M. (2002). Social capital as process: The meaning and problems of a theoretical Metaphor. *Sociological Inquiry, 72*(2), 285–317.

Belfield, C., Britton, J., Buscha, F., Dearden, L., Dickson, M., van der Erve, L., Sibieta, L., Vignoles, A., Walker, I., & Zhu, Y. (2018). *The relative labour market returns to different degrees*. IFS Research Report.

Benton, T. (2012). *Do I really need a degree? The impact of tuition fee increases on young People's attitudes towards the need for qualifications*. NFER.

Benson-Egglenton, J. (2019). The financial circumstances associated with high and low wellbeing in undergraduate students: A case study of an English Russell Group institution. *Journal of Further and Higher Education, 43*(7), 901–913.

Bhopal, K. (2010). *Asian women in higher education: Shared communities*. Trentham.

Bhopal, K. (2016). British Asian women and the costs of higher education in England. *British Journal of Sociology of Education, 37*(4), 501–519.

Bhopal, K. (2018). *White privilege: The myth of a post-racial society*. Policy Press.

Bhopal, K., & Myers, M. (2020). *The impact of COVID-19 on A level students in England*. https://doi.org/10.31235/osf.io/j2nqb

Bhopal, K., & Myers, M. (2023). The impact of COVID-19 on a level exams in England: Students as consumers. *British Educational Research Journal, 49*(1), 142–157.

Bhopal, K., Myers, M., & Pitkin, C. (2020). Routes through higher education: BME students and the development of a 'specialisation of consciousness'. *British Educational Research Journal, 46*(6), 1321–1337.

Blanden, J., & Machin, S. (2013). Educational inequality and the expansion of United Kingdom higher education. *Scottish Journal of Political Economy, 60*, 597–598.

Bourdieu, P. (1984). *Distinction: A social critique of the judgement of taste*. Harvard University Press.

Bourdieu, P. (1986). The forms of capital. In J. Richardson (Ed.), *Handbook of theory and research for the sociology of education* (pp. 241–258). Greenwood.

Brown, R., & Carasso, H. (2013). *Everything for sale: The marketization of UK higher education*. Routledge.

Browne Review. (2010). *Securing a sustainable future for higher education: An independent review of higher education funding and student finance*. HMSO.

Burke, P. (2013). *The right to higher education: Beyond widening participation*. Routledge.

Callender, C. (2008). The impact of term-time employment on higher education students' academic attainment and achievement. *Journal of Education Policy, 23*(4), 359–377.

Callender, C., & Jackson, J. (2005). Does the fear of debt deter students from higher education? *Journal of Social Policy, 34*(4), 509–540.

Callender, C., & Jackson, J. (2008). Does the fear of debt constrain choice of university and subject of study? *Studies in Higher Education, 33*(4), 405–29.

Chowdry, H., Crawford, C., & Goodman, A. (2011). The role of attitudes and behaviours in explaining socio-economic differences in attainment at age 16. *Longitudinal and Life Course Studies, 2*(1), 59–76.

Collini, S. (2012). *What are universities for?* Penguin.

Connell-Smith, A., & Hubble, S. (2018). *Widening participation strategy in England.* House of Commons Briefing Paper.

Crawford, C., & Greaves, E. (2015). *Socio-economic, ethnic and gender differences in higher education participation* (Research Paper No. 186). BIS.

Dearden, L., Fitzimons, E., & Wyness, G. (2011). *The impact of tuition fees and support on university participation in the UK.* Institute of Education.

Dearden, L., Fitzsimons, E., & Wyness, G. (2014). Money for nothing: Estimating the impact of student aid on participation in higher education. *Economics of Education Review, 43*, 66–78.

Department for Business, Innovation & Skills. (2011). *Students at the heart of the system.* The Stationery Office.

Esson, J., & Ertl, H. (2016). No point worrying? Potential undergraduates, study-related debt, and the financial allure of higher education. *Studies in Higher Education, 41*(7), 1265–1280.

Gani, A. (2016, March 13). Tuition fees 'have led to surge in students seeking counselling'. *The Guardian.* https://www.theguardian.com/education/2016/mar/13/tuition-fees-have-led-to-surge-in-students-seeking-counselling

Gov.UK. (1998). Teaching and Higher Education Act. HMSO.

Gov.UK. (2004). Higher Education Act 2004. Retrieved October 1, 2024, from https://www.legislation.gov.uk/ukpga/2004/8/introduction

Gov.UK. (2022). *Graduate labour market statistics.* https://explore-education-statistics.service.gov.uk/find-statistics/graduate-labour-markets

Harrison, N., & Agnew, S. (2016). Individual and social influences on students' attitudes to debt: A cross-national path analysis using data from England and New Zealand. *Higher Education Quarterly, 70*(4), 332–353.

Harrison, N., Chudry, F., Waller, R., & Hatt, S. (2015). Towards a typology of debt attitudes among contemporary young UK undergraduates. *Journal of Further and Higher Education, 39*(1), 85–107.

Higher Education Policy Institute/Higher Education Academy. (2017). Student Experience Survey 2017. HEPI/HEA.

Hillman, N., Dickinson, J., Rubbra, A., & Klanann, Z. (2018). *Where do student fees really go? Following the pound.* Higher Education Policy Institute.

Hubble, S., & Bolton, P. (2018). *Higher education fees in England.* House of Commons Briefing Paper.

Hunt, A., Lincoln, I., & Walker, A. (2004). Term-time employment and academic attainment: Evidence from a large-scale survey of undergraduates at Northumbria University. *Journal of Further and Higher Education, 28*(1), 3–18.

Hussain, Y., & Bagguley, P. (2007). *Moving on up: Asian women and higher education.* Trentham.

Institute for Fiscal Studies. (2017). *Higher education funding in England: Past, present and options for the future.* IFS.

Jessop, D., Herberts, C., & Soloman, L. (2005). The impact of financial circumstances on student health. *British Journal of Health Psychology, 10*(3), 421–39.

Johnson, C., Pollard, E., Hunt, W., Munro, M., Hillage, J., Parfrement, J., & Low, N. (2009). *Student income and expenditure survey 2007/08: English-domiciled students. DIUS research report 09–05.* Institute for Employment Studies.

Macleod, D. (2004, March 30). Academics attack 'divisive' fees bill. *The Guardian.* Retrieved July 20, 2023, from https://www.theguardian.com/education/2004/mar/30/tuitionfees.students

Marsh, S. (2017). Number of university dropouts due to mental health problems trebles. *The Guardian*, May 23. https://www.theguardian.com/society/2017/may/23/number-university-dropouts-due-to-mental-health-problems-trebles

Menzies, V., & Smyth, C. (2024, March 25). Russell Group gets most of its fees from overseas; UK students now account for less than 25% of some leading institutions' income, analysis shows Russell Group gets most of its fees from overseas; UK students now account for less than 25% of some leading institutions' income, analysis shows. *The Times*. p. 1.

Millburn, A. (2012). *Fair access to professional careers: A progress report by the independent reviewer on social mobility and child poverty.* https://assets.publishing.service.gov.uk/government/uploads/system/uploads/attachment_data/file/61090/IR_FairAccess_acc2.pdf

Mishra, S. (2020). Social networks, social capital, social support and academic success in higher education: A systematic review with a special focus on 'underrepresented' students. *Educational Research Review, 29*, 1–24.

Murphy, R., & Wyness, G. (2015). *Testing means-tested aid* (CEP Discussion Paper No. CEPDP1396). Centre for Economic Performance, London School of Economics.

Neves, J., & Hillman, N. (2019). *Student academic experience survey.* AdvanceHE/HEPI.

OFS. (2024). *Financial sustainability of higher education providers in England 2024.* Office for Students.

Portes, A. (1987). Social capital: Its origins and applications in modern sociology. *Annual Review of Sociology, 24*, 1–24.

Reay, D. (2018). *Miseducation: Inequality, education and the working class.* Policy Press.

Richardson, T., Elliott, P., & Roberts, R. (2015). The impact of tuition fees amount on mental health over time in British students. *Journal of Public Health, 37*(3), 412–418.

Richardson, T., Elliott, P., Roberts, R., & Jansen, M. (2016). A longitudinal study of financial difficulties and mental health in a national sample of British undergraduate students. *Community Mental Health Journal, 53*(3), 344–352.

Roberts, R., Golding, J., Towell, T., Reid, S., Woodford, S., Weinreb, I., & Vetere, A. (2000). Mental and physical health in students: The role of economic circumstances. *British Journal of Health Psychology, 5*(3), 289–297.

Russell Group. (2024). *Russell Group response to The Times article on international student fee income.* https://russellgroup.ac.uk/news/russell-group-response-to-the-times-article-on-international-student-fee-income/

Shah, B., Dwyer, C., & Modood, T. (2010). Explaining educational achievement and career aspirations among young British Pakistanis: Mobilizing 'ethnic capital'? *Sociology, 44*(6), 1109–1127.

Tempest, M. (2004, March 27). Government wins top-up fees vote. *The Guardian.* Retrieved July 20, 2023, from https://www.theguardian.com/politics/2004/jan/27/publicservices.uk5

Tomlinson, M. (2014). *Exploring the impact of policy changes on Students' attitudes and approaches to learning in higher education.* Higher Education Academy.

University and College Admissions System (UCAS). (2017). *End of cycle report.* UCAS.

Wilkins, S., Shams, F., & Huisman, J. (2013). The decision-making and changing behavioural dynamics of potential higher education students: The impacts of increasing tuition fees in England. *Educational Studies, 39*(2), 125–141.

Wiseman, J., Davies, E., Duggal, S., Bowes, L., Moreton, R., Robinson, S., Nathwani, T., Birking, G., Thomas, L., & Roberts, J. (2017). *Understanding the changing gaps in higher education participation in different regions in England.* DFE.

Zhou, M. (2005). The multifaceted experiences of the children of Asian immigrants. *Ethnic and Racial Studies, 27,* 376–402.

Zhou, M., & Bankston, C. (1994). *Growing up American: How Vietnamese children adapt to life in the United States.* Russell Sage Foundation.

6

FAMILY SUPPORT, SOCIAL CAPITAL, AND RESOURCES

Black and minority ethnic (BME) students in our study talked about the different types of support they received from their families, and for many, this support was crucial in how they experienced their time at university. These family networks also played an important role in influencing the decisions students made about career paths *after* they had graduated. The support took different forms and was received from a wide range of people, nuclear and extended family as well as friends of the family and others. Students spoke about four types of support that influenced their experiences, choices, and performance whilst at university. These were financial, emotional, and professional support, and access to networks. In this chapter, we explore these different kinds of support and argue that students from wealthy, middle-class backgrounds tended to receive greater levels of often better-quality support compared to those from working-class backgrounds. These types of support have a significant impact on the choices and decisions young people make during their final year as undergraduates at universities. The choices available to them during this transitionary period have a significant impact on later access to the labour market and postgraduate study, future life chances, and social mobility.

Parental support

Many of the students in our study described their desire to become more independent by leaving home to study at university. Independence for students in this context is understood in terms of having the ability and opportunity to take responsibility for their own lives, when living away from the family home (Holdsworth, 2009; Lewis et al., 2014). As discussed in Chapter 5, the hopes and expectations for a number of students to pursue this traditional pathway towards

DOI: 10.4324/9781003097211-6

independence did not always materialise. For some, this was the consequence of limited economic resources and for others, it reflected familial demands that limited their independence including expectations that students remain at home. More generally, there is evidence to suggest that parents' level of involvement in their children's education, whilst away from home has been increasing with more students remaining dependent on parents' support when they leave home to go to university (Wartman & Savage, 2008). There is a range of conflicting evidence suggesting that higher levels of parenting and different parenting styles result in less autonomy for students and that greater autonomy may limit educational achievement but that such support has generally positive outcomes (Hofer & Moore, 2010; Hwang & Jung, 2021; Jeynes, 2024; Padilla-Walker & Nelson, 2012). Studies have found that frequent contact between parents and children is beneficial in terms of providing regular support to children who have left home but that new social networks are also vital sources of support for students (Nieuwoudt & Pedler, 2023; Sarigiani et al., 2013; Spence, 2012).

During their first year of study, students may feel disillusioned and consider withdrawing from their studies if they do not receive enough support from their family, particularly if they have experienced difficulties during the transition from school to university (Longden, 2006; Yorke & Longden, 2008). Various reasons for withdrawal from the university include illness, mental health issues, workload, difficulties with assessment and academic writing, time management, family commitments, and unforeseen problems, but these become most problematic for students who experience multiple rather than a single issue (Nieuwoudt & Pedler, 2023; Williams & Roberts, 2023). This is more likely to be a factor for students from disadvantaged backgrounds (Yorke & Thomas, 2003), mature students (Johnson & Watson, 2004), students in part-time employment (Broadbridge & Swanson, 2005; Longden, 2006), and first-generation students. Students need support to develop their 'learner identity' which includes making connections and forming new relationships with other students and staff (Briggs et al., 2009, 2012; Harvey & Drew, 2006; Johnson & Watson, 2004; Wainwright & Marandet, 2010). Many students feel emotional support from their families is most vital in times of academic stress, such as approaching assignment deadlines or during exam periods, and also, when dealing with personal stress linked to friendships and other relationships (Bland & Stevenson, 2018). Others have explored the importance of family support for low-income students (Roska & Kinsley, 2018; Sax & Wartman, 2010; Tinto, 2007; Wartman & Savage, 2008). Students who attend university can also have the effect of encouraging learning for their peers and family members when they receive family support at university (O'Shea, 2015; Wainwright & Watts, 2019).

Ethnicity and family support

There is evidence to suggest that families of students from BME backgrounds invest a great deal in their children's education particularly whilst at university, and they provide their children with high levels of different kinds of support, particularly financial support (Bhopal et al., 2020). BME students often identify the value of the social support they receive from their friends and family and identify this has a positive impact on their academic success (Cotton et al., 2016; Yorke & Longden, 2008). There is also evidence that students from BME backgrounds, particularly those from Black backgrounds are less likely to spend time socialising whilst at university, but more time on their studies, and this is related to the types of support they receive from their families focused around doing well and achieving (Bhopal, 2010; Rhamie, 2007; Stuart et al., 2008).

Different ethnic groups experience a range of family support measures, and some research has challenged stereotypical assumptions about BME communities and education that are commonly held to be true. Muslim students, for example, often report receiving support for their educational journeys from their parents and family, and this is related to the high expectations that Muslim parents place on their children's success in higher education (Khattab & Modood, 2018). It is also argued that Muslim families use 'Islamic capital' to ensure their children succeed in higher education to gain access to the labour market (Fernández-Reino, 2016; Franceschelli & O'Brien, 2014). At the same, time many Muslim students use the educational space of universities to reinvent themselves and to challenge traditional notions of the 'Muslim other' (Bagguley & Hussain, 2014; Harris et al., 2017). This does not suggest a contradictory pattern of behaviour, rather it is the evidence that family networks and social relations are highly complex and multifaceted. In our research, similar patterns emerged and this often highlighted how students were navigating within the competing demands of their family relations, friendship networks, the university, and their own personal ambitions (see Chapter 5 for a discussion of the ambiguous relationships between ethnic, social, and economic capitals for students).

Family support for education has been used as a site of empowerment in the experiences of Muslim men (Haywood & Mac an Ghaill, 2013), Muslim women (Mirza, 2015), Asian women (Basit, 2013), and Black groups (Bhopal & Danaher, 2013). Many BME communities draw on their families for different kinds of support during their experiences of studying at university. This support has been found to be fundamental and critical for students as they navigate higher education (Bhopal & Danaher, 2013). Recent research suggests that Black families, particularly those from middle-class backgrounds, provide high levels of support for their children's schooling, in which they use specific strategies to ensure their children succeed whilst they continue to experience racism and marginalisation (Rollock et al., 2013; Vincent et al., 2013).

Access to social networks has also been shown to have a significant impact once students have left university and seek employment. Parental networks have been shown to be highly beneficial in finding a job (Kadushin, 2012; Patacchini & Zenou, 2012). However, BME students are less likely than White students to have access to such networks (Bhopal et al., 2020; Flap & Völker, 2008; Zuccotti, 2015). Furthermore, students who have access to parental financial resources have the freedom to be more selective in the types of employment they will accept, as well as access to unpaid internships, compared to others with less choice and the need to find work for financial necessity (Zwysen & Longhi, 2016). Some BME groups may also have access to community networks, which may increase their chances of finding employment (Bayer et al., 2008; Patacchini & Zenou, 2012). They are more likely to rely on community networks (Battu et al., 2011; Dustmann et al., 2011), particularly in relation to cultural values linked to the importance and value of education (Shah et al., 2010; Zhou, 2005). Zwysen and Longhi (2016) have argued that such opportunities can affect access to good jobs in the labour market (for a further discussion on the labour market, see Chapter 8).

The following sections explore our qualitative findings in relation to the different kinds of support respondents received. These included the often gendered emotional support identified by Black students, the advantages family connections could have when securing placements or internships, how more affluent families' access to more and better forms of social and cultural capital was an advantageous resource, and the broader professional and academic support available to middle-class students.

'Mums are great': Black students, emotional support, and gender

All of the students in our study spoke about the emotional support they received from their families. In the previous chapter, we discussed how family support for Asian students was often associated with discussions about financial support. This was less the case for Black students who were more likely to mention emotional support compared to students from other ethnic groups. One consistent finding was the gendered nature of support with many students emphasising how much they valued the support they received from their mothers. Jennifer (female, Black, Russell Group) described how she relied on her mother during a difficult time at university,

> I had a tricky time when I came here and left home. I felt very lonely and suffered some mental health issues in my second year, but it was my mum who was the one who I could contact and who was there for me and who told me who I should contact here at the uni, but she was my first point of contact.

In Jennifer's account, her mother's support was invaluable and contributed to her sense of well-being. Other students highlighted similar examples of their mother providing emotional support at particularly difficult times, but more generally students described ongoing emotional support as they navigated more mundane aspects of university life. Isaac (male, Black, Plate Glass) talked about the continued emotional support he received from his parents, specifically his mother.

> My mum is great, she's a really good person to talk to and I always turn to her. She is a wise woman and she gives me good advice on all sorts of things and sometimes when I feel down like I know I could have got a better mark on something, she just tells me to learn from the experience and do better next time. She is a great person to talk to because she makes me see the bigger picture, rather than the now. She always tells me to think of the long term goals and the bigger plan, that the degree is just the beginning. It will open up all sorts of doors me and put me in a better position compared to other people who don't have a degree.

Shelby (female, Black, Plate Glass) also spoke about how her mother was her source of emotional support and inspired her to do well.

> My mum is a really strong woman and she has made sure we are the same way, she does talk about how we have to be a certain way and that is because she's very proud. She keeps us all in check and gives us lots of different kinds of support. For me, it is that she is always there for us and sometimes she will tell me things that I don't want to hear. And that is ok because she's my mum and I think she knows best. Most of the time. She wants me to do really well at uni and reminds me of the cost and that I should make the most of it, and that ultimately it will help me get a good job.

In Isaac and Shelby's account, it is clear that both mothers provide support that is practical, hard-headed, and will contribute usefully to their academic development (e.g. focusing on what can be achieved not dwelling on work that has gone less well or being clear that the cost of a degree is part of a longer-term strategy). They also flag up the other qualities (being wise, being proud) that relate to academic achievement more tangentially and suggest more holistic forms of support.

Many Black respondents emphasised that it was their mothers who were the ones who pushed them and provided them with greater levels of support compared to their fathers or other members of their family. Mothers played a key role in ensuring their children were working hard in order that they could achieve the best outcomes from their time at university. Rachel (Black, Plate

Glass) said her mother was the one who provided her with emotional support because she was the primary caregiver.

> I don't know why but it seems to be my mum who is the one who I always turn to when I need to talk about something. She is the one who has always been there. My dad works away a lot but my mum is always here. She is also the one I am closer to, but I think mothers in the Black community play a much stronger role and seem to be the ones who we turn to.

This was also echoed by Ethan (Black, Plate Glass),

> My mum is the one I go to for advice, but it depends on what I need to talk about. There are some things I will talk to my dad about, but it's mainly my mum who I speak to the most. She comes up with good suggestions for all sorts of things and most of the time she gives me good suggestions because she knows me and knows what I'm like. She's also quite pushy and wants to know everything about what is going on in my life, so she always give me the advice even when I might not want it or ask for it.

Many of the Black students spoke about how the emotional support they received from their parents and extended families was part of their coping mechanism in a society in which they often felt excluded, particularly in relation to experiences of racism (see Chapter 4 for a detailed discussion of racism). The type of support identified by Ethan highlights the contradictory nature of the relationship between family networks and his personal student independence. On the one hand, Ethan notes his mother is intrusive (she is 'quite pushy'), but he still values and actively seeks out her advice (to be clear, in the interview being 'quite pushy' was recounted as an affectionate characteristic). In Ethan's account, his mother's interest in his life and the advice (asked for and unasked for) she proffered were valuable resources that bolstered his independence away from home and maintained his investment in his family life. Ethan's account most resembled that of Shelby, who lived at home. Shelby also discussed how living at home resulted in an inevitable intrusiveness of family life but explained this was largely mitigated by the value of parental support. An overarching pattern emerged from all students that ready access to family support was a vital resource in their educational journeys. Even students who identified over-protectiveness or interference in their personal lives invariably tempered these accounts by acknowledging how much they valued close relationships with their parents.

The extended family

Many Black students also described the support they received from their nuclear and extended families as having a positive influence on their university life. Olivia (female, Black, Plate Glass) spoke about how she would often seek support and advice from her grandmother and her aunts and uncles,

> I do find I have lots of people who I can turn to for emotional support, that's what makes me feel I am really supported emotionally. I will often talk to my grandmother or my aunts – they all live close by – so it's easy to talk to them. They tend to give me similar advice to my mum, I don't know if that's because they think the same way and know me or because they think that's the kind of advice my mum would give me. It's good to know they are there and I can speak to them. I have cousins who have gone to university and they also give me advice and tell me about their own experiences and all this has helped me in different ways. I feel very lucky that I have lots of different family members I can ask.

Similarly, Kyle (male, Black, Plate Glass) always felt there was someone he could turn to in his extended family if he was unable to speak to his mum. This additional support was an added source of support for Kyle when he needed it.

> We are a large extended family and we are a close family. We see each other a lot and so if I need to speak to someone there will always be someone around, if mum can't speak to me. We have big gatherings at Christmas and Easter and we make sure we stay connected with each other.

Our research supports previous studies which have shown that Black mothers are significant sources of support for their children's education (Erel & Reynolds, 2014; Reynolds, 2005) and advocate for success during their children's educational trajectories (Reynolds, 2013). The relationships that Black students had with their families, specifically their mothers, and extended families were influential in how they experienced university life. If they had a problem, they felt there was always someone they could turn to. They received a significant amount of emotional support from their families, and this helped them to make decisions and choices whilst they were at university.

Work experience, family networks, and social capital

In our study, we asked respondents about the support they received in terms of having access to different social networks through family connections. Most students were required to complete an element of work experience as an internship during the second year of their degree studies. These were often highlighted (by both the university and by students) as an opportunity for students to gain valuable experience and make connections within their chosen profession or career path. When securing suitable placements students described how these were often facilitated by family connections rather than by the university.

Consequently, students from middle-class backgrounds whose parents were themselves working in professions or industries, characterised as being 'graduate jobs', were more likely to secure better placements through their family networks. This outcome was reported regardless of student's ethnic backgrounds. It was also an outcome that was identified to extend beyond the specific parental profession; so, whilst it might be anticipated that the children of solicitors could readily be offered internships within legal firms, in addition to this, the same families were able to draw upon connections to other professions, e.g. the media or medicine. Bourdieu describes social capital as a collectively owned form of capital that is accrued and fostered through social relationships over time, it is 'the product of investment strategies, individual or collective, consciously or unconsciously aimed at establishing or reproducing social relationships that are directly usable in the short or long term' (Bourdieu, 1986, p. 22). This account of social capital was evident in the descriptions students gave of how effectively they could access placements and internships. Whilst universities provided support in identifying and arranging these internships, they were often limited in scope. Students like Bharati (female, Bangladeshi, Plate Glass) relied upon the university to secure a placement. She explained how work placements were overseen by an administrator whose role was to build networks with employers in the local area,

> To be honest she was great. Really interested in me. She tried very hard but it was a dead end. I ended up shadowing an estates manager at [local council office] which was a waste of time. It wasn't about design we just spent all day measuring desks and planning office moves.

Bharati was training to be an architect and the internship she accepted was the best her university could find. Her parents were very supportive of her going to university, but their own networks were limited; her mother was a nurse and her father worked as a security guard. For other students, if the university was unable to find a better option for their placements they could draw upon their parental networks. One such student was Sam (male, Black, Russell Group), he did not arrange his internship through the university but instead relied on family connections. Both his parents had been to university and both were in professional employment (his mother was an accountant and his father was a solicitor). Sam spoke about how his dad's connections led to him securing an internship in the London office of a top solicitors firm,

> I was lucky because of my dad's job. He's a solicitor and he knows lots of people, not just people he works with, but the people they work with. So to be honest in some ways I was spoilt in the amount of choice I had as

to where I could go to do my internship. I could have worked in any area of law, because of the access my dad had to different firms. In the end, I worked with a solicitor who deals with family law because that was what I was interested in. It was one of the best things I did because it made me think about what I want to do in the future, it also made me have more connections. The people I worked with know me now and will contact me again if something were to come up.

Sam's suggested he was *lucky* to have access to this opportunity, but in reality, he was drawing upon his, and his family's reserves of pre-existing social capital. He evidenced how belonging within a more affluent family with connections to professional networks ensured that his personal interests were privileged within the collective interests of *people like himself and his family*. Sam's recognition of his belonging within this well-connected collective was also the recognition that he was entitled to the 'credential' of their collective resources (Bourdieu, 1986). By drawing upon this collective resource, he was simultaneously accruing social capital to extend his own interests and also reinforcing the social capital of the collective. Sam went on to explain how his outcomes compared to his less 'lucky' friends,

I know I am very fortunate to have had the internship, some of my friends were not so lucky. They ended up doing their internship in rubbish places, even like the local council which didn't sound very good, which was wasn't even that related to our degree. I was able to put the degree with the internship, it was related and I got a lot out of it.

Sam was very self-aware that because of his family connections he was able to secure a highly advantageous internship and that this had real material benefits for his career. He explained that the experience of his internship was something that would stand out on his CV and that the personal connections he had made would be valuable in the future. At the same time, his allusion to luck felt misplaced. Some other students, who also had access to such networks gave more explicit accounts that their access to social capital positioned them in very advantageous positions compared to their fellow students who did not have similar resources to draw upon. Ipsita (female, Indian, Russell Group) whose parents both went to university (her mother was a teacher and her father was a doctor), explained,

I know how fortunate I am to be able to have both parents who are professionals and who understand some of the hard stuff at university. I knew I had to just ask them if they could get me access to work placements. I could work in a school or get my dad to get me something in a surgery. He knows lots of other doctors so it wouldn't have been hard. In the end I did work in a school and it was great. I got that connection through my mum.

Ipsita was convinced her mum's access to schools would affect her future choices and open up opportunities for different types of employment linked to education. She also described how different types of capital intersect; the value attached to her social connections was also reflected in valuable knowledge about the professions themselves,

> My mum knows a lot about the different schools in our area and she has worked in some of them. So I know she could get me into them if I needed more experience and it could be that if I wanted to get a job there later that would work in my favour. She also knows other kinds of jobs I could do. If I wanted to stay and work in education but not be a teacher.

Ipsita intended training as a teacher following graduation. However, she also explained that she had doubts about working in schools based on the stress her mother experienced in her current role. Talking this through with her mother, she had identified one possibility of working temporarily in a school but later transitioning to a role teaching trainee teachers in a university. Ipsita made the point that her knowledge of career options was greater than some of her peers also planning to become teachers. She framed that knowledge within the entitlements of social capital predating her time at university,

> It was the same when I applied to [university]. My dad then was 'you have to go to this uni or this uni'. I never wanted to go to London or to Oxford so he was like, 'ok. But you do have to go to a Russell Group'. Which now I get. He was right. One of my friends at school went to [local university] and it's not good.

Rachel (Black, Plate Glass) also spoke about the connections her mum had with different universities where she did her internship.

> My mum works in a university, she's a careers officer and so knows lots of different people in the university. She was able to get me something in a different department. It was working with HR [Human Resources] which is actually something I want to do after I graduate.

Rachel, Ipsita, and Sam, all described how social capital was useful to them, but there were marked differences in the value of the social capital each could draw upon. In particular, the contrast between Sam and Rachel highlighted how some students had access to more valuable social capital than others depending on their parents' class and status.

Other students, however, were unable to draw upon any such connections. They struggled to find suitable internships related to the type of employment they intended to pursue after they graduated. Students like Zainab (female, Pakistani, post-1992) recognised they were disadvantaged,

> I have had real problems finding an internship to give me some kind of work experience, it has been extremely hard for me and I have ended up being in a place that I think isn't really going to help me in the long term for what I do after I have left university. I am working in an office which is the education department for the area, I might go into something like this but in the end it's just office work. It's nothing to do with education and I could have done it anywhere.

Zainab went on to describe some of the benefits her peers enjoyed in terms of the connections they had through their parents or their extended families.

> I was very naïve and used to think it was a certain type of family. Well mainly white middle class families who were the ones who had all the contacts to people who could help them in the future. But it seems that there are lots of wealthy and middle class Asian students who have access to all kinds of things which places them in a better position to someone like me. None of my parents went to university and they are not in professional jobs so they wouldn't know who to contact.

For both Zainab and Bharati, the university was the main resource they could access to make connections with a potential employer. They both noted that their respective departments made considerable efforts to find them suitable internships but that this did not materialise in practice. As first-generation students, they were heavily invested in the potential for a university degree to transform their life chances, but it appeared that the opportunities they were hoping for were more likely to be open to students who came from more privileged backgrounds. Dilip (male, Bangladeshi, post-1992) was in a similar position and explicitly described feeling disadvantaged because his parents had not been to university and did not have professional careers. His dad was a taxi driver and his mum was a housewife.

> If I wanted to do taxi driving or be a Uber driver then yeah that would be pretty simple for me to do that. I would just ask my dad. But I don't want to do that, I'm doing this degree to get me out of that. I don't know who I could ask if they could have me in their company or firm to give me a helping hand. I have to join the list where you get what you're given and that isn't usually much. If my parents were doctors or even if they worked in some professional jobs it would be much easier for me. But it isn't and that's it.

Bharati, who felt her choice of a work placement had been compromised because she relied on the university to find her a position, identified inequalities that access to networks had on her future and current choices. She framed these as being longstanding social relations that reproduced the same inequalities. In particular, she identified how some students were privileged by their prior educational experiences,

> I think a lot of the students have those connections from way back. So a lot of them went to the really good schools – not necessarily private schools – but the good grammar schools and so they have that advantage under their belt. They are able to use those experiences when they come to university and portray themselves in a certain way, which some of us don't have. I didn't go to a grammar school, I went to my local school which was under funded and not in a good area. So you realise you start at different starting points, which are good for some and not so good for others.

Bharati, like Ipsita, highlighted that the materialisation of privileged social capital was not a singular occurrence. So it was not just that one student secured a better internship because their parents had a particular social connection but rather that those parents had been continuously advantaged throughout their lives. They accrued social capital (just as they accrued other forms of capital) because they had access to better and more valuable forms of capital from the outset. Their collective membership of affluent and successful families was protected through the collective sharing of connections and networks of similar families to provide collective opportunities for their children. Some students who had access to more valuable social networks seemed unaware of these privileges, often appearing to regard the experience of privilege as so natural to their life course that it was unquestioned. Maitri (female, Russell Group, Indian) who had attended a grammar school prior to attending university saw her connection to networks as something she expected everyone to have access to.

> Doesn't everyone have access to those kinds of things [networks]? I don't see that as being any different to what my friends have as well. We all went to the same kind of schools and all of our parents had similar jobs and so we all have had access to these kinds of things.

Maitri's assumption was that all students had access to networks and connections that helped them gain access to jobs. Her perception of her accumulation of social capital was almost that this happened without any conscious endeavour on her own or anyone else's part. Maitri described how her father (a self-made businessman) was a well-known figure,

> in the community. If there's a wedding he's invited. Every week he's on a guest list. Or something at the Gudwara. He knows everyone and vice versa everyone knows him.

Our findings suggest that those students who had no or limited access to networks, also tended not to have attended grammar or independent fee-paying schools and their parents were less likely to be in professional occupations. By contrast, more affluent, middle-class students whose parents were more likely to have been to university and more likely to be employed in professional careers had access to a ready-made 'network of knowns' (Bhopal, 2016). This provided them with access to multiple resources including social networks that benefited them in the short and long terms. In the short term, it secured a well-placed internship that, at a later date, translated into opportunities and advantageous positioning in the labour market. Access to more and better forms of social capital had a direct relationship to gaining better experience within the labour market and as a consequence resulted in more impressive *CVs*.

Social capital and professional support

Students also discussed how they might access professional or academic support through their social networks. This included having someone read their essays and coursework, provide advice on significant elements of academic work such as dissertations, and help with drafting *CVs* and job applications. Students from middle-class, professional backgrounds received a great deal more academic support from family members. These regularly included parents, or other close family members, reading their assignments or providing academic advice. Students with access to these sorts of networks were able to draw upon the collective capital of their families to assist them to achieve higher grades. For other students, their families were unable to provide comparable support even if they wanted to do so. Talika's (female, Indian, post-1992) older brother was studying for his MA degree and she explained how she would often ask him to comment on her assignments,

> My brother went to Newcastle to do this degree and he's super clever so I am always asking him to look at stuff for me. He always proofreads my work and tells me if he thinks it makes sense and then he edits it for me sometimes. He will also be looking at my dissertation so that I can get a good mark on that as well.

Other students mentioned their parents who would often read their work and provide them with comments. Nicole (female, Black, Russell Group) said she always asked her mum to provide her with comments about her work and did not necessarily see this as an advantage and felt it was something all of her fellow students would have access to.

> Sometimes I don't get the time to show my mum my work, my essays or coursework but when I do she gives me really good comments. She did an English degree and so knows how things should come across and if they have a coherent argument to them, so I always show my work to her. I think this is what everyone does and should do, it doesn't mean that you are cheating or in a better position in any way, it just means you are getting some help along the way. Everyone does it.

For students like Nicole, asking their parents for advice or help was no different to her expectations that she could, 'reach out to my lecturers' if she needed support with an assignment. However, for other students like Cody (mixed White/Black, post-1992), this was not an option and he identified this put him at a disadvantage,

> I've never had any kind of help with my work at uni. My parents wouldn't know where to start if I showed them my work so I have to do it all myself. I know that other students ask their parents but I don't have anyone. I think they will be in a better position than me. They will get better marks in the end and in their finals, which means they will probably end up with the better jobs. So yes, to a big extent if you don't have that support then you are placed at a disadvantage compared to your peers.

Another student who was unable to draw upon family support was Anthony (male, Black, post-1992), who identified as working class. Anthony characterised attending university as a personal choice and one that he had largely undertaken without family support. Prior to university, he worked for two years as a bicycle courier in London to accumulate some savings. He categorised the types of support received by Talika and Nicole as unfair,

> I don't ask anyone to help me with my work because it's **my** work. If I asked for help, then it wouldn't be my work would it? I think that those people who do ask for support are actually cheating, which means the final grade they get won't be all down to them. What will that be worth in the end? *It's not their own work but at the same time they will benefit from it*, but at the end of the day it's still cheating.
>
> (*original emphasis*)

Other students discussed showing their CVs and job applications to their parents and members of their extended families in order that they could make the best possible impression when applying for jobs. Hamza (male, Pakistani, Russell Group) spoke about how his family connections could be used to his advantage in multiple ways,

> My mum has this friend who works in a big law firm in Scotland, at first I was going to do my internship there but it was too far but now I'm going to see if I can apply for a job there. She [mum's friend] is going to look at my CV first and see if there's anything I can add. I think that will make all the difference and will place me in a better position than other people and the fact that she knows me will also work in my favour.

He was able to draw upon both the extended network of his family connections and also shared access to knowledge or cultural capital to help draft a better application. Hamza did not see this as *cheating* in any way but rather as a beneficial collective relationship,

> How can it be seen as cheating? She is only helping me because she wants to and she knows my family and knows the kind of family we are. I know my mum would do the same for her and her kids, it's just helping each other that's all. This is what everyone does, some people might not want to admit it, but everyone does it.

The notion of *just helping each other* was something that was considered the norm for many students in our sample who were from middle-class, professional backgrounds. Connections with personal and professional networks enabled the transformation of cultural and social capitals between families to ensure individuals from similar backgrounds became part of an in-group of which membership included different advantages, including first refusal and access to jobs. Students clearly recognised social capital as a shared resource in which mutual interests were protected. This was rarely understood as a problematic or inequitable process. Anthony, for example, was unusual in describing the benefits of social capital as 'cheating'. Social capital tended to be understood as playing the more positive role identified in Putnam's (2000) work of building collective, mutually beneficial resources. It was less likely to be identified, particularly by students with the most access to better forms of social capital, as a competitive resource deployed within a competitive field. Those students who did identify social capital as an advantageous resource that was not distributed evenly described it in terms of 'cheating' or in more general terms as inequitable. Chakir (male, Pakistani, Russell Group), for example, explained,

> Even if I do well in my degree and get a good 2:1 or first, I still won't have the same access to advantages that some of those students have. I don't know – neither does my family know – anyone who works in a big law firm who could help me climb the ladder or get a good job there. I have to do the normal route and apply for that job that I want and that means I am competing with lots of other people who I am just as good as them but I don't have the connections. The connections get you far, they mean at least you get a look in. Which some of us won't even get.

Implications for future choices/decisions

All respondents said the types and levels of support they received would have implications for their future choices and decisions after graduation. These included whether they would apply for postgraduate study (such as an MA or PGCE) or access the labour market. For some students, it was clear multiple factors shaped their options. Zainab who had struggled to secure a useful internship, whose parents did not go to university, and who experienced financial insecurity whilst at university explained,

> I feel limited in knowing what I can do after I graduate. I don't know as much as I need about what options I have because I don't have anyone to tell me what I can do. Other than the services we have here [name of university] there isn't anyone out there telling me, this is the best thing you should be doing that will be of the most benefit for you.

Amy (female, Black, post-1992) felt her lack of knowledge about future choices significantly disadvantaged her. Neither of her parents went to university and she identified this as an ongoing problem when making decisions about her career. Amy talked about wanting to pursue further postgraduate studies and described a conversation with her personal tutor discussing her suitability to be a PhD candidate in the future. The only advice she could draw upon was that provided by her university and she expressed doubts about the reliability of that advice,

> My personal tutor told me I should do a Masters at [other local, Russell Group university]. It would be a better experience. She seemed to say that [Amy's university] is rubbish. She burst my bubble when she said that. I've been really happy here and there's a discount on the fees [for current undergraduate students]. Even though I know I would like to do a Masters,

I'm not sure about the scholarships that are available to me. I wouldn't know where to start with them and I have been looking for jobs but that seems to be pretty tough anyway. My parents want me to get a job. They always help me out but they can't get their head around a Masters. Or a PhD. I talk to friends about it but we're all the same we don't really know how it works. If it's worth it even.

Unlike Amy, Nicole (Black, Russell Group) did not feel nervous about her decisions following graduation,

I am looking forward to graduating, it has been a long 3 years but I have really enjoyed it. I'm going to have a little break before I decide what to do. My parents are fully supportive of that decision and will support me in whatever I want to do. I know I will probably go back home before I decide what to do and can stay there for as long as I want. We've talked about the sort of jobs I want to do. My mum just wants to sit down with me and blitz it. It will be like a little project for her. Finding Nic a great job!

Nicole's parents had both been to university themselves and when Nicole discussed her time at university and plans for the future, she drew upon a greater reservoir of knowledge about her opportunities. Nicole was not simply following a career path defined by her parents. She was actively pursuing her own ambitions. She was, however, supported to succeed in these ambitions more effectively because of her family background. By contrast, Amy, even when discussing an apparently supportive conversation about postgraduate study, lacked both practical knowledge and also the same level of self-confidence that students like Nicole could draw upon.

Conclusions

Our research found significant differences in the experiences of BME students driven by a range of competing factors including ethnicity and class backgrounds. Middle-class BME students whilst they shared disadvantages with their working-class peers (such as their experiences of racism discussed in Chapter 4) still occupied more advantageous positions. Their previous educational experiences and their access to family connections and social networks worked in their favour and provided them with access to advantages that their working-class BME peers did not have. One overwhelming finding was that students from more affluent backgrounds tended to have access to a range of advantageous resources that were sedimented within their life chances. These resources can readily be understood in terms of social, cultural, and economic capitals (Bourdieu, 1986). The narratives of student transitions from school to university to the labour market are shaped by student's access to these resources. It was also clear that the uneven distribution cuts across different types of capital. Students from wealthier backgrounds would benefit from their access to economic capital, but at the same time, this would inevitably be associated with better social networks and more informed levels of parental knowledge. The significance of social capital as a resource that was not just being drawn upon by students but also simultaneously being generated anew cannot be underestimated. Students' recognition of entitlement to these collective resources was also a process of extending the reach of socially shared capital: accepting a valuable internship, for example, was a moment in which the social entitlement to that resource extended. Taken together, having more or better forms of capitals was associated with better outcomes. That is unsurprising but it does unsettle the claims to meritocracy that underpinned all three universities mission statements and commitments to widening participation policy.

Surprisingly, few students identified the competitive practice of universities (competing for better grades and degree classifications, for example), or their competitive outcomes (such as more rewarding or better paid jobs), as being a competitive field in the Bourdieusian sense. They did not, for example, provide accounts in which they identified being explicitly in competition with their peers. More generally, students identified universities as broadly supportive places in which they were positioned inequitably by dint of their social circumstances, but not unfairly by the university *per se*. The sense that students recognised (or misrecognised) the legitimacy of their positioning as a natural outcome would resonate within Bourdieu's account of doxa, as 'an uncontested acceptance of the daily lifeworld' (Bourdieu & Wacquant, 1992, p. 73). From a sociological perspective, we might anticipate students recounting their transitions through their life course as likely to be understood as a natural progression that goes largely unchallenged. However, more problematic is the role played by universities faced by circumstances in which inequity can easily be identified. If students are better positioned because of their pre-existing capitals, it would be reasonable to anticipate universities would actively adopt the fundamentals of widening participation to redress the uneven distribution of resources. In the next chapter, we discuss how the forms of cultural capital that Amy identified as being missing in her experience are not necessarily being fostered by the university. If anything, we identify that the same inequalities are reproduced by universities suggesting the institutional willingness to embrace a natural order in which some better placed students are always more likely to succeed, and conversely, less well-placed students are more likely to do badly.

Whilst the overarching pattern of outcomes suggests that inequality is largely unchallenged, our interviews also revealed how personal relationships, such as supportive parents, were a significant factor for students' wellbeing. The strength of these relationships cut across the range of different family experience with both more and less affluent students and students from different ethnic backgrounds highlighting the value of supportive parents. Despite being a shared trait, the complexities of family support were revealed in the differential weighting that accrued between being supportive parents in a general sense and being supportive parents in both a general and specifically academic sense by being able to offer support around academic work. One line of demarcation was the distinction between parents who had themselves attended university (or elder siblings who had been to university) and those with less educational experience. The accrual of more specific knowledge within families bolstered the value of the more general support they could offer (just as social networks bolstered access to specific outcomes such as work placements or internships).

References

Bagguley, P., & Hussain, Y. (2014). Negotiating mobility: South Asian women and higher education. *Sociology, 50*(1), 43–59.

Basit, T. (2013). Educational capital as a catalyst for upward social mobility amongst British Asians: A three-generational analysis. *British Educational Research Journal, 39*(4), 714–732.

Battu, H., Seaman, P., & Zenou, Y. (2011). Job contact networks and the ethnic minorities. *Labour Economics, 18*, 48–56.

Bayer, P., Ross, S., & Topa, G. (2008). Place of work and place of residence: Informal hiring networks and labor market outcomes. *Journal of Political Economy, 116*, 1150–1196.

Bhopal, K. (2010). *Asian women in higher education: Shared communities.* Trentham.

Bhopal, K. (2016). *The experiences of BME academics in higher education: A comparative study of the unequal academy.* Routledge.

Bhopal, K., & Danaher, P. (2013). *Identity and pedagogy in higher education.* Bloomsbury.

Bhopal, K., Myers, M., & Pitkin, C. (2020). Routes through higher education: BME students and the development of a 'specialisation of consciousness'. *British Educational Research Journal. 46*(6), 1321–1337.

Bland, B., & Stevenson, J. (2018). *Family matters: An exploration of the role and importance of family relationships for students in UK higher education.* Stand Alone/UK Council for International Student Affairs: Sheffield Hallam University.

Bourdieu, P. (1986). The forms of capital. In J. Richardson (Ed.), *Handbook of theory and research for the sociology of education* (pp. 241–258). Greenwood.

Bourdieu, P., & Wacquant, L. (1992). *An invitation to reflexive sociology.* University of Chicago Press.

Briggs, A., Clark, J., & Hall, I. (2009). *Bridging the gap: Project report on student transition.* Newcastle University.

Briggs, A., Clark, J., & Hall, I. (2012). Building bridges: Understanding student transition to university. *Quality in Higher Education, 18*(1), 3–21.

Broadbridge, A., & Swanson, V. (2005). Earning and learning: How term-time employment impacts on students' adjustment to university life. *Journal of Education and Work, 18*(2), 235–49.

Cotton, D., Joyner, M., George, R., & Cotton, P. (2016). Understanding the gender and ethnicity attainment gap in UK higher education. *Innovations in Education and Teaching International, 53*(5), 475–486.

Dustmann, C., Glitz, A., & Schonberg, U. (2011). *Referral-based job search networks* [Discussion Paper 1–47]. Norface Migration.

Erel, U., & Reynolds, T. (2014). Black feminist theory for participatory theatre with migrant mothers [Special issue 'Black British Feminism']. *Feminist Review, 108*, 106–111.

Fernández-Reino, M. (2016). Immigrant optimism or anticipated discrimination? Explaining the first educational transition of ethnic minorities in England. *Research in Social Stratification and Mobility, 46*, 141–156.

Flap, H., & Völker, B. (2008). Social, cultural, and economic capital and job attainment: The position generator as a measure of cultural and economic resources. In N. Lin, & B. H. Erickson (Eds.), *Social capital: An international research program* (pp. 65–80). Oxford University Press.

Franceschelli, M., & O'Brien, M. (2014). 'Islamic capital' and family life: The role of Islam in parenting. *Sociology, 48*(6), 1190–1206.

Harris, P., Haywood, C., & Mac an Ghaill, M. (2017). Higher education, de-centred subjectivities and the emergence of a pedagogical self among black and Muslim students. *Race Ethnicity and Education, 20*(3), 358–371.

Harvey, L., & Drew, S. (2006). *The first-year experience: A review of literature for the higher education academy*. The Higher Education Academy.

Haywood, C., & Mac an Ghaill, M. (2013). *Education and masculinities: Social, cultural and global transformations*. Routledge.

Hofer, B., & Moore, A. (2010). *The iconnected parent: Staying close to your kids in college (and beyond), while letting them grow up*. Free Press.

Holdsworth, C. (2009). "Going away to uni": Mobility, modernity, and independence of English higher education students. *Environment and Planning A, 41*, 1850–1864.

Hwang, W., & Jung, E. (2021). Parenting practices, parent–child relationship, and perceived academic control in college students. *Journal of Adult Development, 28*, 37–49.

Jeynes, W. H. (2024). A meta-analysis: The relationship between the parental expectations component of parental involvement with students' academic achievement. *Urban Education, 59*(1), 63–95.

Johnson, G., & Watson, G. (2004). "Oh gawd, how am i going to fit into this?" Producing [mature] first-year student identity. *Language and Education, 18*(6), 474–487.

Kadushin, C. (2012). *Understanding social networks*. Oxford University Press.

Khattab, N., & Modood, T. (2018). Accounting for British Muslim's educational attainment: Gender differences and the impact of expectations. *British Journal of Sociology of Education, 39*(2), 242–259.

Lewis, J., West, A., Roberts, J., & Noden, P. (2014). Parents' involvement and university students' independence. *Families, Relationships and Societies: An International Journal of Research and Debate. 4*(3), 417–432.

Longden, B. (2006). An institutional response to student expectations and their impact on retention rates. *Journal of Higher Education Policy and Management, 28*(2), 173–187.

Mirza, H. (2015). Decolonizing higher education: Black feminism and the intersectionality of race and gender. *Journal of Feminist Scholarship, 7*(8), 1–12.

Nieuwoudt, J. E., & Pedler, M. L. (2023). Student retention in higher education: Why students choose to remain at university. *Journal of College Student Retention: Research, Theory & Practice, 25*(2), 326–349.

O'Shea, S. (2015). Filling up the silences – First in family students and university talk in the home. *International Journal of Lifelong Learning Education, 34*, 139–155.

Padilla-Walker, L., & Nelson, L. (2012). Black hawk down? Establishing helicopter parenting as a distinct construct from other forms of parental control during emerging adulthood. *Journal of Adolescence, 35*(5), 1177–1190.

Patacchini, E., & Zenou, Y. (2012). Ethnic networks and employment outcomes. *Regional Science and Urban Economy, 42,* 938–949.

Putnam, R. (2000). *Bowling alone: The collapse and revival of American community.* Simon and Schuster.

Reynolds, T. (2005). *Caribbean mothers: Identity and experience in the U.K.* Tufnell Press.

Reynolds, T. (2013). 'Them and us': 'Black neighbourhoods' as a social capital resource among black youths living in inner-city London. *Urban Studies, 50*(3), 484–498.

Rhamie, J. (2007). *Eagles who soar: How black learners find the path to success.* Trentham.

Rollock, N., Gillborn, D., Vincent, C., & Ball, S. (2013). *The colour of class: The educational strategies of the black middle classes.* Routledge.

Roska, J., & Kinsley, P. (2018). The role of family support in facilitating academic success of low-income students. *Research in Higher Education, 60,* 415–436.

Sarigiani, P., Trumbell, J., & Camarena, P. (2013). Electronic communications technologies and the transition to college: Links to parent-child attachment and adjustment. *Journal of the First-Year Experience and Students in Transition, 25*(1), 3560.

Sax, L., & Wartman, K. (2010) Studying the impact of parental involvement on college student development: A review and agenda for research. In L.W. Perna (Ed.) *Higher education: Handbook of theory and research* (pp. 219–255). Springer.

Shah, B., Dwyer, C., & Modood, T. (2010). Explaining educational achievement and career aspirations among young British Pakistanis: Mobilizing "ethnic capital"? *Sociology, 44,* 1109–1127.

Spence, P. (2012) Parental involvement in the lives of college students: impact on student independence, self-direction, and critical thinking [Dissertations, Paper 315, Loyola University].

Stuart, M., Lido, C., Morgan, J., & May, S. (2008). *Student diversity, extra-curricular activities and perceptions of graduate outcomes* (Report of a Higher Education Academy Grant 2007–2008). The Higher Education Academy.

Tinto, V. (2007). Research and practice of student retention: What next? *Journal of College Student Retention, 8*(1), 1–19.

Vincent, C., Rollock, N., Ball, S., & Gillborn, D. (2013). Raising middle-class black children: Parenting priorities, actions and strategies. *Sociology, 47*(3), 427–442.

Wainwright, E., & Marandet, E. (2010). Parents in higher education: Impacts of university learning on the self and the family. *Educational Review, 62,* 449–465.

Wainwright, E., & Watts, M. (2019). Social mobility in the slipstream: First generation students' narratives of university participation and family. *Educational Review. 73*(1), 111–127. https://doi.org/10.1080/00131911.2019.1566209

Wartman, K., & Savage, M. (2008). *Parental involvement in higher education: Understanding the relationship among students, parents, and the institution.* Jossey-Bass.

Williams, H., & Roberts, N. (2023). 'I just think it's really awkward': Transitioning to higher education and the implications for student retention. *Higher Education, 85*(5), 1125–1141.

Yorke, M., & Longden, B. (2008). *The first-year experience in higher education in the UK, report on phase 1 of a project funded by the higher education academy.* Higher Education Academy.

Yorke, M., & Thomas, L. (2003). Improving the retention of students from lower socio-economic groups. *Journal of Higher Education Policy and Management, 25*(1), 63–74.

Zhou, M. (2005). Ethnicity as social capital: Community-based Institutions and embedded networks of social relations. In G. C. Loury, T. Modood, & S. M. Teles (Eds.), *Ethnicity, social mobility and public policy* (pp. 131–159). Cambridge University Press.

Zuccotti, C. (2015). Do parents matter? Revisiting ethnic penalties in occupation among second generation ethnic minorities in England and Wales. *Sociology, 49,* 229–251.

Zwysen, W., & Longhi, S. (2016). *Labour market disadvantage of ethnic minority British graduates: University choice, parental background or neighbourhood?* [No. 2016-02]. ISER Working Paper Series.

7

INSTITUTIONAL SUPPORT

Who gets it and why?

In the previous chapter, we discussed how family support was often differentiated along the lines of class, ethnicity, and family expectations. In addition to family support, some participants also discussed other forms of support they had received. In particular, this included advice from schools prior to admission and also support received during their time at university. Such institutional support is particularly significant in the current higher education context with greater numbers of students being recruited, many of whom are the first in their family to attend university. Such students inevitably are less able to draw upon their social capital to inform decision-making.

The introduction of widening participation policies has seen a significant increase in the numbers of students attending university from a wide range of diverse backgrounds. In the context of neoliberal policy making, this has led to a related interest in measuring the success of higher education institutions not just in their initial recruitment but also in their retention of students to completion of their degrees. In effect understanding, or at least quantifying, how first-generation or non-traditional students transition into becoming graduates who embark on graduate careers. This evaluation of success in measurable terms is one consequence of the shift from elite to mass to universal university education that has characterised developing nations (Trow, 1973). At the same time, third-way understandings of social organisation have tended to situate reflexive individuals as exercising agency in order to navigate transitions through the life course including taking greater individual responsibility for managing risk and challenges throughout their lives (Bauman, 2012; Giddens, 1991; Field et al., 2009). The analysis of more liquid forms of modernity parallels the emergence of neoliberal political and economic structures. Despite the optimism of theorists such as Ulrich Beck (1992, 2006) that individuals'

DOI: 10.4324/9781003097211-7

potential to navigate more equitable pathways towards greater social mobility within globalised economies would increase, the evidence of the last 20 years has been that individual life courses have often been adversely impacted by structural inequalities (Dorling, 2015; Wilkinson & Pickett, 2010). Although this highlights the inequity of neoliberal economies when delivering services that might have previously been regarded as public goods, it is worth noting that neoliberal economies do not represent a break from an earlier golden age when inequalities were not embedded within education. One depressing conclusion would be that the same forms of inequality characterise the provision of higher education within both modernity and postmodernity. As Bourdieu notes, the evolution of neoliberalism is inevitably linked to the reproduction of different forms of the same inequitable social structures and the emergence of different forms of legitimisation for those same inequalities (Bourdieu, 1984, 2003).

In Chapters 5 and 6, we discussed the importance of financial and family support and how this is often differentiated along the lines of ethnicity and class. In addition, universities themselves provide a range of support for their students. How the provision of such services is affected by the needs of an increasingly diverse student body is the focus of this chapter. In particular, we interrogate how the provision of university practices designed to provide evidence of measurable effective support might still be skewed along class and racial lines to reproduce longstanding inequalities and, at the same time, is used as evidence that legitimises these inequalities. In a Bourdieusian sense, this creates the circumstances in which dominated or subordinated factions accept their subordination, while dominant groups recognise the validity of their dominant positions (Bourdieu, 1977, 1984).

Who needs support?

There is evidence to suggest that the type of institutional support students receive can have a significant impact on their university experience. Both academic and pastoral support have been shown to affect the learning experience and improve academic progress and achievement for students (Cahill et al., 2014; Ning & Downing, 2012; Thomas, 2012). However, the types of support that are most effective for students often vary between individual needs, and the level and expectation of support required by students vary as they progress through their studies (Eaton et al., 2000; Fu, 2010).

Universities have found greater diversity a challenge when providing support for students. Students from non-traditional and marginalised backgrounds often have different needs and require different and greater pastoral and academic support compared to those from traditional backgrounds (Ellis & Allan, 2010; Kennett & Reed, 2009; Kitzrow, 2003; Rolfe, 2002).

Whilst there is evidence to suggest differences in academic attainment for different ethnic groups, this varies by different institutions as well as differences in teaching and assessment practices (Richardson, 2015), and the expectations of different students, with non-traditional students unclear of what is expected from them (Burke et al., 2013). Black and minority ethnic (BME) students are less likely to be satisfied than white students with their university experiences and a more targeted approach with specific activities which offer support to marginalised students in order that they can reach their full potential is needed (Mountford-Zimdars et al., 2017). Mahmud and Gagnon (2023) identify a relationship between racist academic mindsets and the attainment gap for BME students enacted through the types of support White academics provide for non-White students.

The quality and quantity of support that students receive varies both within and between institutions with many students reporting poor support from academic staff (Leese, 2010; Lowe & Cook, 2003). There is also evidence to suggest that the type of university students attend has a significant impact on levels and the quality of support offered to students (Byrne et al., 2012; Leese, 2010; Telford & Masson, 2005). Money et al. (2017) have argued that academic staff must work to connect with students in order to cement a relationship in which they belong within the university community. This is particularly true for first-year students who tend to require the greatest amount of support. It is important they quickly form positive relationships with staff tutors, to ensure attendance and participation in lectures and seminars and successful progression to the second year of study (Carter & McNeill, 1998; Cooke et al., 2006; Keup & Barefoot, 2005; Pitkethly & Prosser, 2001; Westlake, 2008). Academic support is crucial to support and engage students and this must focus on building student engagement into the university experience through clear initiatives with focussed outcomes (Krause, 2011; Thomas, 2012). Yorke and Thomas (2003) have argued that students from non-traditional backgrounds and those recruited through widening participation schemes require detailed formative assessment during their first year of study in order that they can advance and maximise their chances of success throughout their degree programmes. This includes thinking about their own identities as learners in order that they can form positive relationships with staff and their peers (Briggs et al., 2009; Johnson & Watson, 2004).

Different expectations between staff and students affect whether students feel engaged during their time at university and whether they decide to continue with their studies (Borghi et al., 2016; Byrne et al., 2012; Leese, 2010; Lobo & Gurney, 2014). In order to provide adequate support, students need to be treated as individuals and their specific needs must be addressed for successful transitions and journeys through higher education (Briggs et al., 2012). For the student-lecturer relationship to be successful, mutual trust and understanding are needed to create a partnership between both parties (Cahill et al., 2010). Identifying the need for universities to adopt more holistic understandings of students' needs, Mountford-Zimdars et al. note this is in a context where many institutions were 'surprised when they discover how many of their students combine study with work, caring or family responsibilities, the numbers living at home, and how they access information and support' (2017, p. 105).

One striking consequence of the changing higher education landscape is the apparent disconnect between universities' recruitment of greater numbers of more diverse students and their simultaneous inability to recognise their differing identities and needs. With students understood as consumers of education, it is arguable that universities can choose what support they offer different groups of students. Problematically, more elite or prestigious universities invested in restricting access could in effect choose to offer very little support to students who do not match their preferred demographics.

Differences in support: accessibility and satisfaction

Ethnic and gender differences have been identified in how students engage with academic and pastoral support from lecturers, with some evidence that BME students seek more academic support compared to their peers (Angrist et al., 2006; ECU, 2012; Stock et al., 2002). However, Miller (2016) has argued that BME students feel less confident than their peers to ask lecturers for academic support and feel less able to build trusting relationships with them. Furthermore, BME students do not feel adequately supported by their institutions or individual departments (Bernard et al., 2014; Masocha, 2015; *Race for Equality*, 2011), particularly in relation to the quality and quantity of academic and pastoral support they receive from tutors compared to their white peers (*Race for Equality*, 2011). BME students have also reported feeling their psychological needs are not met whilst at university. This results in greater stress and anxiety (Parkman, 2016) and has a negative impact on their motivation, hindering their chances to reach their full potential (Bunce et al., 2019). A greater investment from academic staff based on tailored needs for BME students is needed to create positive experiences for students to address inequalities based on teaching, learning, and assessment strategies (Richardson, 2015; UUK/NUS, 2019). A further benefit of creating positive relationships with personal tutors is the successful integration of students into the academic and social world of the university (Wilcox et al., 2005). This depends on the quality of the relationships between students and their personal tutors, as well as other academic staff (Thomas, 2002; Tinto, 2002). Initiatives to improve such relationships include effective induction courses and regular staff student contact (Lowe & Cook, 2003; Yorke & Thomas, 2003).

Support for mental health

Increasing numbers of students attend student counselling services, particularly in relation to mental health concerns, and this has been linked to drop-out rates at university (Auerbach et al., 2016; Broglia et al., 2023; Nevers & Hillman, 2016; Thorley, 2017). The research that has explored students and how they cope with different kinds of stress whilst at university has focussed on white students, with research suggesting that students from BME backgrounds are less likely to report mental health problems to counsellors compared to those from white backgrounds (Kerr, 2013; Mind, 2013). It has also been argued that many BME students feel they do not have a sense of belonging at university and feel alienated (Johnson et al., 2013), reporting a lack of understanding regarding the additional roles they may have such as those associated with caring responsibilities and having to juggle university with part-time employment (Van der Riet et al., 2015). There is also some evidence that BME students who are suffering from mental health may use self-help techniques rather than consult a counsellor (Fuchs et al., 2013; Kelly & Gleeson, 2018).

The following sections explore why respondents chose a particular university and the types of support they received from their university. It specifically examines how the type of university respondents' attended affected the quality and quantity of support they received.

Choosing the institution/course

Participants offered a variety of reasons for choosing their particular university. These included the attractiveness and reputation of the location, experiences of open days and students' assessment of the atmosphere of the campus, advice given by schools and family members. The proximity of the university to the family home was also a factor with some students preferring to remain close to home and study at their local university, whilst others identified moving away from home as a significant attraction. In addition, students discussed the advice or support from their schools when explaining their choice of university and how this often reflected school advisors' understanding of their personal circumstances. Students who attended the Russell Group university were more likely to suggest institutional status was a significant factor when considering their applications. They often identified the prestige and status of Russell Group universities as having a positive impact on their future careers. For these students, greater weight was given to the status of the university than its location, and sometimes more than the actual course of study. Students studying at the Russell Group university showed a greater awareness and understanding of the different types of universities. This included knowledge about league tables, the TEF,[1] and distinctions around research and teaching focussed universities. Students at all institutions were largely unaware of the

REF[2] as a means of identifying research excellence. However, a number of students at the Russell Group institution explained that their choice was largely driven by entirely different reasons such as the university location. These students often noted they only became aware of their university's status after they were admitted. Students studying at the post-1992 university (and to a lesser extent the Plate Glass institution) displayed less knowledge about the characteristics associated with university status and prestige.

Sam (male, Black, Russell Group) whose parents previously attended university explained how he drew upon both his parents' knowledge and also his school's sixth form advisor,

> For me, the main thing first and foremost was the reputation and status of the university. That was the key message the school drummed into me. I was going to get good grades so don't blow that by going to a naff university. I was told about Russell Group universities. Their reputation. So I checked the league tables with my parents to see where this university came and it seemed the best one for me. The reputation of the university mattered more to me than the actual course. If the reputation of the university was really good and the course was ok, then I would have still chosen this university.

Sam made clear that his family had a detailed knowledge of the higher education landscape and this aligned with the advice received at school meant he had a very clear plan about where he would apply. In Sam's case, he was predicted three A's at A level,[3] he applied for four Russell Group institutions, and as a safety net, he applied for a Plate Glass university with a good reputation in his subject area. Identifying the expansion of student numbers, Sam suggested, thinking about the future, that his main aim was 'to stand out from the crowd' by securing 'a good degree from a good uni'. Whilst Sam was well positioned, receiving good advice from his school and having knowledgeable parents, other students had fewer resources to draw upon. Riya (female, Indian, Russell Group) who was the first in her family to attend university explained,

> My parents don't know that there are different types of universities with different reputations, for them, university is university. I didn't have a clue myself, it was only when I was in sixth form when I was given really good advice about where I should apply that I found out. Our careers teacher was really good, she said that I should only apply to Russell Group universities because they expected me to do well in my 'A' levels.

Riya also made clear that she herself had taken a lot of initiative by researching her options. She also noted that within her friendship group,

> There was quite a lot of pressure for us all to apply to the same uni. Its ten minutes away. So we would all be together and that would have been fun.

My parents thought that was a good idea as well. They were thinking we could move into uni halls but still be close enough. I just had to keep on saying no, no, no! No way this is such a better uni. I literally had to sit them down with [sixth form careers advisor] to explain I could come here and that was the best option.

Another student whose parents had not been to university was Pavani (Indian, Russell Group), she explained how her parents wanted her to attend university but were not able to offer any real advice on which university. Unlike Riya, she did not feel her school gave her useful support

I had a little idea that X was a good university, but I didn't realise how good it was and that it had such a high status until I came here. We were told that when we started and we were told that they only take really good students here. Then when I looked at the league tables it seems that we are at the top and the courses are all really rated highly as well. The advice we were given at school was to think about where you wanted to spend the next three years. It was sort of if you want to be in the city or do you want to live in the country. One boy was a surfer and they said 'oh you should go somewhere by the sea'. At the time it sounded quite sensible. Quite grown-up. Making plans. You know what I mean? But I look back and think what were they talking about?

Pavani cited the location as the main reason she had applied and noted this was to some extent a decision informed by the advice she received at school. She had lived all her life in the same city and had spent most of her time at university living at home. Pavani was pleased with her final choice of a Russell Group university and felt it had been a good choice for her. However, she also made the point that she had applied to four other universities that were similarly close to her home and it was 'random, good luck' that she ended up in a Russell Group university.

Those students who attended the post-1992 university were generally not as knowledgeable about the status of different types of universities. In some part, this might be explained by Pavani's account; she only became aware of different types of universities and their respective status after being admitted to a Russell Group university, which was keen to ensure that all their students were aware of their status. The majority of participants chose the post-1992 university for reasons associated with its location. The university is located in a small compact city. It has a reputation for being a relatively inexpensive place to live and for having a lively, student-orientated nightlife. Many students mentioned it was commutable for them which limited their financial costs of not having to leave the parental home to attend university. Others mentioned the welcoming atmosphere and community atmosphere at the open days which convinced them to attend.

Amy (Black, post-1992) whose parents did not go to university explained that she lived close by and as a teenager, she and her friends would come for nights out in the city.

> I mean for me, the place [name of city] is a really big persuader, it's the city itself that I really like and a place where I want to live. I like the fact that the uni is spread out over the city. I just liked the area. You have to think about the area, it is a place you want to live because you are going to be here for 3 years and spend a lot of your time here.

Amy suggested that she had taken little advice from her school when applying to university as she had already decided that it was the only place she wanted to go to. Aaron (male, Black, post-1992) also mentioned the importance of the university location,

> The city itself, I just love it. There's so much to do here and for me it was about adding up all the little things. Do I like the city? Is there a lot to do here for someone like me? What is the student life like? That totally swung it for me, it had to be somewhere I knew I would enjoy living and somewhere that would be fun for me.

Aaron also recalled being advised at school to balance his decision-making to take account of both his academic and social interests. His university was a popular choice for pupils from his school in part because of its proximity to London (Aaron lived in a London suburb). This factor was stressed by his school aligned with advice that it was a cheap place to live. Aaron did not recall any specific advice from his school on different types of universities but he was told during careers advice session that it was one of the best universities. Aaron's parents did discuss alternatives,

> Not going to uni would be a deal breaker. They'd go ballistic. My dad thought I should go to Cambridge. And mum went along with that. But it was never an option. He suggested some other, classier places. [names two Russell Group universities]. But they were asking for better grades than I was ever likely to get. In the end they're pleased I'm here.

Bharati (female, Bangladeshi, Plate Glass) and several other Asian female students who attended the Plate Glass university discussed the expectations their families placed on them.

> My parents didn't want me to leave home, but they wanted me to go to university so I chose my local university which is good anyway. So that didn't matter so much. It also means I can go out with my friends and I don't have a large amount of debt when I leave. It works better that way for me.

Bharati discussed the support she received from her school when choosing a university. She was unsure whether different types of universities had been discussed. Her main memory was of one-to-one interviews with a careers advisor,

> they were quite useful at the time. I wasn't sure about uni at all. He was really helpful. Said go somewhere I would be happy. If I wanted to stay at home that would be sensible.

In some respects, it felt that students held slightly sketchy recollections of the advice they received from schools. This was probably unsurprising, several participants made comments to the effect that we were asking them about something that was, or at least felt as though, it was a long way in the past. Despite this, two significant conclusions did emerge. Firstly, the advice received by different students was not consistent in terms of the academic status of different institutions. Some students reported being given clear advice that there are differences between universities, but many were unaware of this at the time they applied to university. Secondly, in the recollections of students attending the post-1992 and Plate Glass institution, there was a stronger emphasis on advice to choose around location and social interests but less significance attached to the academic status of institutions. For students whose parents had a good knowledge of higher education, this was probably less of an issue, but for many other students, it meant the decisions they made about university were limited by a lesser awareness of different institutional reputations.

Institutional support

When students were asked about the types of support they received from their institution, they mentioned support in relation to coursework, from personal tutors, and about future decision-making. Students reported some variance in the usefulness of support they received and also, in their personal willingness to access support. Consequently, a slightly ambiguous picture emerged about the effectiveness of institutional support both between different institutions and within the same universities. Broadly, students at the Russell Group and Plate Glass university reported receiving the most practical, useful, and meaningful support compared to those at the post-1992 university. The Russell Group students specifically mentioned support other than academic support that they found to be useful. This included emotional support such as mental health counselling and careers advice. One consequence of the research focussing on final-year students was that many participants discussed the support they received from their departments and the university in relation to future careers, postgraduate options, and employment. For students like Josh (male, Black, Russell

Group), this included invaluable advice about the options available to him after graduation,

> I did have a lot of support, we all received a lot of emails about other things we could do when we finish, like a Masters or a PGCE.[4] They also had a lot of talks and workshops you could go to and I think they made a real difference to me. The department set out the different options for you and you could make your own decision.

Riya (female Indian, Russell Group), who previously discussed relying on her school for advice about applying to universities, similarly mentioned the value of support she received from her personal tutor when she applied for master's programmes.

> He helped me with my applications and gave me lots of different advice which was really useful. He gave me practical advice and if he didn't know, he told me where I could go to get the correct advice and that was really useful for me, otherwise I would not have known what to do.

Riya also commented that her tutor had been the same throughout her time at university and during that time he had got to know about her future plans and ambitions before her final year. He had previously offered Riya advice about opportunities offered by the British Council to work abroad and improve her language skills. Whilst this was not directly relevant to her academic studies it was something she felt would facilitate her future ambitions. Riya identified a deficit in her knowledge about higher education and her example highlights the positive impact of school and university support in building her reserves of cultural capital. Pavani also talked about how she discussed her degree journey with her personal tutor which helped her decide whether she wanted to continue with postgraduate study or enter the labour market.

> Talking with my personal tutor and other staff – people who are specialist in the things I am interested in – made me go through the whole degree and think about what I had learnt, both in the academic way and in my practice, that just made it much more easier for me to say this is what I can do, and this is what I want to do. Speaking to the tutors made me see that there are different options. I could carry on and do more studying or get a job. It was being able to discuss the pros and cons of this with people who had lots of experience. That was very useful for me.

Students like Pavani and Riya explained how they had relied on advice from their schools and from the university because their parents were unable to draw upon knowledge of higher education. Both referred to elements of luck in their outcomes. This was not a narrative universally shared by other participants.

Careers and employability support

It has been evidenced that BME students do not receive adequate support to make successful transitions into the labour market. They are less likely to secure work experience (Smith et al., 2019; Social Mobility Commission, 2016) compared to their white peers, which affects their chances of finding future paid employment and access to the labour market (Borghi et al., 2016; Shadbolt, 2016). Black students are more likely to report receiving inadequate careers advice or support from their universities resulting in disadvantages in accessing jobs and once in the labour market they experience discrimination and marginalisation (*Race to the Top*, 2012).

Students spoke about staff providing them with a range of different options that were available to them, and many mentioned that the university had staff who were experts in their fields and this helped them and gave them the confidence to trust staff when making their future decisions. Kuldeep (Indian, post-1992) said,

> The lecturers gave us lots of different information in terms of what we could do and I think because they know the subject really well, they were able to give us advice. One of my lecturers has studied Psychology, so she advised me to think about educational psychology which is something I didn't really consider before she mentioned it. I am now thinking of taking that forward.

Students also mentioned that staff were willing and available to read their applications for Masters courses, or jobs. In addition, the department and university offered students workshops and lectures on careers and employability. Dipak (male, Indian, Russell Group) said,

> We had quite a few careers advice lectures which we attended and they were very good and very informative. Some of them were by the staff here in the department and there were others that were by the actual careers service. They also had people coming in from the outside from big companies telling us the sorts of things they were looking for if we wanted to apply to their graduate scheme. These have all been extremely useful for me because I didn't have any idea what I wanted to do after I graduate.

One noticeable difference between the Russell Group and post-1992 institution was the more structured, multi-agency approach taken by the Russell Group university. In effect, a variety of careers advice was integrated between different arms of the university and delivered at different times within the overarching delivery of its curriculum. By contrast, the post-1992 university offered a more *ad hoc* approach that relied on students choosing to access different services themselves.

Hamza (male, Pakistani, Russell Group) emphasised how his department worked in conjunction with other academic departments as well as the careers network, employability, and library services to ensure that students had access to a wide range of knowledge when making their future decisions after graduation.

> The guidance that I have been given from the department and the university has been very good. There are lots of different avenues you can go to, so it's not just the department it's the whole university. They have several careers networks and these focus on different things. The first one I attended was on writing a good job application and CV. There was another on well-being and then one on future careers.

The careers network was also emphasised by respondents as being a useful and informative service, which helped respondents make their future decisions after graduation. Haley (female, mixed Black/White, Russell Group) said she would not have been able to make her decisions without the support she received from the careers service,

> We were given lots of information – handouts and websites we could look at – that was so good for me, because I didn't have a clue where to start. At the end of every year, and not just this year we had employability sessions we could attend, workshops, all part of the careers network. They would come in and tell us about the types of jobs we could get in the social sciences, and there were jobs they mentioned that I didn't think I could apply for with my degree but now I know there are lots of different options out there for me.

Leela (female, Indian, Russell Group) mentioned the specific support she received around graduate recruitment schemes,

> I wasn't sure what I was going to do after this year but the university has put on lots of different events about the different graduate schemes that are available to us. This has helped me a lot because it has made me realise that I know the different options that are available to me, otherwise I would think the only thing I can do is a Masters or get a job but here are lots of different graduate schemes you can go into, like the Banking industry, or fast track civil service jobs which I've been looking at.

The support on offer was often related to finding future employment within better rewarded corporate sectors or fast-track opportunities designed to promote rapid career advancement. It was unclear (from our participant accounts) whether the access to advice being offered and these particular opportunities was a consequence of the university's own practice. Or as seems likely, the higher status of the Russell Group institution meant those opportunities were more specifically targeted by employers to the university. However, the accounts of students at the post-1992 (and to some extent the Plate Glass) university did not tend to mention the same level of opportunities being offered. Unlike the participants from Plate Glass and post-1992 universities, the Russell Group students also discussed receiving advice on internships across a range of corporate sectors that offered bursaries to support applicants. In some respects, this suggests that the level of institutional support is constrained by institutional reputation rather than by the commitment of universities to providing support itself.

Other students found the support available to be less effective. In particular, a common concern of students at the post-1992 university was the limited nature of the information provided about postgraduate study. Respondents were unsure about how to find out about their options for postgraduate study and many lacked the confidence to do so. Usha (female, Indian post-1992) said students were left to their own devices when they made inquiries about future options.

I asked about what we could do to find out about careers fairs and Masters courses but I didn't get much information from anyone, the lecturers were very vague. I don't think they knew themselves what we could do.

She also explained that,

When I have asked about an MA everyone says that's a great idea but they just mean about doing a Masters here. There's a discount for students who go on to the MA programme and that's the first thing any of my lectures say. If I ask about going somewhere else it's just 'go and do some research'.

Usha's complaint about being pushed towards postgraduate study at the same university was one repeated by other students at the post-1992 university. By contrast, students at both the Plate Glass and Russell Group university described being encouraged and given advice and assistance to apply to other universities. This seemed to fall within a more general pattern in which students at the post-1992 university identified being less well-supported.

One consequence of the difference in types of support received was that whilst most Russell Group students had clear future plans for when they left university, the same was not as true for post-1992 students. One Black student, Lauren (female, mixed Black/White, post-1992), explained that, in large part, this was related to her university's lack of commitment,

> We are told by our lecturers and we were told this when we started that we would get support in making our decisions regarding employment and what we would do when we leave here. But that support has not been forthcoming and when we have asked for it, we get directed somewhere else. Some of the lecturers have actually told us, that it's not their job to sort this out for us. That has been disheartening. The lecturers are trying to disconnect themselves from what we are going to do when we leave, when I think they should be responsible and play a part in helping us make these decisions.

Yogita (female, Indian, post-1992) also spoke about the lack of support she had received,

> I don't get anything from my parents because they don't know about these things and they didn't go to uni so I have to rely on my lecturers but they don't seem to be interested in what we are going to do when we leave. They don't seem very committed to that aspect of our journey.

Yogita and Lauren both made the point that when they had discussed their career plans with their personal tutors, they were directed towards the university careers service. Students reported mixed views about the careers service, often explaining that the advice received was excellent but that it was often difficult to access. In particular, students noted receiving very helpful feedback on CVs, job applications, and personal statements. One specific area in which the post-1992 careers service appeared limited in comparison to the Russell Group was in the provision of support for applications for internships and bursaries. Students at the Russell Group were much more likely to have accessed the careers service prior to their final year in order to secure internships and similar opportunities that would be valuable additions to their *CV*.

Students at the post-1992 described the *ad hoc* nature of the careers service. Students often described they would access the service by independently visiting the building in which it was housed rather than through a more formal process in which all students were invited to access their services. Brianna (female, Black, post-1992) expressed a common concern that her careers service appeared to be underfunded. However, she explained that,

> I had to wait ages because there were so many people waiting, but when I did see someone they were really good. They gave me lots of different information on websites I could look at and I saw someone else about my CV. She helped me change it and make it better.

Other students were less convinced by the quality of the advice they received. Christian (male, mixed Black/White, Indian, post-1992) noted that many of the advisors were former students including some who had only finished their undergraduate study the previous year. He questioned whether or not 'they have the real sort of knowledge' necessary to secure a job and went on to suggest.

> a lot of students will lose out because of it, because they have nowhere else to go to get that sort of information. Their parents or family may not know what to do or where to go. So we rely on the university for that kind of information, it's not been as good as it could be compared to some of my friends who are at better unis. They have had much more information, advice and support than we have.

Students at the Plate Glass university explained how their careers service was understood to be an 'opt-in service' and not seen as something that was expected of all graduates (compared to the expectation of students who attended the Russell Group university). The responsibility was placed on the students. If they wanted to be part of the careers scheme, this was their choice and they were not necessarily encouraged to do so by their tutors and lecturers. The careers service was an independent service which did not necessarily work in partnership with academic departments. Daniel (male, Black, Plate Glass) emphasised the value of some online activities as he could pick and choose when and what he wanted to be part of.

> We have a careers service here, and you get sent an email and have to decide if you want to be part of it. They have a lot of online activities and workshop types of things you can access – I'm thinking that may be for the international students. They also have a "You Tube" channel you can watch. I have used some of the services for writing CVs, but it's not compulsory, it's kind of up to you if you want to use it.

A number of students discussed the possibilities for securing placements through the careers service. Many suggested these were poorly communicated and noted they only became aware of these opportunities too late in the day to participate. Several students emphasised the importance of having the option to apply for placements to give them experience when applying for future employment but also suggested the opportunities on offer were fairly limited. Kyle (male, Black, Plate Glass) said

> the placements are really good because they give you on the job training but you don't get paid for them. They give you that experience that you need. But I think they are very limited in what they offer you. The university only has a handful of connections to employers which means we as students are limited in where we can go. If there was more choice, that would be better.

Rachel (female, Black, Plate Glass) explained that not having a placement was a significant disadvantage when applying for jobs, not least because many other students would have a placement on their *CV*,

> I think all courses should offer students a placement. I know people who have done their degree and had no work experience whatsoever and they are then disadvantaged in getting a job. This university should make it compulsory that everyone does a placement, regardless of their degree. I know people at other universities who can do a placement if they want to are encouraged to do it, because they know that people are disadvantaged when they look for a job and they have no experience.

In summary, it often appeared that the support and opportunities for students at post-1992 and Plate Glass universities were less valuable than that at the Russell Group university. It tended to be delivered in a less well-organised fashion often relying on students being proactive. It was also noticeable that the opportunities Russell Groups could offer students, such as bursaries and internships, were more prestigious and more valuable in real terms. This reflected a degree of reciprocity between more prestigious institutions and higher status career options. For some companies, their graduate recruitment, premised on recruiting from Russell Group institutions, is a mutually beneficial relationship for these universities to foster. This reflects the process by which inequalities of class and race embed across multiple parts of society including education (Bhopal & Myers, 2023).

Conclusions

Our study found that students who attended different institutions displayed different experiences in relation to the type of support they received when making decisions regarding their transitions from university into employment, future study, or other options that were available to them. At the same time, the opportunities available to students were often starkly differentiated. The most valuable opportunities such as bursaries and internships were more likely to be accessible to students at the Russell Group university. Those students who attended the Russell Group university (irrespective of their social class or ethnic background) were on an upward trajectory compared to other students once they engaged in the support that was available to them. They were able to make key, informed decisions regarding their transitions out of university. As a result, they were able to demonstrate a greater understanding of and 'consciousness' around the choices that were available to them after they graduated. This included access to postgraduate study and labour market transitions. They were given better and more structured information to make informed decisions about their future trajectories. They were made aware of the barriers, systems, and the current labour and education market, which contributed to them making informed decisions.

In effect, what emerged was that the hierarchical structuring of different universities, by their reputation, institutional rankings, and so on, had a direct impact on the likely employment outcomes of students. This is largely unsurprising. The evidence that students attending elite and non-elite universities benefit differentially within higher education is well evidenced (Bhopal & Myers, 2023). By far, the biggest concern raised within this study is the very overt manner in which institutional support mirrors and reinforces other patterns of inequality. The support received by some students when applying for university would in effect make them more or less likely to attend universities where they are more or less likely to progress to better rewarded, more fulfilling, or higher status employment. The parents of many first-generation students are ill-placed to provide advice because they lack knowledge of the university sector. If these same students also receive poorly informed advice from schools or advice tarnished by biases around race and ethnicity or class, then the opportunities for many of these students will be further limited along multiple lines. If, in addition, they progress to universities that offer more limited support and fewer opportunities, then the same patterns of inequality are sedimented into student outcomes. This is a familiar pattern of the evidence that underpins the reproduction of inequalities within, and by, education (Bourdieu, 1998; Bourdieu & Passeron, 1990; Ladson-Billings & Tate, 1995; Yosso, 2005).

One way of interpreting Bourdieu's different forms of capital is when cultural capital can be understood in terms of 'qualitative differences in *forms* of consciousness *within* different social groups' (Moore, 2014, p. 99) rather than just an arbitrary attribution of value based on social class. We argue that those students attending elite Russell Group universities are developing a 'specialisation of consciousness' in which they are mastering techniques and gaining the knowledge they need to be *more* successful than their peers at other institutions in moving into further study or entering the labour market. At the same time, students attending less prestigious universities are themselves developing a 'specialisation of consciousness', one in which they are less equipped to navigate the different choices and options available to them. Whilst Yosso (2005) has argued students from ethnic minority backgrounds can draw upon community cultural wealth to develop other valuable forms of cultural capital, this perhaps unsurprisingly does not materialise in an effective way within the spaces of higher education. Instead, the practice of education prepares students for a range of different outcomes that are continually reinforced not by individual aptitude or ability but by prior access to opportunity. Universities privilege very narrow forms of capital that can be characterised as being White middle-class capitals (Bhopal & Myers, 2023; Myers & Bhopal, forthcoming). The participants in our research did not have the exclusive access to White capital typically possessed by White students, and this shaped the overall pattern of outcomes: many were less likely to be at a Russell Group university and most were less likely to graduate with a first or 2:1 because they were not White. Yosso identifies how other more marginalised, outsider capitals (including aspirational, linguistic, familial, social, navigational, and resistant capitals) have value particularly within communities. This provides a non-deficit view of capital held by communities and is a useful critical race theory standpoint to understand the world through a non-White lens. In the language of the twenty-first-century university, it can be distinguished as *non-traditional capital*, the capitals non-traditional students bring to the table. Throughout our re-search, elements of non-traditional capital were apparent, within accounts of family support for example shaped by specific community values. Those capitals undoubtedly impact student experience, often in a very positive way, but they do so within an overarching pattern of educational systems premised on reproducing outcomes beneficial to all White students. They might miti-gate those outcomes but they did not change the direction of traffic.

In the next chapter, we discuss students' expectations of the labour market. We argue that the groundwork for their expectations, for their anticipation of what sort of employment will be available for them, has been determined through their progressive earlier encounters with education limiting individual opportunities. In the context of higher education, a 'specialisation of con-sciousness' is a process that ensures the acceptance of these limited outcomes as a natural and expected outcome.

Notes

1 The Teaching Excellence and Student Outcomes Framework is a national frame-work which assesses excellence in teaching at universities and colleges, resulting in a gold, silver, bronze, or provisional rating (https://www.officeforstudents.org.uk/for-providers/quality-and-standards/about-the-tef/
2 The Research Excellence Framework is a process of expert review which assesses a university's research outputs, impact, and environment, which informs the selective allocation of research funding. (https://www.ref.ac.uk/about/what-is-the-ref/).
3 Advanced level exams are public exams taken by students at age 18 in England; they are required to gain entry into universities.
4 A postgraduate certificate in education is an academic qualification to become a qualified teacher.

References

Angrist, J., Lang, D., & Oreopoulous, P. (2006). *Lead them to water and pay them to drink: An experiment with services and incentives for college achievement.* National Bureau of Economic Research.
Auerbach, R. P., Alonso, J., Axinn, W. G., Cuijpers, P., Ebert, D. D., Green, J. G., Hwang, I., Kessler, R. C., Liu, H., Mortier, P., Nock, M. K., Pinder-Amaker, S., Sampson, N. A., Aguilar-Gaxiola, S., Al-Hamzawi, A., Andrade, L. H., Benjet, C., Caldas-de-Almeida, J. M., Demyttenaere, K., … & Bruffaerts, R. (2016). Mental

disorders among college students in the world health organization world mental health surveys. *Psychological Medicine, 46*(14), 2955–2970.

Bauman, Z. (2012). *Liquid modernity.* Polity.

Beck, U. (1992). *Risk society.* Sage.

Beck, U. (2006). *Cosmopolitan vision.* Polity.

Bernard, C., Fairtlough, A., Fletcher, J., & Ahmet, A. (2014). A qualitative study of marginalised social work Students' views of social work education and Learning. *The British Journal of Social Work, 44*(7), 1934–49.

Bhopal, K., & Myers, M. (2023). *Elite universities and the making of privilege: Exploring race and class in global educational economies.* Routledge.

Borghi, S., Mainardes, E., & Silva, É (2016). Expectations of higher education students: A comparison between the perception of student and teachers. *Tertiary Education and Management, 22,* 171–188.

Bourdieu, P. (1977). *Outline of a theory of practice.* Cambridge University Press.

Bourdieu, P. (1984). *Distinction: A social critique of the judgement of taste.* Harvard University Press.

Bourdieu, P. (1998). *The state nobility: Elite schools in the field of power.* Stanford University Press.

Bourdieu, P. (2003). *Firing back: Against the tyranny of the market 2* (Vol. 2). Verso.

Bourdieu, P., & Passeron, J. C. (1990). *Reproduction in education, society and culture* (Vol. 4). Sage.

Briggs, A., Clark, J., & Hall, I. (2009). *Bridging the gap: Project report on student transition.* Newcastle University.

Briggs, A., Clark, J., & Hall, I. (2012). Building bridges: Understanding student transition to university. *Quality in Higher Education, 18*(1), 3–21.

Broglia, E., Ryan, G., Williams, C., Fudge, M., Knowles, L., Turner., A, & on behalf of the Score Consortium. (2023). Profiling student mental health and counselling effectiveness: Lessons from four UK services using complete data and different outcome measures. *British Journal of Guidance & Counselling, 51*(2), 204–222.

Bunce, L., King, N., Saran, S., & Talib, N. (2019). Experiences of black and minority ethnic (BME) students in higher education: Applying self-determination theory to understand the BME attainment gap. *Studies in Higher Education. 46*(3) 534–547. https://doi.org/10.1080/03075079.2019.1643305

Burke, P. J., Crozier, G., Read, B., Hall, J., Peat, J., & Francis, B. (2013). *Formations of gender and higher education pedagogies.* NTFS Final Report.

Byrne, M., Flood, B., Hassall, T., Joyce, J., Montano, J., Gonzalez, J., & Torna-Germanou, E. (2012). Motivations, expectations and preparedness for higher education: A study of accounting students in Ireland, the UK, Spain and Greece. *Accounting Forum, 36,* 134–144.

Cahill, J., Bowyer, J., & Murray, S. (2014). An exploration of undergraduate students' views on the effectiveness of academic and pastoral support. *Educational Research, 56*(4), 398–411.

Cahill, J., Turner, J., & Barefoot, H. (2010). Enhancing the student learning experience: The perspective of academic Staff. *Educational Research, 52,* 283–295.

Carter, K., & McNeill, J. (1998). Coping with the darkness of transition: Students as the leading lights of guidance at induction to higher education. *British Journal of Guidance and Counselling, 26*(3), 399–415.

Cooke, R., Bewick, Barkham, M., Bradley, M., & Audin, K. (2006). Measuring, monitoring and managing the psychological well-being of first year university Students. *British Journal of Guidance and Counselling, 34,* 505–517.

Dorling, D. (2015). *Injustice: Why social inequality still persists.* Policy Press.

Eaton, N., Williams, R., & Green, B. (2000). Degree and diploma student nurse satisfaction levels. *Nursing Standard, 14*(39), 34–39.

Ellis, R., & Allan, R. (2010). Raising aspiration and widening participation: Diversity, science and learning styles in Context. *Journal of Further and Higher Education*, *34*(1), 23–33.

Equality Challenge Unit (2012). *Male students: Engagement with academic and pastoral support services*. ECU.

Field, J., Gallacher, J., & Ingram, R. (Eds.). (2009). *Researching transitions in lifelong learning*. Routledge.

Fu, F. (2010). Comparison of students' satisfaction and dissatisfaction factors in different classroom types in higher education. In P. Tsang, S. K. S. Cheung, V. S. K. Lee, & R. Huang (Eds.), *Hybrid learning* (pp. 415–426). Springer.

Fuchs, C., Lee, J., Roemer, L., & Orsillo, S. (2013). Using mindfulness- and acceptance-based treatments with clients from non-dominant cultural and/or marginalized backgrounds: Clinical considerations, meta-analysis findings, and introduction to the special series. *Cognitive and Behavioural Practice*, *20*, 1–12.

Giddens, A. (1991). *Modernity and self-identity: Self and society in the late modern age*. Polity.

Johnson, G., & Watson, G. (2004). "Oh gawd, how am I going to fit into this?" Producing [mature] first-year student identity. *Language and Education*, *18*(6), 474–487.

Johnson, S., Scammell, J., & Serrant-Green, L. (2013). Degrees of success. Safeguarding an ethnically diverse nursing workforce in nursing education. *Journal of Psychological Issues in Organisational Culture*, *3*(s1), 321–45.

Kelly, M., & Gleeson, H. (2018) 'Factors affecting black and minority ethnic students decisions to access mindfulness based support at university'. *Mental Health Nursing*, December 2018–January 2019, 1–5.

Kennett, D., & Reed, M. (2009). Factors influencing academic success and retention following a 1st-year post-secondary success course. *Educational Research and Evaluation: An International Journal on Theory and Practice*, *15*(2), 153–166.

Kerr, H. (2013). *Mental distress survey overview*. NUS.

Keup, J., & Barefoot, B. (2005). Learning how to be a successful student: Exploring the impact of first-year seminars on student outcomes. *Journal of the First-Year Experience and Students in Transition*, *17*(1), 11–47.

Kitzrow, M. (2003). The mental health of today's college students: Challenges and recommendations. *Journal of Student Affairs Research and Practice*, *41*(1), 167–181.

Krause, K. (2011). Transforming the learning experience to engage students. In L. Thomas & M. Tight (Eds.), *Institutional transformation to engage a diverse student body* (pp. 199–212). Emerald.

Ladson-Billings, G., & Tate, W. F. (1995). Toward a critical race theory of education. *Teachers College Record*, *97*(1), 47–68.

Leese, M. (2010). Bridging the gap. Supporting students into higher education. *Journal of Further and Higher Education*, *34*, 239–251.

Lobo, A., & Gurney, L. (2014). What did they expect? Exploring a link between students' expectations, attendance and attrition on English language enhancement courses. *Journal of Further and Higher Education*, *38*, 730–754.

Lowe, H., & Cook, A. (2003). Mind the gap: Are students prepared for higher education? *Journal of Further and Higher Education*, *27*(1), 53–76.

Mahmud, A., & Gagnon, J. (2023). Racial disparities in student outcomes in British higher education: Examining mindsets and bias. *Teaching in Higher Education*, *28*(2), 254–269.

Masocha, S. (2015). Reframing black social work students' experiences of teaching and Learning. *Social Work Education*, *34*(6), 636–49.

Miller, M. (2016). *The ethnicity attainment gap: Literature review*. University of Sheffield: Widening Participation Research and Evaluation Unit.

Mind. (2013). *Mental health crisis care: Commissioning excellence for black and ethnic minority ethnic groups. A briefing for clinical commissioning groups.* Mind.

Money, J., Nixon, S., Tracy, F., Hennessy, C., Ball, E., & Dinning, T. (2017). Undergraduate student expectations of university in the United Kingdom: What really matters to them? *Cogent Education, 4*, 1–11.

Moore, R. (2014). Capital. In M. Grenfell (Ed.), *Pierre Bourdieu: Key Concepts* (pp. 98–113). Routledge

Mountford-Zimdars, A., Sanders, J., Moore, J., Sabri, D., Jones, S., & Higham, L. (2017). What can universities do to support all their students to progress successfully throughout their time at university? *Perspectives: Policy and Practice in Higher Education, 21*(2–3), 101–110.

Myers, M., & Bhopal, K. (forthcoming). Capital blanc et diversité dans Les universités d'élite: Les ruses de la raison méritocratique. *Journal Sociologie Et Sociétés.*

Nevers, J., & Hillman, N. (2016). *HEPI/HEA student academic achievement survey.* London: HEPI.

Ning, H., & Downing, K. (2012). Influence of student learning experience on academic performance: The mediator and moderator effects of self-regulation and Motivation. *British Educational Research Journal, 38*(2), 219–237.

Parkman, A. (2016). The imposter phenomenon in higher education: Incidence and Impact. *Journal of Higher Education Theory and Practice, 16*, 51–60.

Pitkethly, A., & Prosser, M. (2001). The first year experience project: A model for university-wide change. *Higher Education Research and Development, 20*(2), 185–98.

Race for equality. (2011). NUS.

The race to the top. (2012). Department for Innovation, Universities and Skills.

Richardson, J. (2015). The under-attainment of ethnic minority students in UK higher education: What we know and what we don't know. *Journal of Further and Higher Education, 39*, 278–291.

Rolfe, H. (2002). Student demands and experience in an age of reduced financial Support. *Journal of Higher Education Policy and Management, 24*(2), 171–182.

Shadbolt, N. (2016). *Shadbolt review of computer sciences degree accreditation and graduate employability.* BIS.

Smith, S., Taylor-Smith, E., Bacon, L., & Mackinnon, L. (2019). Equality of opportunity for work experience? Computing students at two UK universities "play the game". *British Journal of Sociology of Education, 40*(3), 324–339.

Social Mobility Commission. (2016). *State of the nation: Social mobility in Great Britain.* Social Mobility Commission.

Stock, C., Willie, L., & Kramer, A. (2002). Gender specific health behaviours of German university students predict the interest in campus health promotion. *Health Promotion International, 16*(2), 145–154.

Telford, R., & Masson, R. (2005). The congruence of quality values in higher education. *Quality Assurance Education, 13*, 107–119.

Thomas, L. (2002). Student retention in higher education: The role of institutional habitus. *Journal of Education Policy, 17*(4), 423–442.

Thomas, L. (2012). *What works? Student retention and success.* Paul Hamlyn Foundation.

Thorley, C. (2017). *Not by degrees: Improving student mental health in the UK's universities.* https://www.ippr.org/articles/not-by-degrees

Tinto, V. (2002). *Establishing conditions for student success* [Paper presentation]. The 11th Annual Conference of the European Access Network, Monash University, Prato.

Trow, M. (1973). *Problems in the transition from elite to mass higher education.* Carnegie Commission on Higher Education.

UUK/NUS (2019). *Black, Asian and minority ethnic student attainment at UK universities: #Closing the gap*. UUK/NUS.

Van der Riet, P., Rossiter, R., Kirby, D., Dluzewska, T., & Harmon, C. (2015). Piloting a stress management and mindfulness program for undergraduate nursing students: Student feedback and lessons learned. *Nurse Education Today*, *35*, 44–9.

Westlake, C. (2008). Predicting student withdrawal: Examining the reasons through a preliminary literature review. *Newport CELT Journal*, *1*, 29–33.

Wilcox, P., Winn, S., & Fyvie-Gauld, M. (2005). 'It was nothing to do with the university, it was just the people': The role of social support in the first-year experience of higher education. *Studies in Higher Education*, *30*(6), 707–722.

Wilkinson, R., & Pickett, K. (2010). *The spirit level. Why equality is better for everyone*. Penguin.

Yorke, M., & Thomas, L. (2003). Improving the retention of students from lower socio-economic groups. *Journal of Higher Education Policy and Management*, *25*(1), 63–74.

Yosso, T. J. (2005). Whose culture has capital? A critical race theory discussion of community cultural wealth. *Race Ethnicity and Education*, *8*(1), 69–91.

Web references

National Student Survey. https://www.thestudentsurvey.com/

What is the REF? https://www.ref.ac.uk/about/what-is-the-ref/

TEF and Student Outcomes Framework. https://www.officeforstudents.org.uk/for-providers/quality-and-standards/about-the-tef/

8

FEARS OF THE FUTURE

Labour market inequalities

This chapter draws upon students' aspirations for the future and examines the choices available to them when they transition into the labour market. Discussing future prospects for employment following graduation, all students discussed their fears of exclusionary practices in the labour market (including being unemployed, competition for jobs, and underselling based on their qualifications). These fears were often nuanced around a number of different factors including ethnicity, class, type of university, and parental background. Within that mix of different experiences, we found that students from some Black and minority ethnic (BME) backgrounds are better equipped than others to make the transition into the labour market. We found that the type of university students attended and parental background made a significant difference to future transitions and choices. Many students reported two particular fears that emerged from their university experiences and had a profound impact on their expectations for the future. The first, which is discussed in Chapter 5, being concerns about the high levels of debt incurred whilst a student. The second, touched upon in the previous chapter but discussed more fully now, being concerns about what the labour market offered BME students.

The transition from university to the labour market has become increasingly complex as graduates navigate a wide range of pathways within an increasingly diversified graduate labour market (Tomlinson & Nghia, 2020; Isopahkala-Bouret et al., 2023). Successfully navigating the graduate job market entails entry into a complex field in which degree subject, type of institution, social class, gender, and ethnicity all influence employment outcomes including types of jobs, level of salary, and status (Belfield et al., 2018; Britton et al., 2021; Gov.UK, 2023a; Hunt et al., 2023; IFS, 2020; Reiss et al., 2023; Walker

DOI: 10.4324/9781003097211-8

& Zhu, 2018). Consequently, the experience of graduates entering the job market is often characterised by encountering recruitment strategies framed within segregated pathways that prefer candidates based on specific class, gender, or ethnic background. This is exacerbated by corporate employers placing a premium on identifying and nurturing a graduate 'elite' in a bid to win the 'war for talent', which tends to favour graduates from higher socio-economic backgrounds and graduates who are more mobile (Brown et al., 2011; Marini, 2024). In the UK, there is evidence that BME students are less mobile than their White counterparts which restricts employment outcomes. However, there is also evidence of BME graduates being more likely to migrate out of the UK for employment because they identify systemic racism in the UK labour market (Bhopal, 2016; Marini, 2024). Consequently, graduate perceptions of the job market tend to be framed by wider socio-cultural dynamics relating to their social class, gender, and ethnicity. This is potentially damaging for many students as decisions made during this period have been shown to have a significant impact on social mobility and future life choices.

Within an increasingly competitive job market, graduates face the challenge of accessing jobs commensurate to graduate-level qualifications whilst also demonstrating their so-called 'employability' (Tomlinson, 2012). Employability in these terms is a form of capital shaped by relations between individual experiences of education and the employment market that include students' 'values, identities and other life narratives beyond the accrual of private good human capital' (Tomlinson, 2024, p. 2). The relational nature of capitals meaning its value when competing for other capitals, such as higher status or greater financial reward, is determined by multiple structural factors. One obvious concern is that 'employability' is likely to be associated with demonstrating those characteristics that are valued more in the labour market such as being a White candidate from a middle-class background. Tomlinson identifies graduate's occupying a liminal space and time transitioning from student to employment. This moment can be both fraught with difficulties and opportunities; however, he notes that,

> it can also constitute a form of cruel optimism, experienced as a schism between an idealised state of being (being a publicly affirmed graduate) and here-and-now realities of joblessness, delay or underemployment.
>
> *(Tomlinson, 2023, p. 15)*

Graduates in our study were cognisant of the transition Tomlinson describes. However, they often framed their understanding of the disappointments of job-hunting against previous experiences of inequity across the life course. Consequently, despite their apparent optimism for the future, they often described being already prepared for disappointment.

Ethnic inequalities in the labour market

Unemployment rates in the UK are higher for all other ethnic groups than the White ethnic category (Powell & Francis-Devine, 2023). In 2022, the rate of White unemployment stood at 3.1% compared to mixed/multiple ethnic groups 11.3%, Pakistani 8.7%, Black/African/Caribbean/Black British 8.5%, Chinese 7.8%, Bangladeshi 7.3%, and Indian 5.9% categories. Unemployment is higher for those in the 16–24 years age group, and within that category, there is significantly greater unemployment based on ethnicity. The unemployment rate for White 16-to-24-year-olds is 9%; by comparison, Bangladeshi or Pakistani and Black young people unemployment rates stand at 20% and 19%, respectively.

BME employees are disadvantaged when applying for jobs as they are more likely to be rejected at application based on their ethnicity, less likely to be promoted compared to White colleagues, experience prejudice from employers including both conscious and unconscious bias, and experience wage inequalities based on their ethnicity (Bhopal, 2018; Gov.UK, 2023b; McGregor-Smith, 2017; Mirza & Warwick, 2022). The Office for National Statistics (ONS, 2022) consistently identifies ethnic pay gaps in their raw data, with 'White and Black Caribbean', 'Bangladeshi', 'Pakistani', 'other Black', 'other Asian', and 'Black African' groups earning the least compared to the White population. The ONS refined their analysis of the raw data and concluded, 'After holding personal and work characteristics constant, to provide an adjusted pay gap based on a like-for-like comparison, we find that UK-born White employees earn more on average than most ethnic minority employees' (ONS, 2022).

BME employees are over-represented within blue-collar, manual, and more poorly paid occupations and under-represented in professional and managerial roles (Li & Heath, 2018). In addition, they experience an ethnic penalty in terms of reward, being paid less than White employees in similar jobs (Li & Heath, 2018; Longhi & Brynin, 2017).

Despite the narrative that racism is a less significant factor in British social life, research by the Trades Union Congress (TUC) in 2022 found two in five BME workers have faced racism at work in the last five years (CRED, 2021; TUC, 2022). Amongst workers who experienced racism, four out of five felt unable to report their experience fearing they would not be taken seriously or that to do so would have further negative impacts on their working lives. The TUC Research, which included polling of 1750 BME workers and regional focus groups, concluded,

> Racism does not exist in a vacuum. It is multi-faceted, multi-layered and emerges from established values and practices that are deeply embedded within our institutions and structures. Often workplace racism is wrongly reduced to either a series of random one off events and/or the implicit attitudes and unconscious biases of an individual.
>
> *(TUC, 2022, p. 6)*

Whilst BME groups continue to experience racism in the labour market at all levels, particularly in relation to career progression and promotions, it is particularly apparent at the most senior manager levels and board membership (McGregor-Smith, 2017; Parker Review, 2024). There is a significant under-representation of BME groups on the boards of FTSE 100 and FTSE 250[1] organisations starkly at odds with the ethnic diversity of the UK (Green Park, 2017; Parker Review, 2024).

Despite evidence that diversity is beneficial for organisations and increases performance (Hunt et al., 2015), employers continue to employ workers from similar ethnic and social classes to those of current employees (Smith & Smith, 2016; Social Mobility Commission, 2016). In her review *Race in the Workplace* commissioned by the Department for Business and Trade, McGregor-Smith found that the 'potential benefit to the UK economy from full representation of BME individuals across the labour market through improved participation and progression is estimated to be £24 billion a year, which represents 1.3% of GDP' (2017, p. 7). This has led to calls for a more targeted approach to support the education-to-work transition of BME young people (particularly graduates) to redress such inequalities (Rolfe et al., 2015). Chapman et al. (2023) argue that although the 'baseline expectation is that greater workforce gender and racial diversity is associated with better organizational outcomes' measured across different outcomes this comes at a cost. They find an association between greater ethnic diversity and increased staff turnover caused by intergroup biases and lower levels of social integration. To mitigate problems of turnover related to diversity they suggest there is a long-term value in introducing diversity charters. However, some measures to foster diversity, including diversity charters and unconscious bias training have been criticised as performative exercises designed to disguise continuing racism and inequality within organisations (Bhopal, 2024; Bhopal & Pitkin, 2020; Myers, 2022; Noon, 2018).

Researchers found that BME employees have to change aspects of their behaviour to 'fit in' with organisational practices and be accepted resulting in poor career progression and development opportunities (CIPD, 2017; BITC, 2018). There is also clear evidence that the glass ceiling effect in the labour market and affects different ethnic groups in different ways (Saggar et al., 2016). Black, Pakistani, and Bangladeshi groups experience the most disadvantages in the labour market, facing higher risks of unemployment and lower levels of earnings compared to White groups, and unemployment affects their future likelihood of re-entering the labour market and wage penalties (Breach & Li, 2017; Li & Heath, 2018; Zucotti & Platt, 2016). This is the result of cumulative discrimination in the labour market and continuing ethnic disadvantages (Li & Heath, 2018).

Ethnic inequalities in the graduate labour market

Overall, all graduates see a positive economic return in comparison to non-graduate earnings but the scale of that difference is often differentiated along multiple lines including ethnicity. The Department for Education's Longitudinal Education Outcomes (LEO) statistics for graduate outcomes reveals that White students are more likely to be in sustained employment, further study, or both, one, three, five, and ten years after graduation (Gov.UK, 2023c). The same data show consistent differences in earnings over a ten-year period with Indian and Chinese graduates earning the most and Black and Pakistani graduates earning the least. Three years after graduation, Indian and Chinese graduates' average (median) earnings were £27,800; White graduates £24,900; Black Caribbean graduates £23,400; and Pakistani graduates £23,100. Ten years after graduation, the same pattern is apparent with Chinese graduates averaging £36,500, Indian £35,300, White £32,200, Black Caribbean £23,900, and Pakistani £25,600. To some extent, these statistics disguise more complex and nuanced differences within groups associated with other characteristics including gender and private education; degree class, subject, and type of institution; historic and regional differences; and changing socio-economic conditions (Britton et al., 2021; Mirza & Warwick, 2022). Some of these are themselves adversely impacted by ethnicity. This includes BME students often graduating with lower class degrees from less prestigious universities, less likelihood of coming from higher class backgrounds with access to associated economic resources and social networks, a higher likelihood of coming from regions with poorer educational provision, and less mobility when searching for employment (Bhopal et al., 2020; Richardson, 2015; Zwysen & Longhi, 2016). So, for example, the attainment gaps in degree classes discussed in Chapter 3 will further disadvantage BME students entering the labour market because they are less likely to possess more valuable first or 2:1 class degree. Comparisons of BME and White groups with similar levels of educational attainment have also identified inequitable outcomes and a greater likelihood of BME graduates employed in jobs for which they are overqualified (EHRC, 2016; TUC, 2016; Zwysen & Longhi, 2018).

Race and class inequalities

The participants in our research consistently reported being aware they were entering a labour market that was rigged against them. Those from working-class backgrounds were aware of the different ways in which class was a factor when applying for jobs and getting interviews. They identified indicators of their social class background, such as their accent, language, and presentation of self, led to overt discrimination. Respondents from the post-1992 university were more likely to identify class as a discriminatory factor when applying for jobs. Paige (female, Black, post-1992) whose parents did not go to university emphasised this,

> None of my parents went to university and I would say I am working class. I find people have stereotypes of working class people and what that means to them, so they make certain judgements about you. They will make certain judgements about me when I go for an interview, certain assumptions based on the way I speak, because I speak in a certain way and have an accent. Because of my working class accent they will think I'm not clever or affluent, I'm not la di da like some middle class people are. People will make judgements about me because of how I speak, my upbringing and my level of education. They won't do that for a middle class person who is well spoken.

Similarly, Usha (female, Indian, post-1992), whose parents also did not attend university, felt that she was at a disadvantage because of her race and her class.

> I do feel generally I am at a disadvantage definitely based on who I am. I have a double or even a triple disadvantage. First I'm not white, then I am working class and then I am a woman. Employers have these ways of making assumptions that are based on bias and how they think certain groups are and what they expect from them. So they go on those assumptions and immediately make judgements about you. I believe, they have in some ways, already made their decisions about you before they meet you. So they will give jobs to certain kinds of people who speak like them and who they want working for them.

Students spoke about the impact of racism and how this was a defining factor in whether they would gain employment and how they would be judged, once in employment. Their understandings of racist prejudice, unconscious bias, and stereotyping in the labour market mirror research that has explored the experiences of BME employees (TUC, 2022). Other middle-class students shared similar expectations. Thanh (female, Vietnamese, Russell Group) said,

> We have to be realistic and know that racism is out there and exists and it happens when you go for a job. I don't know what we can do to challenge that because people doing the hiring and firing have that power. We do have laws in place, but how do we know these laws are being followed?

Students were aware that their ethnic background would impact on how they were judged when applying for jobs. Even those who expected to achieve a first class or 2:1 degree[2] felt this would make little difference to their chances of actually *securing* employment; they felt their ethnic identity would trump their degree classification. Sam (male, Black, Russell Group) said,

> I have been told that I should get a First but I still think that I will be disadvantaged in getting a job because people will look at me see I am a Black man first, not a student who has achieved a First class degree. Do they want someone who looks like me to work for them? I think there are real divisions about what kind of people companies want and they can pick and choose because there are more graduates looking for jobs than there are jobs. They won't choose the Black male, they will choose the white, middle class well spoken, well dressed male over me.

It was striking that Sam should make these comments. He came from a supportive, affluent family and both his parents worked in professional occupations. He had readily drawn upon his parents' social capital to secure a prestigious internship. Despite all these factors, he still voiced his concerns that he could be disadvantaged because of his ethnicity. Other Black students also felt that divisions of class (defined in relation to background, wealth, connections, and accent), in conjunction with ethnicity, were used to separate workers who were employable in certain types of occupations. Josh (male, Black, Russell Group) said,

> Employers stereotype young Black males in a certain way, they use racial profiling and think do we want him here? What will our clients think about him, do we want a Black man representing us? It happens all the time, my parents would tell me stories about how they would get to the interview and not get the job and they thought it was because they were Black. I know that still happens.

BME respondents whose parents worked in manual and non-professional occupations, and who had not attended university, felt disadvantaged particularly in relation to specific ways of *doing* and *being* needed to excel in the labour market. Alyssa (female, mixed Black/White, Plate Glass) said,

> There are certain ways you have to behave and you have to act to be accepted for a job. This even comes down to the types of clothes you wear and what you look like. I believe the qualifications are the last thing that certain employers look for. They want to do see how you behave and whether you will fit in and be like them.

Students' accounts of their future prospects were often understood to be constrained by the same limitations that students had already outlined in terms of experiencing racism and inequality whilst at university and before then (at school or college). Obviously, the actual paths their lives would take in the future, including any successes or disappointments, were unknown. In conjunction with findings about experiencing racism and inequality at university, it becomes apparent that BME students are also learning that the institutional production of such inequality is itself an ordinary, everyday occurrence. This acceptance or complicity in the processes of fostering acceptance/complicity in producing inequalities characterises the 'specialisation of consciousness' through which students remained largely pragmatic about their unequal outcomes. Bourdieu's description of competitions for capitals within institutional fields is useful in this respect because it highlights the complexities of structures and individual practice in which inequalities are reproduced. Bourdieu is perhaps less adept at understanding how racism functions and how it is particularly understood by BME individuals who are themselves experiencing racism. It often appeared in our research that racism materialised both within the fluid social relations that structured the institutional field including covert institutional or systemic racisms, and, at the same time, as a less fluid, structuring element in the wider institutional field of play. This second form of racism could be characterised as a precise, limiting set of barriers clearly demarcated in plain sight. Students recognised the existence of such racisms as inequitable and unacceptable but did not appear to challenge them.

Access to social networks

Many respondents spoke about how access to social networks was a significant factor that affected entry into particular jobs. Respondents from post-1992 and Plate Glass universities felt they lacked access to such networks and this would disadvantage them. Madison (female, Black, post-1992) spoke about this in relation to different types of capital,

> If for example my dad was a lawyer, I could get a job as a lawyer quite easily. More easily because he would have the right sort of connections and people to put me in touch with. In that way, it wouldn't matter what kind of degree I had, it would mean I could rely on him getting me that job. I don't have parents with those connections. They didn't go to university. They don't have those connections full stop. Realistically they don't know people who know people, to make those connections. So regardless of having the degree, people like me would be disadvantaged because they don't have those connections.

Olivia (female, Black, Plate Glass) spoke about this in relation to social advantages and access to specific social contacts,

> If you have those social advantages that some families have, like for example if your mum is successful in business or your dad has his own

business, then you have connections with other people. They will put you in touch with other social contacts. It just goes on and you then have this wide range of people you can draw on, and this means you have access to progress and different opportunities and careers after you graduate. But some students won't have parents who have been to uni or even a career and so they won't have the same sort of opportunities as that person who has the parents with all the contacts. It just makes you question, is it worth doing the degree if it means you don't get anywhere with it?

Students like Madison and Olivia identified how their specific lack of social capital put them at a disadvantage within the labour market. More generally, this lack of capital was something that sat within the broader pattern of their family backgrounds and the types of schools they had attended, and also was emblematic of the differences in opportunity offered to students based on the universities they attended. Unlike Madison and Olivia, students at the Russell Group university were far more likely to speak about fostering their social networks in relation to the job market through bursaries, placements, and internships that allowed them to spend time in higher status corporate environments during their studies.

A competitive labour market

Black respondents, in particular, spoke about inequalities related to ethnicity and felt that processes of discrimination continued to exist in the labour market. The idea that respondents would be discriminated against despite earning a good university degree demonstrated how race trumped class. We argue that Black students experience a 'Black graduate tax'. Whilst they may achieve high outcomes from their degree this alone does not compensate or replace the racism they anticipate they will experience when applying for jobs and whilst in employment. Several respondents outlined employer bias when they had attended interviews. Isaac (male, Black, Plate Glass) discussed how he was treated after being accepted into a graduate training scheme,

I was really pleased when I was accepted onto this fast track graduate employment scheme and I think the employers when they interviewed me were also a bit shocked. I had passed the exam and got a place, which was a followed by a formal interview. But you got on it automatically when you passed the exam. I think the employers were a bit shocked that I had got on. They were not expecting to see me. I was really pleased for myself that I did well. I should feel more confident about my own abilities rather than think about how employers will judge me.

Many participants discussed the prejudice they felt employers would have towards them, including towards different types of universities and degree courses. Gul (Bangladeshi, Plate Glass) felt he would experience discrimination because he would not graduate from a Russell Group university,

> I have heard how employers look at the type of university that you've been to. So they will look more favourably at the students who went to better universities like the Russell Group. And if there were two candidates then they would choose the student and favour the one who went to the Russell Group. I have heard this happens even if you get a first from [name of their university]. So a 2:2 or 2:1 from a good university has more value than say a first from here.

Students at the post-1992 university described being disadvantaged compared to other students at more prestigious universities. Bikram (Indian, post-1992) explained this fell within a wide pattern of biases,

> I feel that there are lots of different inequalities to do with where you went to university, what degree you did and what you got at the end of it. You have to have a degree to get a job, and if you don't then you are against people who have more and more experience than you. So your options are very limited. On top of that there are further ways of dividing people because employers want people to be from certain universities.

Other respondents felt they would be competing against students who would have better grades from better, prestigious institutions. Brianna (female, Black, post-1992) emphasised this in relation to selection based on discriminatory processes,

> Getting a job is always going to be competitive but if you have a degree you are at least ahead of the game. It means you can be selected for the job. But there are going to be different types of inequalities based on what degree you did and where you did it, but that doesn't mean you can't try to get that job. There are other discriminations like racism and so if you look at it in that way the whole labour market is not equal for everyone. It works better for some groups than it does for others.

Students at the Russell Group university recognised the advantages associated with gaining a degree from a prestigious, elite university. They felt this put them one step ahead of other students who attended non-Russell Group universities. As Maitri (Indian, Russell Group) said,

> I chose this university for a reason because I know it has a good reputation, so when I finish I want to make sure I am able to get a good job.

If employers look at where I did my university and the placement that I had, I think that puts me in a better position. At an advantage compared to other students who may not have gone to such a good university. I know also that this university does well on their employability. Lots of students leave here and have a plan, they get good jobs or they do a Masters degree.

The notion of 'having a plan' was outlined by several students who felt prepared for life after their degree. Nicole (Black, Russell Group) emphasised this in relation to the guidance she received at university,

I know what I'm going to do because my uni has prepared me for life after graduation. So lots of us know what we are going to do, we are either going to get a job or do a Masters, there are none of us who don't know. I think that may be because we know we have to be prepared, but it could also be that we have been given lots of guidance to make sure we just don't leave here and have no idea. I felt I was well prepared and supported in that process. They were not just concerned about me when I was there, they want to make sure I know what I'm doing when I leave.

Other students felt less confident regarding their degree course and options for their future. They did not share Nicole's clear vision for life after university. Lauren (mixed Black/White, post-1992), for example, highlighted concerns about the academic quality and the broad nature of her courses, and the potential implications this may have for the different types of jobs that would be available to her. Lauren (mixed Black/White, post-1992) found this concerning,

I am worried about the degree I am getting, it seems the qualification itself is so broad so you can't say you have specialised in anything. It's not really classified as a 'specialised' degree or a degree that's really 'wanted' by employers. So on job applications it comes across as too broad and not specialist enough.

Paige (Black, post-1992) emphasised how early on in her degree she had contacted the careers service to enquire about the types of jobs that would be available to her, only to be told they were limited. She also described feeling her degree course (psychology) was not as focussed on career opportunities as she would have liked. Despite having enjoyed her studies, she described a 'sudden lack of confidence' as she came to the end of her third year. She noted that,

I think now it would have been better for me to do something more focussed because that would have helped me to get a job. Having a degree that is general probably means it will be harder for me to get a job, more so if there are other people who are applying for a job who have that particular specialism related to the job.

Zainab (Pakistani, post-1992) also argued that the academic value attached to her degree was less than she needed suggesting she had, 'to go and get more qualifications and do another course to actually get a real job'. Zainab went on to describe feeling slightly cheated by her time at university,

> I've spent over nine grand a year for a degree that's going to give me limited job prospects.

Chandra (Indian, Plate Glass) made similar points to Zainab about the perceived value of her degree course. Her main aim upon graduating was to get a well-paid job, but she explained that,

> I sometimes think about whether coming to university has really been worth it, the main point of coming to university for me was to get a good job out of it but I don't know if that is going to happen. I look at all the other people I am competing with, who have better degrees from better institutions and also work experience, I think I am disadvantaged. On top of that, I think about the amount of money it has cost and I have to ask myself, has it been worth it?

Throughout the research, students like Chandra often explained their knowledge of the differences between universities and the respective value that might be conferred upon degrees from different types of universities only became apparent after they had begun their studies. This was most noticeably the case for students at post-1992 universities but not exclusively so. Despite the progressive shift towards marketised higher education and their positioning as consumers of education, it often appeared that students' understanding of the 'markets' in which universities compete was often fairly limited when they had first applied. This was particularly apparent for students whose own parents had less knowledge about higher education and/or those who attended schools that provided limited advice. Some students felt they had invested in, or at least incurred substantial debt from, the wrong institution. Russell Group students were less likely than other students to question the value of their degree and often emphasised the long-term financial investment returns of their degree. Dipak (male, Indian, Russell Group) said,

> It is worth doing the degree, of course it's worth it. After you graduate you will be able to get some kind of job, it might not be the job you want first but that will help you get another job. I don't think we will see the value of the benefits of having a degree until we are doing the job we want to do. But it's definitely better to have done a degree than not having one.

Leela (Indian, Russell Group) felt the benefit of her degree was the knowledge she acquired and the transferable skills that would enable her to get a job,

> I have really enjoyed my degree, I think of all the new things that I've learnt and how I can use them in the job market. When I go for an interview or decide to do a Masters, I can talk about my degree. Saying that I went to [name of university] which has a really good reputation in my area of study means people will see that I have a good degree which has been worth paying the fees for.

Students at the post-1992 and Plate Glass universities often described being at a disadvantage compared to their peers who were studying at Russell Group universities. A key factor that many respondents at post-1992 and Plate Glass universities emphasised was the value of their degrees. Talika (female, Indian, post-1992) emphasised this in relation to the competitive nature of the job market,

> I feel that you need more and more and I don't think my degree from [name of university] is going to be enough. I think you need to stand out from the crowd, so you need more than a Bachelors degree, you need to think about having a Masters. A Masters from [name of well-known elite university]. That will get you up on the job ladder and it will make you stand out from the crowd, but that comes with more debt.

Conclusions

Throughout our research, it was clear that when making decisions about their future employment, further education, and training, students were influenced by a whole range of cultural experiences, access to social networks and resources, and in addition, their awareness and experience of their peers differing experiences and access to networks and resources. Despite the anticipation that students, acting as consumers of education, within a free market should be able to best serve their own interests by making neutral and rational decisions (Ball et al., 2001), this was not reflected in their lived experiences. Their decision-making sat within a framework of past experience in which BME students face multiple forms of racism, exclusion, and marginalisation within education. This includes the mapping of wider patterns of geographical inequality of class and race, mirrored in the concentration of BME students attending inner-city post-1992 universities and associated deficits of cultural and social capital, a narrative which, in turn, is consistently distorted and misinterpreted within public discourse (Connor et al., 2004; Bhopal, 2018; Gillborn et al., 2018). A pattern emerges of poorer BME students experiencing repeated and multiple disadvantages and this is an experience that positions their individual expectations of the transition into the labour market. In this respect, the universities in this research were not redressing those patterns of disadvantage but rather reproducing them and at the same time preparing students to accept them. It is therefore unsurprising that similar stratification is also apparent in employment outcomes experienced by students from different types of institutions (Wakeling & Savage, 2015). Progression into postgraduate study is also heavily skewed towards students who previously attended research-intensive universities, with a concomitant relationship towards the likelihood that they will be White and middle-class (AdvanceHE, 2018; Bhopal & Myers, 2023; Bhopal & Pitkin, 2018; HEFCE, 2017).

Whilst there was a clear sense that the students we were interviewing were excited and looking forward to entering the labour market, for many students, this was also tainted by lingering concerns and fears that their time at university might not match their aspirations. They did not share the optimism of Beck's reflexive individuals (Beck, 2006), well-equipped by a university education to manage the challenges ahead. Instead, they identified real and persistent barriers likely to limit their opportunities. Undoubtedly this was partly an inevitable consequence of the pressures associated with their final year of study and uncertainties about future employment or further education. However, it was also a result of students' own processes of reflection on their past lives and what they could expect in the future. Many students identified how difficulties associated with their personal circumstances impacted upon their opportunities and suggested institutional processes reinforced these difficulties. The economies of higher education and the labour market are often characterised as wracked by change and upheaval demanding rapid adaptation by individuals and institutions. In Bourdieu's account, there is a degree of fatalism about individual's futures marked by 'the unchosen principle of all "choices"' (Bourdieu, 1990, p. 61); individual *habitus* apparently producing strategies to cope with change but institutions reproducing identities in the image of pre-existing structures. A picture emerged in our research in which universities, despite their public commitments to widening participation, are engaged in imbuing students with characteristics that reinforce their prior status as they enter the labour market.

Obviously, the actual paths their lives would take in the future, including any successes or disappointments, were unknown. However, it was noticeable that accounts of prospects were often understood to be constrained by the same limitations that students had already outlined in terms of experiencing racism and inequality whilst at university and previously. In conjunction with the earlier findings about experiencing racism within university, it becomes apparent that BME students are both experiencing racism and inequality and also learning that the institutional production of such inequality is itself an ordinary, everyday occurrence. It reflects how the experience of racism is a 'normal, not aberrant' experience, in universities as in society more generally racism 'looks ordinary and natural to persons in the culture' (Delgado & Stefancic, 2000, p. 12).

Notes

1 The Financial Times Stock Exchange Group is an independent organisation which specialises in creating index offerings for the global financial markets. The FTSE 100 consists of blue chip stocks which are listed on the London Stock Exchange, and the FTSE 250 consists of mid-blue chip organisations ranked 101–350.
2 Degree classifications in England are awarded in five different categories. These consist of first class, 2:1, 2:2, third, and fail, with first class being the highest award.

References

AdvanceHE. (2018). *Statistical report: Students.* AdvanceHE.
Ball, S., Davies, J., David, M., & Reay, D. (2001). 'Classification' and 'judgement': Social class and the 'cognitive structures' of choice. *British Journal of Sociology of Education, 23*(1), 51–72.
Beck, U. (2006). *Cosmopolitan vision.* Polity.
Belfield, C., Britton, J., Buscha, F., Dearden, L., Dickson, M., van der Erve, L., Sibieta, L., Vignoles, A., Walker, I., & Zhu, Y. (2018). *The impact of undergraduate degrees on early-career earnings.* Institute for Fiscal Studies (IFS).
Bhopal, K. (2016). *The experiences of black and minority ethnic academics: A comparative study of the unequal academy.* Routledge.
Bhopal, K. (2018). *White privilege: The myth of a post-racial society.* Policy.
Bhopal, K. (2024). The (un)equal university: Training programmes and the commodification of race. *Higher Education Quarterly.* Early online. publicationhttps://doi.org/10.1111/hequ.12518
Bhopal, K., & Myers, M. (2023). *Elite universities and the making of privilege: Exploring race and class in global educational economies.* Routledge.
Bhopal, K., Myers, M., & Pitkin, C. (2020). Routes through higher education: BME students and the development of a 'specialisation of consciousness'. *British Educational Research Journal, 46*(6), 1321–1337.
Bhopal, K., & Pitkin, C. (2018). *Investigating higher education institutions and their views on the race equality charter.* UCU.
Bhopal, K., & Pitkin, C. (2020). 'Same old story, just a different policy': Race and policy making in higher education in the UK. *Race Ethnicity and Education, 23*(4), 530–547.
Bourdieu, P. (1990). *The logic of practice.* Polity.
Breach, A., & Li, Y. (2017). *Gender pay gap by ethnicity in Britain – Briefing.* Fawcett Society.
Britton, J., Dearden, L., & Waltmann, B. (2021). *The returns to undergraduate degrees by socio-economic group and ethnicity.* Department for Education and IFS.
Brown, P. et al. (2011). *The global auction: The broken promises of education, jobs and incomes.* Oxford University Press.
Business in the Community (BITC). (2018). *Race at work.* BITC.
Chapman, G., Nasirov, S., & Özbilgin, M. (2023). Workforce diversity, diversity charters and collective turnover: Long-term commitment pays. *British Journal of Management, 34*(3), 1340–1359.
Chartered Institute of Personnel and Development (CIPD). (2017). *Addressing the barriers to BAME employee career progression to the top.* CIPD.

Connor, H. et al. (2004). *A closer look at higher education minority ethnic students and graduates.* HMSO.

CRED. (2021). *Commission on racial and ethnic disparities: The report.* HMSO.

Delgado, R., & Stefancic, J. (2000). *Critical race theory: The cutting edge.* Temple University Press.

DIUS. (2006). *Statistical release: Participation rates in higher education, academic years 2000-2007.* HMSO.

EHRC. (2016). *Healing a divided Britain.* EHRC.

Gillborn, D. et al. 2018. QuantCrit: Education, policy, 'Big Data' and principles for a critical race theory of statistics. *Race Ethnicity and Education, 21*(2), 158–179.

Gov.UK. (2023a). *Graduate labour market statistics.* https://explore-education-statistics.service.gov.uk/find-statistics/graduate-labour-markets

Gov.UK. (2023b). *Ethnicity facts and figures: Employment.* https://www.ethnicity-facts-figures.service.gov.uk/work-pay-and-benefits/employment/employment/latest/

Gov.UK. (2023c). *Work and study after higher education.* https://www.ethnicity-facts-figures.service.gov.uk/education-skills-and-training/after-education/destinations-and-earnings-of-graduates-after-higher-education/latest/

Green Park. (2017). *Leadership 10,000.* Green Park.

Higher Education Funding Council for England (HEFCE). (2017). *Higher education in England: Students.* HEFCE.

Hunt, W., Baldauf, B., & Lyonette, C. (2023). Horses for courses: Subject differences in the chances of securing different types of graduate jobs in the UK. *Journal of Social Policy.* https://doi.org/10.1017/S0047279423000041

Hunt, V., Layton, D., & Prince, S. (2015). *Why diversity matters.* McKinsey & Company.

Institute for Fiscal Studies. (2020). *The impact of undergraduate degrees on lifetime earnings.* IFS.

Isopahkala-Bouret, U., Tholen, G., & van Zanten, A. (2023). Introduction to the special issue: Positionality and social inequality in graduate careers. *Journal of Education and Work, 36*(1), 1–8.

Li, Y., & Heath, A. (2018). Persisting disadvantages: A study of labour market dynamics of ethnic unemployment and earnings in the UK (2009–2015). *Journal of Ethnic and Migration Studies, 46*(5), 857–878.

Longhi, S., & Brynin, M. (2017). *The ethnicity pay gap* (Research Report 108). EHRC.

Marini, G. (2024). Brexit and the war for talents: Push & pull evidence about competitiveness. *Higher Education.* https://link.springer.com/article/10.1007/s10734-024-01186-1

McGregor-Smith, R. B. (2017). *Race in the workplace: The McGregor-Smith review.* HMSO.

Mirza, H., & Warwick, R. (2022). *Race and ethnicity* (Institute for Fiscal Studies [IFS] Report No. R230). IFS.

Myers, M. (2022). Racism, zero-hours contracts and complicity in higher education. *British Journal of Sociology of Education, 43*(4), 584–602.

Noon, M. (2018). Pointless diversity training: Unconscious bias, new racism and agency. *Work, Employment and Society, 32*(1), 198–209.

ONS. (2022). *Ethnicity pay gaps, UK: 2012 to 2022.* https://www.ons.gov.uk/employmentandlabourmarket/peopleinwork/earningsandworkinghours/articles/ethnicitypaygapsingreatbritain/2012to2022

Parker Review. (2024). *Improving the ethnic diversity of UK business. An update review of the parker review March 2024.* Department for Business and Trade.

Powell, A., & Francis-Devine, B. (2023). *Unemployment by ethnic background* (Research Briefing No. 6385). House of Commons Library.

Reiss, L. K., Schiffinger, M., Rapp, M. L., & Mayrhofer, W. (2023). Intersectional income inequality: A longitudinal study of class and gender effects on careers. *Culture and Organization.* https://doi.org/10.1080/14759551.2023.2232505

Richardson, J. T. E. (2015). The under-attainment of ethnic minority students in UK higher education: What we know and what we Don't know. *Journal of Further and Higher Education, 39*(2), 278–291.

Rolfe, H., Portes, J., & Hudson-Sharp, N. (2015). *Local authority schemes supporting people towards work.* National Institute of Economic and Social Research.

Saggar, S., Norrie, R., Bannister, M., & Goodhart, D. (2016). *Bittersweet success: Glass ceilings for Britain's ethnic minorities at the top of business and the professions.* Policy Exchange.

Smith, C., & Smith, S. (2016). Matching and mismatch: Understanding employer expectations of work placement applicants. In *ACEN 2016 conference supporting work-integrated learning in Australia* (p. 32). ACEN.

Social Mobility Commission. (2016). *Socio-economic diversity in life sciences and investment banking.* Social Mobility Commission.

Tomlinson, M. (2012). Graduate employability: A review of conceptual and empirical themes. *Higher Education Policy, 24*(4), 407–431.

Tomlinson, M. (2023). Conceptualising transitions from higher education to employment: Navigating liminal spaces. *Journal of Youth Studies, 27*(8), 1079–1096.

Tomlinson, M. (2024). A paradigm shift in the dialectical relationship between higher education and the labour market: Reconstructing human capital, value, and purposeful work. *Peking University Review, 21*(3), 1–27.

Tomlinson, M., & Nghia, T. (2020). An introductory overview of the current policy and conceptual landscape of graduate employability. In H. N. Tran, T. Pham, M. Tomlinson, & D. Jackson (Eds.), *Developing and utilizing employability capitals: Graduates' strategies across labour markets.* Routledge.

Trades Union Congress (TUC). (2016). *Black, qualified and unemployed.* TUC.

TUC. (2022). *Still rigged: Racism in the UK labour market 2022.* Trades Union Congress.

Wakeling, P., & Savage, M. (2015). Entry to elite professions and the stratification of higher education in Britain. *The Sociological Review, 63*(2), 290–320.

Walker, I., & Zhu, Y. (2018). University selectivity and the relative returns to higher education: Evidence from the UK. *Labour Economics, 53*, 230–249.

Zucotti, C., & Platt, L. (2016). Does neighbourhood ethnic concentration in early life affect subsequent labour market outcomes? A study across ethnic groups in England and Wales. *Population and Space, 23*, 6.

Zwysen, W., & Longhi, S. (2016). *Labour market disadvantages of ethnic minority British graduates: University choice, parental background or neighbourhood.* University of Essex: Institute for Social and Economic Research.

Zwysen, W., & Longhi, S. (2018). Employment and earning differences in the early career of ethnic minority British graduates: The importance of university career, parental background and area characteristics. *Journal of Ethnic and Migration Studies, 44*(1), 154–172.

9

A 'SPECIALISATION OF CONSCIOUSNESS'

In this final chapter, we argue that students from Black and minority ethnic (BME) backgrounds remain disadvantaged in their experiences of higher education. Historic racisms underpinning UK education remain entrenched but have adapted to work within the current higher education socio-economic model. This model presents itself as a free market in which students, understood as consumers of education, can choose to invest an accumulation of debt in the pursuit of a degree qualification. Choice in this context is a debatable concept not least because as many students in our research explained they felt they had *little choice other than to go to university*. They are a generation of students whose entire lifetimes have been spent under the expectation that half of all school leavers will progress to higher education to secure the credentialised capital of a degree in order to secure a *graduate job*. The expansion of student numbers is a clear indication there has been a reciprocal increase in numbers of jobs defined as *graduate jobs*. An obvious conclusion would be that as the scarcity of degrees has declined so too has their value (Bourdieu, 1984, 1986).

Making some allowance for the extent of student choice generally, BME students are still more likely to choose to study in universities that limit their educational and employment outcomes because they are not White. In principle, this should provoke outrage, particularly in the context of marketized universities competing for students as consumers. Proponents of the free market could presumably argue that the nature of such a market would be to encourage universities to adopt a package of anti-racist measures in order to generate greater recruitment of BME students. In reality, a meaningful free market has never materialised, and if it ever does, it remains unlikely that its first step would be to redress structural racism.

DOI: 10.4324/9781003097211-9

There are a number of reasons why the economies in which UK universities currently operate do not resemble a free market. Firstly, university fee levels have been consistently regulated by successive governments with no uplift to the £9250 cap since 2017. Freezing fees at this level is undoubtedly a political decision designed to avoid alienating parents by placing greater financial burdens on their children. This highlights the problem of regulating education as a consumer service when there is a widespread belief it is a public good. Any increase in fees, by politicians of any party, and loaded with any number of protections in place to make an argument that no one will be disadvantaged, will still be deeply unpopular.

The cap also signals an ostensibly democratic principle that does not align with the rationale for a free market by failing to acknowledge there are differences between universities. One irony of marketisation has been the increasing need for rankings, including those created by the government like the Teaching Excellence Framework (TEF), to provide the information necessary for students to be consumers. Despite the publication of information distinguishing universities, all students still pay the same £9250 fees. If they attend the University of Oxford or Oxford Brookes; Southampton or Southampton Solent; Leeds or Leeds Beckett, the fees remain the same. Sadly, this is not indicative of a democratising spirit because *degrees from different universities do hold different values*. A degree from a prestigious or elite university is more likely to lead to more rewarding, better paid employment. That difference in the value of degrees from different universities is not a new feature of the free market; it has always been the case. The recognition of value associated with different institutions has flourished in other parts of HE, such as the variations in fees for international students. Central government does not regulate these, and the greater prestige associated with some institutions enables them to charge significantly higher fees. In essence, the market for international students would be replicated for home students if they were to be treated genuinely as consumers. If that was to happen, many poorer home students would not be able to afford to attend the most prestigious universities. It is indicative of the inequalities fostered by UK universities that international student recruitment is partly based on wealth.

One final reason for making the claim that the free market is not a reality is the position of students themselves. Despite the claims they are engaged in making market-led decisions, this is not entirely true. Many students believe they have little choice other than to embark on undergraduate studies. Successive governments have prompted them down this path as the means of securing graduate jobs at times when other options have been severely limited. In principle, a degree adds value as evidenced in the earnings potential for graduates compared to non-graduates. In a precarious economy, many students will understand they have little other choice than to go to university.[1] In this respect, *students as consumers* and a *free market* for UK universities are misnomers. In its bastardised form the UK university economy is, however, a perfect example of the social formation of multiple inequalities including racism. Within the enlarged field of higher education institutions, first-generation and BME students are more likely to attend less prestigious universities.

We found that universities were producing students who understand their opportunities are limited but accept that process as a reality of twenty-first-century education and life. We describe these outcomes as the production of a 'specialisation of consciousness'. Throughout this process, the university is just one cog, albeit a significant cog, within social structures that reproduce White supremacy. As discussed in the previous chapters, racism is a normal, not an unusual, feature of university life. It materialises in multiple ways including racist abuse, violence, and systemic institutional practice. In and of itself, this is not a new finding but rather the evidence of longstanding histories of racism embedded within all aspects of social life including educational institutions; it is, 'ordinary, not aberrational – "normal science," the usual way society does business, the common, everyday experience of most people of color' (Delgado & Stefancic, 2012, p. 7). Delgado and Stefancic go on to draw the obvious conclusion that such normalcy has concrete benefits for White people at the expense of people of colour, both in terms of material gains and how they are able to perceive such gains as legitimate and equitable. The economies in which universities operate function to normalise racism. This is evident in the public-facing accounts universities give of themselves that stress their commitment to equality and diversity. Such commitments are not matched by equitable outcomes. At the time of our research, all three universities were committed to addressing attainment gaps for BME students. Whilst the narrative of action to address inequality is intended to signal a positive institutional commitment to equity, it also signals their systems are creating racist outcomes. That has not changed in the intervening years. It has *remained a normal state of affairs for universities to be committed to addressing racism without delivering any positive change to existing evidence of racism.*

The normalcy of racism within universities also flags up the evidence that this is not a new phenomenon. It is not the case, for example, that racism has materialised in the last 40 years as a consequence of massification, marketisation, and the emergence of a neoliberal mindset in which universities have succumbed to managerialist profiteering rather than serving the public good. Instead, racism has adapted and reinvented itself within these developments. The massification of universities, for example, has seen a pattern in which the increasing number of BME students are channelled into less prestigious institutions. The 'value' of their degrees within economies of higher education is consequently systematically devalued. And, the new breed of university leaders, the bean-counters and the profit-mongers, are inevitably driven by the unfailing cynicism of a free market (including one in its current bastardised form). It is in their collective interests to profit from this economy rather than critically challenge the erosion of education as a public good. If we do turn our gaze back to examine eras when education was valued as a public good, we do not find a golden age in which racism was not an issue. It was *business as usual then*, just as it is *business as usual now*.

This has remained the case despite the commitments of successive governments, policy-makers, and universities to widen university participation. Despite the growth in numbers of students from increasingly diverse classes and ethnic backgrounds attending university, there remains clear evidence that the twenty-first-century university is a White university that disproportionately services the interests of more affluent White people. On the basis of the evidence of our research, *we make the argument that such inequality is out in the open*. In other words, the narratives of our participants are not revealing something that is happening in a covert fashion. Rather these are accounts of racism as a well-established characteristic of university life; it is neither hidden nor new but stands in plain sight sedimented into institutional structures and practice. Depressingly the research at the heart of this book is less concerned with the empirical evidence of the existence of racism and far more interested in why racism in universities is openly tolerated. How, in effect, can universities get away with their indifference to addressing everyday occurrences of racism and why do BME students *choose* to incur large debts for the privilege?

In answer to that question, we have argued students develop a 'specialisation of consciousness'. They are able to understand the world around them, including its overt inequalities, but display an acceptance of the limitations imposed upon them. In Fanon's account of consciousness or knowledge of the self ('La connaissance' Fanon, 1952), consciousness includes the acquisition of empirical information about the individual body and also the understanding of one's own identity, history, and place in the world (Fanon, 2008). In the context of colonialism, this is a distorted form of consciousness imposed by the colonisers to reproduce inequalities, stereotypes, self-alienation within the mindset of the colonised. Only through a process of the decolonization of knowledge, and of consciousness, can the colonised reclaim the agency in which other forms of knowledge about the realities of their experience can be recognised.

In the context of twenty-first-century universities, the promise of Fanon's account of decolonisation rings hollow. The processes of 'decolonising the curriculum' have become shorthand for performances of diversity. 'Decolonising the curriculum' and other examples of equality and diversity initiatives championed by universities clearly do not deliver on the promise of challenging racism in universities, but they do remain a central tenet of universities' presentation of their institutions' commitment to redressing inequality. It is hard not to conclude this reflects an awareness within the university that in order to profit within a free market by, for example, recruiting large numbers of BME students, it is necessary to be seen to be progressive. The students we interviewed often appeared cognisant of equality policy being little more than a smokescreen. They recognised the failings of equality policies as another normal feature of their education. Unlike Fanon's colonised they understood the practices by which racism was engrained in university life and beyond; their accounts were of universities seen from a BME not a White gaze. They were under no illusions about racism and how it materialised throughout university systems and practice. This seemed to inform the means by which they understood forms of liberation from daily inequalities were not the political or psychological confrontations that would characterise Fanon's resistance. They often proffered more practical or mundane solutions such as having greater access to economic or social capitals. Such solutions rang true. Students whose work was suffering because they always had to work during term time would see an immediate levelling up if they received more financial support. Students whose parents were unable to secure useful job placements would benefit from better interventions by the university to generate those connections. These sorts of interventions are relatively easy to envisage within funding arrangements and university support processes but they do not materialise because the systemic processes of students attending university are predicated on producing racist outcomes. The production of White supremacy is intrinsic to the institutional practice of universities. We would argue that recognition of racist outcomes being normal is a key element legitimising universities' reproduction of inequality whilst maintaining a façade of liberalism. It also points to a key understanding within critical race theory that liberalism has always failed to address racism (Bell, 1992; Warmington, 2024) because it stabilises a White supremacist social structure.

A 'specialisation of consciousness'

BME students provided accounts of the inequalities they faced before entering university and discriminatory practice encountered whilst at university. One striking feature was the degree to which this became an unchallenged aspect of their lives. Universities often claim they are producing young people capable of challenging and questioning the world; that was less evident in our research than might be anticipated. Although BME students recognised histories and institutional practices of discrimination, they tended to be accepted as a fixed 'reality'. There was a noticeable gulf between the widely publicised actions of students engaged in protest around causes such as 'decolonising the curriculum' and the BME students in our research. This is not to suggest they were disengaged or unaware of such protest; simply it did not feature in their accounts of engagement with the university despite identifying and being critical of discriminatory practice.

Again we describe this conjuncture of an 'awareness of' and 'acceptance of' personal and institutional inequality and the processes of its production as a 'specialisation of consciousness'. By this, we are arguing the legacy of racism within family histories and schooling is sedimented within everyday racisms at university as normal, everyday practice. Even understanding how universities deploy such racism is less a source of overwhelming discomfort or reason to challenge the *status quo*; rather it becomes part of the everyday routine of being a student. BME students entering university bring their *habitus* and access to capitals into play within the university's competition for economic, social, and cultural capitals. It might be anticipated that some students are less at home, less 'fish in water' (Bourdieu & Wacquant, 1992, p. 127) because of their ethnicity or lower social economic status. BME students often described their ability to compete intellectually and socially and, in the case of wealthier students, economically. However, they identified the competition itself was rigged and their efforts were actively disadvantaged by racism. Against a back-drop of more competitive labour markets and increasing university participa-tion, for many students, securing a degree still remains the only game in town. BME students participate because not participating would mean limiting already diminished opportunities.

For Du Bois (2007) or Fanon (2008), such a moment, the production of Black identities understood from a White gaze as holding lesser value, would be a signal of extreme psychic harm but our participants often appeared re-signed to this process. It appeared ironic that students described experiences of 'covert' racism; the ease with which racism was being identified suggested it was clearly an 'overt', and not a 'covert' practice. The 'covert' tag seemed to signal a means of labelling and understanding racisms but removing the pos-sibility of challenging them. In part, this was a process of institutional racism. The university experience trained BME students to recognise the anti-racist trappings of their universities (their equality policies or promotional materials) as being a substantial enough response to meet the basic requirements of in-stitutional life. In part, it was also individuals reconciling their recognition of discriminatory practice as an everyday, reality of their lives. Universities ef-fectively narrowed understandings of racism to specific actions (verbal abuse, for example), rather than wider evidence of racism (systemic attainment gaps or micro-aggressions of lecturers). By participating in the university field BME students became complicit in a process of seeing themselves framed through an 'institutional gaze' that flies under the false colours of a narrative of diversity. Students accepted the university's diversity and equality work was an unproductive smokescreen, but not something they would actively chal-lenge. As consumers of the products on offer, they are effectively investors within the institutional field. Indebted in the most literal sense, BME students' agency to challenge systemic forms of racism is inevitably eroded. To chal-lenge or to actively disengage and not participate would be counterproductive and result in the waste of resources. By accumulating debt in exchange for a university degree, students buy into the institutional ethos. In Bourdieu's terms, they become complicit with the White orientations of its practice and gaze.

The process of generating BME students' acceptance or complicity in these processes (e.g. paying fees, living in university accommodation) signals its *specialisation*. A narrow and specific view of discriminatory practice made acceptable to those most disadvantaged by the practice. Although this research did not explore the perspectives of White students, we might speculate some would be less comfortable with such an account of disadvantage and the acceptance of that disadvantage, despite being its main beneficiaries. At the same time, some White students might understand the performance of equality policies as something more concrete because its perceived benefits are not directed at them. They are less likely to be as aware of the failures of such policies to deliver change whilst recognising the performance of such policies as more meaningful interventions. In other research, we interviewed White students who described equality policies as a source of disadvantage for White students (Bhopal & Myers, 2023b). They claimed that 'contextual offers' or 'affirmative action' policies in the USA meant they experienced discrimination *because of their Whiteness*. These views were held despite abundant evidence that it was both easier for White students to gain entry to more prestigious universities and that they were more likely to be awarded higher classes of degree.

For White students, the potential of university education that broadens knowledge by developing a more *expansive consciousness* remains possible. Entering the labour market, third-year BME students are often burdened with a historic legacy of individual, familial, and institutional expectations lower than White students. This is a burden largely accepted as a 'reality' of daily life, a fixed point rather than an over-riding obstacle. A former Secretary of State for Education, Gavin Williamson, argued that degrees should give all students, 'the knowledge and the skills they need to achieve whatever goals they set themselves' (Gov.UK, 2019). For many BME students, this is not a true reflection of their degree's value. Competing at university for better grades and better degrees they are hampered by racist practice and expectations their experience of university inequalities would be repeated in the labour market. Williamson's optimism was not mirrored by BME students who were not confident their degree qualification would trump inequalities of ethnicity or social class. Their understanding of everyday realities of racism is well-founded and evidenced in patterns of statistical disadvantage related to ethnicity.

Bourdieu describes a 'dialectic between *habitus* and institutions', such as universities, 'in which there is constantly created a history that inevitably appears, like witticisms, as both original and inevitable' (Bourdieu, 1990, p. 57). This is uncannily observable within the 'racial sociodicy' (Bourdieu & Wacquant, 1999) of universities, producing narratives of widening participation whilst simultaneously producing BME students imbued with dispositions and characteristics that disadvantage their futures. These students are never disinterested parties within this process, rather they are engaged and complicit in their engagement with the rules and consequences of the field. Bourdieu recognises their 'interest' as their 'tacit recognition of the value of the stakes of the game and as practical mastery of its rules' (Bourdieu & Wacquant, 1992, p. 117). The unequal nature of such practical mastery for BME students indicates the disjunct between realistic opportunities and outcomes compared to their White peers. Students recognised that the value of the stakes being competed for at university was often diminished because of the 'realities' of ethnicity or 'social class'. This was compounded for many BME students from non-traditional backgrounds who chose less prestigious universities assuming a relative parity between different institutions and the value of their degrees. BME students without the initial access to capital generally enter into a lesser game with lower stakes than those with an excess of capital. The current funding arrangements ensure all students pay the same fees regardless of institution or social background. At the same time, students can access a loan to cover living costs that is means-tested on parental income. Students from poorer families receive a substantially higher living cost allowance than affluent students who are expected to be supported by their parents. This means that poorer students leave university with greater debt. In this model, the transfer of economic capital mirrors transfers of knowledge and cultural capital and the fostering of social networks to benefit already privileged students. In simple terms, poorer students, from non-traditional working-class BME backgrounds tend to leave university with more debt and a less valuable degree from a less prestigious university. This can be understood as a perfect circle of institutional and structural racism ensuring White supremacy is reproduced.

Students in our research often described their acceptance of university practices that appeared inequitable or racist. The flourishing of inequitable practice within any institutional field is commonplace and often identified as symbolic violence, 'the *violence which is exercised upon a social agent with his or her complicity*' (Bourdieu & Wacquant, 1992, p. 167). Participants discussed openly the detrimental impact of such practice upon them, rather than providing accounts that could be interpreted as 'hidden persuasion' (Bourdieu & Wacquant, 1992, p. 168). Instead, they identified obvious, overt discrimination. Their ability to work within everyday racism was partially understandable in terms of their *habitus* and engagement in a competition for capitals shaped by the 'order of things' (Bourdieu & Wacquant, 1992, p. 168), by the underlying social structures of unsaid positioning and status. The acceptance of racism in universities by BME students *aware* of such racism appeared if not entirely contrary to the complex version of complicity suggested by Bourdieu, at least divergent from its tone of unsaid and embodied behaviours.

The role racism played throughout the lives of BME students indicates specific demarcations of potential and lost potential (both readily understood in terms of *habitus* and the competition for capitals). The acceptance of the knowledge of lost potential being enacted upon BME students by those students suggests a different type of fault line in which racism is a visible everyday limit. Racism, unlike other inequalities experienced by the students we spoke to, did not emerge within the same process of social structuring Bourdieu identifies. The legitimation that emerges for a dominated group through a concept like *doxa* as the 'most radical form of acceptance of the world, the most absolute form of conservatism' (Bourdieu & Wacquant, 1992, p. 74) was apparent in some aspects of students consciousness but diverged from how race and racism were perceived. Students provided concrete, complex examples of how racism operates in the twenty-first-century university. Their accounts of class or gender differences were less pronounced unless being discussed in relation to race and racism, e.g., the experience of being a Black woman or a working-class Muslim. In this sense, they shared elements of a construction of a *White doxa*, a conformism with a range of inequalities being normalised within the university but when it came to race and racism this was identified as an explicit, unfair limitation.

This limitation of potential is a limiting of access to education and a narrowing of available knowledge. This inevitably runs counter to the claims made by universities in their mission statements and in commitments to equality and diversity. It also runs counter to the ethos of equality legislation and education policy more generally. Whilst in part, it can be understood through prior histories and family background, within the university it materialises as the reconfirmation of inequalities as natural demarcations. 'Specialisation of consciousness' encompasses a range of racist processes universities implement in order to preserve their institutional and economic standing, whilst training BME students to graduate without challenging overtly inequitable institutions and social inequalities more generally. It generates a form of student consciousness that is deliberately narrowed because the student is a BME student. *It is a form of educational apartheid in which White supremacy is recognised as an uncomfortable truth.* It can be opposed in spirit but it is too normal, ordinary, and banal to expect it to change. The narrowing 'specialisation of consciousness' embodied throughout the acquisition of university degrees ensures students transition into the labour market socialised by their institution into *believing* their lesser positions are inevitable consequences of a normalised racist reality.

Note

1 This became even more apparent during the COVID-19 pandemic, with many students reporting that the consequent downturn in the labour market meant they had no other option than going to university or living at home and relying on their parents (Bhopal & Myers, 2023a).

References

Bell, D. (1992). *Faces at the Bottom of the well: The permanence of racism*. Basic Books.

Bhopal, K., & Myers, M. (2023a). The impact of COVID-19 on a level exams in England: Students as consumers. *British Educational Research Journal*, *49*(1), 142–157.

Bhopal, K., & Myers, M. (2023b). *Elite universities and the making of privilege: Exploring race and class in global educational economies*. Routledge.

Bourdieu, P. (1984). *Distinction: A social critique of the judgement of taste*. Harvard University Press.

Bourdieu, P. (1986). The forms of capital. In J. Richardson (Ed.), *Handbook of theory and research for the sociology of education* (pp. 241–258). Greenwood.

Bourdieu, P. (1990). *The logic of practice*. Polity.

Bourdieu, P., & Wacquant, L. (1992). *An invitation to reflexive sociology*. University of Chicago Press.

Delgado, R., & Stefancic, J. (2012). *Critical race theory: An introduction* (2nd ed.) NY Press.

Du Bois, W. E. B. (2007). *The souls of black folk*. Oxford University Press.

Fanon, F. (1952). *Peau noire masques blancs*. Éditions du Seuil.

Fanon, F. (2008). *Black skin, white masks*. Pluto Press.

Gov.UK. (2019). *Education secretary addresses Universities UK conference*. Retrieved October 3, 2024, from https://www.gov.uk/government/speeches/education-secretary-addresses-universities-uk-conference

Warmington, P. (2024). *Permanent racism: Race, class and the myth of postracial Britain*. Policy.

INDEX